"Blake Snyder has done the single hardest thing there is to do in Hollywood: Produced a sequel to his terrific *Save the Cat!* that is surprising, entertaining, informative, and smart. His genius isn't in telling how to write movies — i.e., laying down clichéd dictates of what has to happen on what page — but rather, it's the way he teaches you how to think about writing movies."
> — Bruce Feirstein, Writer, *GoldenEye*, *Tomorrow Never Dies*,
> *The World Is Not Enough*; Contributing Editor and Writer,
> *Vanity Fair Magazine*

"Even if you've read and analyzed 50 screenplays, you still wouldn't learn half as much as you could from reading this book. *Save the Cat! Goes to the Movies* proves that not only is Blake a great screenwriter, he's also a great screenwriting teacher."
> — Stephanie Palmer, Author, *Good in a Room*,
> *www.goodinaroom.com*

"Blake has created an extremely valuable guide to engaging and entertaining your audience, both in the big idea and moment-by-moment. This amazing book is a window into how successful writers and developers think."
> — Luke Ryan, Vice President, MTV Films; Executive
> Producer, *Harold & Kumar Go To White Castle*

"Blake Snyder unlocks the secret of successful screenwriting by deconstructing the framework of cinematic storytelling and redrawing genre lines along new borders. His revealing analysis shows how seemingly unconnected films are actually related and unveils deeper links between movies that occupy the same traditional genres, offering the reader fresh insight into what makes films tick. Surprising, enlightening, and fun."
> — Kristofer Upjohn, *B-Scared.com*

"Blake has done it again! *Save the Cat! Goes to the Movies* puts his easy-to-digest theories to the test and proves them time after time. With great insight and wit, Blake has identified the key components of good storytelling and presented them in a clear, indisputable form that is at once universal and immediately applicable... no matter where you are in the writing process. Blake is a light-switch in the dank, cluttered basement of story. What an eye-opener."
> — Dean DeBlois, Co-Writer/Director, *Lilo & Stitch*

"Blake's book breaks everything down in a way that pinpoints precise reasons I'm stuck and allows me to fight my way through it. I can't tell you how many times *Save the Cat!* has saved my ass!"
> — Jeremy Garelick, Writer/Producer, *The Break-Up*

"You can't think outside the box until you understand what it is — and nobody understands the box that movies come in the way Blake does. A fantastic book!"
— Jeff Arch, Writer, *Sleepless in Seattle* (Oscar®-nominated), *Saving Milly* (Humanitas Prize Nominee)

"Blake Snyder proves once again that his practical, strategic approach to writing is the foundation for great movies. His wildly informative and entertaining follow-up to *Save the Cat!* is an invaluable guide to foolproof storytelling."
— Craig Perry, Producer, the *American Pie* and *Final Destination* films

"With so much over-emphasis on special effects in today's films, thank heavens for Blake Snyder and *Save the Cat! Goes to the Movies*. Snyder reminds budding screenwriters it's the story that counts — and he does so with plenty of wit and the inclusion of extensive personal knowledge as a screenwriter himself. Bravo!"
— Betty Jo Tucker, Editor and Lead Film Critic, *ReelTalkReviews.com*; Author, *Confessions of a Movie Addict, Susan Sarandon: A True Maverick*

"Blake Snyder does it again! His enthusiasm for film and screenwriting shines through every page of this amazing book. Fantastic!"
— Matthew Terry, Columnist, *www.hollywoodlitsales.com*

"Blake Snyder has managed to reinvent the wheel and improve the way it rolls. His *Save the Cat* books pack a two-fisted punch to help you understand what makes a story work and how to make your story work better. Save your script — read this book!"
— Catherine Clinch, Publisher, *www.MomsMediaWorld.com*

"Funny and genuinely useful, this is a perfect follow-up to a groundbreaking book for screenwriters. You'll never look at films the same way again."
— Jenna Glatzer, Author, *Make a Real Living as a Freelance Writer, The Street-Smart Writer*

"The perfect companion to *Save the Cat!* Blake Snyder again delivers a fun and informative guide that doesn't disappoint. If you think that people in Hollywood don't watch other movies to solve problems in their own scripts, you're already behind the game. This book easily breaks down what makes all of your favorite movies work to their core and will help you apply those principles to your own scripts."
— Luis Guerrero & Chris Lemos, Producers, Vital Pictures

SAVE THE CAT!™
GOES TO THE
MOVIES

THE SCREENWRITER'S GUIDE
TO EVERY STORY EVER TOLD

BLAKE SNYDER

Published by Michael Wiese Productions
3940 Laurel Canyon Blvd., #1111
Studio City CA 91604
Tel. 818.379.8799
Fax 818.986.3408
mw@mwp.com
www.mwp.com

Cover Design: Michael Wiese Productions
Layout: Gina Mansfield Design
Editor: Brett Jay Markel

Printed by McNaughton & Gunn, Inc., Saline, Michigan

Library of Congress Cataloging-in-Publication Data

Snyder, Blake, 1957-
Save the cat! goes to the movies : the screenwriter's guide to every
story ever told / by Blake Snyder.
p. cm.
ISBN 978-1-932907-35-3
1. Motion picture authorship. 2. Motion pictures--Plots,
themes, etc. I. Title.
PN1996.S64 2007
808.2'3--dc22
2007025210

TABLE OF CONTENTS

ACKNOWLEDGEMENTS

So many people contributed to this book. Thanks to Pete Barnstrom (especially for the Kathy Bates line) and Olivia Bohnhoff (for her insight into female superheroes), Hilary Wayne (for getting me started), my manager Andy Cohen (for introducing me to Sheila Taylor), my attorney Chuck Hurewitz (for his continued guidance), Rich Kaplan (for joining our team just when we needed him most), and Jesse, Dana, and Mario at The Writers Store for being supporters of this and all *Cat!* projects. I am also thrilled to thank Naomi Beaty, brilliant researcher and writer, and the one person I can email at 3:00 a.m. to ask who said what when in nearly ANY movie! Thanks too for the amazing Gina Mansfield, whose artistic eye for layout and design made this book, and the first, *Cat!*tastic. Almost last, but not least, are the dynamic duo: publisher Michael Wiese and Ken Lee. But mostly I want to thank my longtime friend, business partner, editor, and *le mot just* genius, Brett Jay Markel, without whom this book, or the last, would not be possible — or even legible. He and his wife, Tanya, step-daughters Deborah and Rebecca, son Noah, and assorted cats are the hearth where I have learned what love really means.

FOREWORD

Sheila Hanahan Taylor
Producer, Practical Pictures

When Blake told me he was rolling up his sleeves to write a second *Save the Cat!* I literally whooped for joy.

I was excited because, while the original book generated amazing feedback and results (there's nothing like getting an email from a CAA-repped writer telling me how much he loved *STC!* and how he retooled and SOLD an idea after reading it!), we both secretly knew Blake's work as a story guru and Sherpa through the mysteries of Hollywood was not yet complete.

Yes, the words of wisdom in *STC!* had enlightened and motivated movie lovers of all types, but as readers across the globe discovered and explored the book, some really smart questions arose. Some people, including my film students at UCLA, couldn't or wouldn't believe Blake's theories on story type held up for all movies, so they asked for more proof. Some gobbled up the comparisons between similar movies and clamored for more to noodle on. Others just needed a few more examples to really get their heads around the approach Blake presented.

And so, *Save the Cat! Goes to the Movies* was born.

I wish I were exaggerating when I say that six or seven years ago I told a co-worker, "Until someone takes the time to help filmmakers see the bones of storytelling from the buyer's point of view, we'll continue to meet writers with great voices but no real chops for surviving in Hollywood."

Well, Blake's taken the time — all to help the next generation of film lovers join the club. He found 50 benchmark films and masterfully walks through the mechanics of their structure and story beats. He shows the reader exactly what I wished for so long ago — all in 3 or so pages per! How delightful is that?

And for those of you who lean more toward the art and less toward the commerce, *STC!2* reveals how some fantastic, beautiful "art house" films such as *Eternal Sunshine of the Spotless Mind* or *Maria Full of Grace* have the same story bones and the same core as their big, fat studio-sized cousins. Because Blake knows that to compete in today's movie-marketplace, *every* filmmaker needs to speak the same language.

I would encourage anyone flipping through this gem to go back and explore the original, but if this is your first stop on the *Save the Cat!* journey, jump right in! The water's fine.

In fact, it just doesn't get any better than this.

Sheila Hanahan Taylor is a partner at Practical Pictures, where she has over 20 feature projects set up at major studios, is an executive producer on hour-long TV series at both AMC and Paramount Television, and recently entered into a first look deal with award-winning producer Scott Rudin at Disney Studios. Along with her producing duties, Sheila is also an associate professor at UCLA's film school, teaching year-round in the MFA Program for Producing.

STC! 2:
THE INTRODUCTION

Godfather 2.

Terminator 2.

Spider-Man 2.

What do these titles have in common?

Each represents that rarity of rarities in the movie business: the sequel that outshines the original!

In movies we always expect the first one to be the best. If the storytellers are doing their job, what more is there to say? And yet if you're a true fan, you know there's always the chance for a curtain call. Do we really believe Freddie Kruger is *dead*-dead? Can't all those dinosaurs be moved to the 'hood for *Jurassic Park 5*? And even though we know he bit the big Rosebud, isn't there maybe a prequel to *Citizen Kane*?

And this time... let's *really* do it right!

So when you author a hit screenwriting how-to titled *Save the Cat! The Last Book on Screenwriting You'll Ever Need*, you can see the tempting of fate that goes with sticking a "2" on the end of it. Well, isn't that just typical Hollywood?! Trying to wangle every last dollar out of us, to squeeze the rag dry!! Is that what this is about?

Well... yes.

But maybe, just maybe, the second one is better.

The reason for a continuation in my case is actual requests from hundreds of readers for more. Somehow, I made the foolish mistake of including my email address in the first book. Since then, I have been deluged with 5 to 10 missives daily from readers, many of whom I've helped by offering advice on their loglines or their movie pitches.

And that's when we get down to the nitty-*gritée*.

In these email interactions, we inevitably wind up discussing "what to do next." Okay, so you have a solid concept and a "poster" for the best movie ever made.

Now what?

As most sequels do, I return to the heroes of the first installment, The League of Extraordinary Gentlemen... and Ladies, my writing partners to whom I dedicate this book. Yes, I am a successful screenwriter who has been writing and selling scripts to Hollywood for over 20 years — and my "war stories" sometimes star only ME — but without Howard Burkons, James Haggin, Colby Carr, Mike Cheda, Tracey Jackson, Cormac and Marianne Wibberley, Sheldon Bull, C. David Stephens, and many others I have met along the way, I'd be nowhere. They taught me everything.

And our process is always the same.

Once we think up the idea, pitch it around, and get the right reaction, we ask: "So what is this movie most like?" — and we proceed to take the next step everyone in Hollywood takes when writing a screenplay.

We cheat.

That's right. You heard me.

We look at every single movie that our story bears any resemblance to and see how other writers did it. We learn what they did right, what they did wrong, and how our script MUST be a big step forward in the evolution of the genre in which we are working. And frankly, to do otherwise strikes me as foolish. I don't just mean surveying the last five years of movie history either, because believe it or not, there are movies made before we were born that beat us to the punch on our "original" idea.

Why not take a look?

Usually if I am working with a partner we'll divvy up the film-watching assignments. I'll take two or three, she'll take two or three, and we'll "screen" them with a timer and a yellow pad to mark down where each "beat" of the story takes place.

And why.

We open up the back of the Swiss watch and take a look at how the mainspring and gears of each movie are put together. We acquaint ourselves with the requirements of the tale we're trying to tell and see if we must use certain conventions or if we can throw them away and create new ones.

And everyone, and I do mean *everyone*, does likewise.

In this book I take the 10 movie genres I coined in *Save the Cat!* and give you five examples of each from the iconic films of the '70s right up to their 21st Century counterparts. I detail the variations in each genre, and also show how a movie from 1975 begat one in 1987, which led to the most recent incarnation. And if you look at this enterprise as a whole, you can start to see the method of my *Cat!* madness.

To paraphrase Jodie Foster in *Contact*, this is an "encyclopedia galactica," a compendium of every story type ever told for film. It is, in short, the most useful tool I can think of for any screenwriter, the "cheat sheets" for 50 of the most instructional movies from the past 30 years, to give you the clues to write *your* movie.

It will reveal how other screenwriters who came before you tackled the same challenges you are facing with the film you want to write — or the one you are currently working on. And to use this book, all you need is a good idea to get started. Right now. Today.

How's *that* for a sequel?

For those of you new to my approach, I realize there is nothing worse that tuning in to a re-run of *The X Files* and seeing that this is Part II of an episode you missed. There is no more sinking sensation than to feel left out, or that you've come in late. To that end, I have tried to make this book complete unto itself. I've given you a second that adds to the first, enhances what came before — yet stands alone. If you've never read *Save the Cat!* (poor soul!), you don't need to in order to use *STC! 2*. But I'm hoping that if this is your first *Save the Cat!* experience, you'll want to go back and see where it all began. And if you're a veteran *Cat!*-ite... this book will blow your mind.

"GENRE" AND "STRUCTURE"

In doing all of my research for *STC!2* — and learning more than I ever expected — I was reminded again what makes for a good movie, whether it's a quirky indie or a big-budget blockbuster. And while many studios greenlight a script based on a point system of star, director, and the last hit like it, in fact the success of any film is based on two far more important factors:

1. A story that surpasses our expectations for the familiar **genre** of movie it is. And...

2. The most crucial element: **structure**.

Genre and structure. These are the two requirements for creating a winning screenplay — and the basis of this book.

Unlike the authors of other how-to's on screenwriting, my job day-in and day-out is writing and selling scripts. I am a screen-writer first and foremost and my daily struggle is figuring out what it takes to turn my ideas into movies that everyone — agents, producers, studio executives, and audience members — will love! And the odd thing is: To have a true hit movie, to please one, is to please all.

This simple mandate, which I want to instill in others, makes up the raison d'etre of the *STC!* oeuvre: Hollywood is not the prob-lem, story is — and I want my story, and yours, to be the very best it can be.

In years of trying to get a better grip on what our stories en-tail, my screenwriting buddies and I have come up with 10 types that have proven to be the ones moviemakers find most popular with audiences. Within these 10 you will see comedy, drama, and action, but that's not what each is about. Tone is not the issue. Neither is subject. It's about story. Only by lumping together movies that are alike as story types have we discovered that others know these tricks, too. They *must*! Otherwise there wouldn't be so many similarities shared by the movies in each category.

Look hard at the films found in the genre I refer to as

"Monster in the House" and see how *Jaws*, *Alien*, *Tremors*, and most "ghost stories" are alike.

And need to be!

Take a peek at what I call "Superhero," and you'll be amazed at how *Gladiator* and *The Lion King* use exactly the same kinds of story dynamics. Both pit a "special being" against us Lilliputians who are jealous of his amazing gifts and want to stop him. These match, identically, stories from the comic-book universe and those of Frankenstein, Dracula, and the Wolfman!

Why? Because it's the same tale.

Told in extremely different and creative ways.

And while they are set miles apart in time, location, and style, these stories keep being told — because audiences across generations always want to hear them.

I have given catchy names to my 10 genres to make them easier to remember and also to deconstruct your ideas about how movies should be categorized. Monster in the House, Golden Fleece, Out of the Bottle, Dude with a Problem, Rites of Passage, Buddy Love, Whydunit, Fool Triumphant, Institutionalized, and Superhero are, to me, so much more indicative of what story you're trying to tell. So when I ask: "What are you writing?" you no longer have to say "It's a western" or "It's a cop drama" — because these responses tell me nothing. I want to know what *story* you're working on, and what these 10 genres provide are indications of story type we all can understand.

Okay, so these categories tell me how movies are different. But how are they the same? Well, after some soul-searching — and years of hard knocks in and around every production office west of Azusa — I figured out a way to codify the similarities too, and that is how movies are structured.

What I wanted to create, in addition to "type" of movie, is a never-fail template that I can lay on top of *any* story as a way to test whether or not it will be satisfying.

Think about that for a minute.

A universal key to unlock every successful movie ever made.

Pretty good if you can do it — and I think I have!

My structure education came slowly. I started my career as a young and eager screenwriter, ill-equipped to pitch to the studio *genii* who'd deigned to see me. I usually had "an idea" and maybe a few "cool" scenes, but early on that was pretty much all I had. These meetings were short. For despite the fact that I had washed my face and brushed my teeth and applied my sparkling personality at every opportunity, sadly... I had no plot. And it didn't take long for both the exec and me to figure that out.

I heard rumors about this Syd Field guy. Once, an equally charming executrix asked me what my "Break into Two" was and hinted that the mysterious Syd could explain it to me. That's how I discovered Field's seminal work, *Screenplay*, and soon I, too, was pointing at movie screens at about Minute 25 of the film, turning knowledgeably to my date and whispering:

"See! Act Break!"

But as cute as this was, it did not solve my problem. I could identify three acts, thanks to Mr. Field. But in actually trying to write my scripts, there was a lot of empty space in between. So I started filling in the rest myself.

After watching hundreds of movies, I soon discovered the "Midpoint" and was amazed at how at page 55 the "stakes are raised" and many a **time clock** appears. Thanks to other books, like Viki King's *How to Write a Screenplay in 21 Days*, I was impressed by the importance of the "All Is Lost" point on page 75 — and saw that something must "die" there. I also made up terminology of my own. One, of which I am unduly proud, is the part of the script that occurs after page 25 that I dubbed "Fun and Games." Soon, I created the "Blake Snyder Beat Sheet" (the BS2), a handy device with the suggested page count indicated in parentheses of each "beat."

It looks like this:

THE BLAKE SNYDER BEAT SHEET

PROJECT TITLE:
GENRE:
DATE:

1. Opening Image (1):

2. Theme Stated (5):

3. Set-Up (1-10):

4. Catalyst (12):

5. Debate (12-25):

6. Break into Two (25)

7. B Story (30):

8. Fun and Games (30-55):

9. Midpoint (55):

10. Bad Guys Close In (55-75):

11. All Is Lost (75):

12. Dark Night of the Soul (75-85):

13. Break into Three (85):

14. Finale (85-110):

15. Final Image (110):

What are each of these so-called "beats" about?

Opening Image — This is fairly self-explanatory; it's the scene in the movie that sets up the tone, type, and initial salvo of a film, a "before" snapshot — and the opposite of the Final Image.

Theme Stated — Also easy. Usually spoken to the main character, often without knowing what is said will be vital to his surviving this tale. It's what your movie is "about."

Set-Up — The first 10 pages of a script must not only grab our interest — and a studio reader's — but introduce or hint at introducing every character in the A story.

Catalyst — The telegram, the knock at the door, the act of catching your wife in bed with another — something that is done *to* the hero to shake him. It's the movie's first "whammy."

Debate — The section of the script, be it a scene or a series of scenes, when the hero doubts the journey he must take.

Break into Two — Act Two, that is; it is where we leave the "Thesis" world behind and enter the upside-down "Anti-thesis" world of Act Two. The hero makes a choice — and his journey begins.

B Story — The "love" story, traditionally, but actually where the discussion about the theme of a good movie is found.

Fun and Games — Here we forget plot and enjoy "set pieces" and "trailer moments" and revel in the "promise of the premise."

Midpoint — The dividing line between the two halves of a movie; it's back to the story as "stakes are raised," "time clocks" appear, and we start putting the squeeze on our hero(es).

Bad Guys Close In — Both internally (problems inside the hero's team) and externally (as actual bad guys tighten their grip), real pressure is applied.

All Is Lost — The "false defeat" and the place where we find "the whiff of death" — because something must die here.

Dark Night of the Soul — *Why hast thou forsaken me, Lord?* That part of the script where the hero has lost all hope...

Break into Three ...but not for long! Thanks to a fresh idea, new inspiration, or last-minute action or advice from the love interest in the B story, the hero chooses to fight.

Finale — The "Synthesis" of two worlds: From what was, and that which has been learned, the hero forges a third way.

Final Image — The opposite of the Opening Image, proving a change has occurred. And since we know **All Stories Are About Transformation**, that change had better be dramatic!

These two sets of organizing principles — "genre" and "structure" — give us everything we need to write our movie and make the idea we're working on more likely to succeed.

I'll say it again.

If you want to sell your script and create a story that pleases most audiences most of the time, the odds increase if you reference these two checklists to write it.

Genre and structure are what buyers *and* moviegoers want.

This is because one of the other things I discovered in selling many scripts to Hollywood — a couple in the million-dollar range — is that executives know this, too. The savvy ones follow the same rules writers do. They want to know the type of story they signed on for, and whether it's structured in a way that satisfies everyone. It's what they're looking for.

Why not give it to them?

And while many of you rebel from "structure" or referencing other films for clues as to how to create and write your story, it has been my experience that mastering these templates is the only way to know if what you have is actually new — or if you are inventing a wheel that has already rolled out of the factory and down the road without you.

What I've done is fully expand on genre by showing the range and breadth of each. And since we learn from all movies, this isn't about the 50 "best," but the ones we can gain the most insight from. Along the way, I'll also point out some of the tricks the directors and writers used. And for those of you who haven't seen these films yet... WARNING: SPOILERS AHEAD!

SOME FINAL WORDS

In this book you will also see terms and phrases you might not be familiar with. If you haven't read the first *Save the Cat!* there is no need for you to feel left out:

Save the Cat! — Not only the title of this series, but a great principle of storytelling. When we meet the hero, he must do something that makes us like him. Save a cat and we will!

Stasis = Death — We know what Death means. Stasis = Things Staying the Same. It is the moment before the journey begins where we know the hero will "die" if his life doesn't change.

Stakes Are Raised — Also known as the "midpoint bump." Those events found at the middle of a movie that supply sudden pressure, new problems, or "bad news" for the hero(es).

The Pope in the Pool — A distracting way to bury exposition, so called for a scene in a script I know where the pope swims in the Vatican pool while boring plot details are told to us.

Booster Rocket – A character that appears for the first time toward the end of a movie and lifts it to its final push, e.g., John Candy in *Home Alone* or Will Ferrell in *Wedding Crashers*.

A Limp and an Eyepatch – When characters lack character, that thing which gives them a unique identifying quirk or habit.

Primal – My favorite word and a guiding force in good stories. To test if your story is so, ask: Would a caveman understand?

These terms and others will be used throughout our discussion. As in the first book, if there's anything that you want to comment on, or need clarification for, email me. My direct email address is the same as it was in the first book: *bsnyder264@aol.com*. You can also check my website at *www.blakesnyder.com*, and contact me at *blake@ blakesnyder.com*.

Please do. I really like to hear from you!

So if you're ready, let's imagine a movie theater. In my mind, whenever I think of the perfect place to see a film, I picture the Arlington on State Street in Santa Barbara, California, where I grew up. With a Spanish motif, like the rest of the town, the interior of that great old movie palace copies that of a classic hacienda: chalky adobe walls with purple shadows painted on them, topped by a rim of red-tile roofing as though you were in the middle of an open-air plaza. Overhead, the cavernous ceiling of the theater is covered by hundreds of pinlights that mimic stars. And like you and everyone who loves the adventure of storytelling, as the stars dim and the plush velvet curtains part, I scrunch down in my seat, and think:

This is gonna be good...

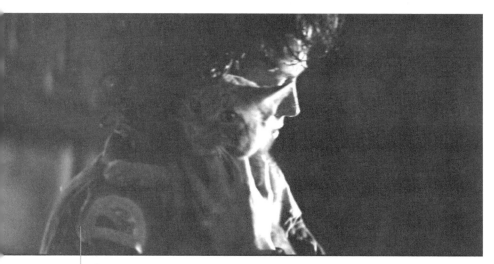

🐾 *In space no one can hear you meow! Sigourney Weaver "saves the cat" in the "Monster in the House" classic,* Alien.

1 MONSTER IN THE HOUSE

Welcome to the wonderful world of genre! What is genre? It's a grouping of stories that share similar patterns and characters. And "Monster in the House" is one of the oldest... and most primal.

It is also the first story type I ever discovered — or at least had pointed out to me. Like many of the insights in this book, the term came from a fellow scribe, in this case my friend and writing partner, Jim Haggin.

We were working on a script and taking a break, standing around the parking lot outside my Dad's office in Santa Barbara when Jim, smoking a Lucky Strike, idly said: "Did you know that *Alien* and *Jaws* are the same movie?"

This was amazing news. And like so much of what Jim knew about film, this little nugget made me stop and think. *Jaws* is the story of a killer shark, *Alien* is set on a starship somewhere in space. I didn't see the connection.

The illustrious Mr. Haggin went on. He said that both movies have a powerful creature intent on eating the cast, an enclosed community into which the beast is let loose to ply his trade, and a third element: sin. It is the sin of greed that lets the shark roam the shores of Amity, greed too that is at the bottom of why *The Nostromo* picks up its titular hitchhiker. In fact, Jim said, sin is what really makes all true "monster" movies work. It's one thing to get eaten, but to be lunch because of something *we* did adds guilt to horror — and the guilt makes it much more juicy.

Wow.

My adventure into finding story patterns had begun.

What I discovered with this genre, one Jim and I started calling "Monster in the House," was that filmmakers weren't just ripping off *Jaws*, but in fact had been stealing from a story type that went all the way back to the Minotaur and the maze, and the dragonslayer myths of the Middle Ages! We've been letting the monster in the house, or going to where the monster lives and invading his abode for centuries.

And yet there is always a way to tell a new version.

So how does this help *you*? You've got a great "monster" movie idea. Or maybe you've got a serial killer whose power comes from insanity, or an evil spirit haunting some kind of dwelling.

Are these Monster-in-the-House tales?

That's why we're here: to fit your ideas into established story forms and, by doing so, better see just what they are. To discover if yours is a true MITH, we should begin with the basics. As hinted at above, movies in the MITH genre have three main components: (1) a "monster," (2) a "house," and (3) a "sin."

Let's dig deeper into these.

When it comes to the "monster" found in every MITH tale, the common denominator is: supernatural power. Whether a "Pure Monster" like the supercharged beasts in *Jaws* and *Jurassic Park*, a "Domestic Monster" like the human kind found in *The Hand That Rocks the Cradle* and *Pacific Heights*, or a "Serial Monster" such as the knife-wielding baddies of many a "slasher" flick, supernatural power is a monster must-have. Look at *Jaws*. That shark isn't just a shark; it's a super-shark with an agenda beyond feeding. It's come for the one person, Chief Brody (Roy Scheider), who is afraid not only of sharks but of water. Thus, the Great White also represents what all good monsters must be... "evil."

There is a sense in many a MITH that what's at stake is not one's life but one's soul. This is why *The Exorcist* and films it begat, such as *Poltergeist* and *The Ring*, are so deeply frightening. At the heart of what I call "Supra-Natural Monster" movies — those starring a monster that represents forces beyond our three dimensions — is the sense that something more than daylight will be lost if we don't survive. This is also why lesser monsters, like the tiny spiders in *Arachnophobia*, or the ones that can be dispatched with a baseball bat in *Signs* or die of the sniffles in *War of the Worlds*, are so unsatisfying.

Lesser Monsters = Lesser Movies.

So what about the "house" we find these monsters in — why is that so important? Well, think about the myth of the Minotaur for a moment and realize that while facing a half-man/half-bull is frightening, more frightening is being trapped with one inside a dark maze. And whether it's an actual house, like the creepy hotel in *The Shining*, a deep-sea diving bell in *The Abyss*, or the basement prison Cary Elwes wakes up in *Saw*, the more cramped the space — the more isolated our heroes — the better.

In *Fatal Attraction*, the family unit is the "house" within which Michael Douglas is trapped. And considering the "monster" he created by his actions, this will be the perfect place to confront it. In films like *Scream*, where a serial monster stalks a whole town, it is the city limits that enclose the horror, and the community that locks its doors at night and becomes the "house" through which the monster roams. Still, isolated enclosures like the spaceship in *Alien* remind us that if there's a choice, lock 'em in. It's scarier knowing you're trapped and have nowhere to go!

As far as the "sin" is concerned, think about all those teen slasher movies in which "Michael Myers" and "Jason" run riot. "Have sex and die," says Jamie Kennedy, who lays out the rules in *Scream*, and speaks to why guilt about sin is important. Sex works in teen-targeted movies because it's new for them — and scary. For adults, "sins" like putting career over family, as Ellen Burstyn does in *The Exorcist* and Naomi Watts does in *The Ring*, or greed over ethics like in *Jaws*, when the town fathers of Amity keep the beaches open to protect their "summer dollars," or even in a dark comedy like *The Cable Guy* when Matthew Broderick tries to get free cable! — these hit a universal guilt button.

Remember: Without a sin of some kind, it's not a total MITH experience. Part of the scare is knowing that one thing the hero did wrong was answer the doorbell and say: "Come on in!"

And yet with the advent of what we'll call the "Nihilist Monster" story, influenced by the trend in Japanese horror films, and represented by a movie like *The Grudge*, there appear to be some MITH movies in which no sin is committed. Films in this category, like *Saw*, *American Psycho*, and *Cabin Fever*, have an otherworldly quality and characters that seem oblivious — but that's the point, for theirs is the sin of ignorance. The heroes of these films are like us, blithely going along when they are suddenly sucked into an evil world long disregarded — which now *must* be dealt with. And as a movie like *Saw* reveals, it's about finding what we did wrong fast — or risk having to hop away!

There are other fine points that go with many a MITH. A character that shows up in a lot of these films is one I call the **Half Man**. This is a survivor who has run into the monster before — or has prior knowledge of the evil — and come away damaged because of it. Robert Shaw as Quint is the Half Man in *Jaws*; Scatman Crothers is the Half Man in *The Shining*; and Ian Holm as Ash in *Alien* is not only Half Man but also half robot! From a practical screenwriting point of view, the Half Man allows us to reveal the myth of the monster — and give the hero a hint about what dealing with the monster entails. Many of these Half Man characters wind up dying at the "All Is Lost" moment on page 75 and are the "flawed mentors" of each story, warning us by their deaths... about the horror that awaits.

Isn't that Half Man thing cool?

If you are writing a Monster in the House story, you're probably itching to race to your computer and start figuring out how to put that character into *your* script.

Well, don't run off just yet.

What started with a buddy telling me about how two movies were the same inspired the first of our genres. But wait! There's a lot more cool stuff to come.

HOW TO TELL IF YOUR HIT IS A MITH!

If your script has these components (and if not, for God's sake try harder!), a MITH film festival is in your future:

1. A "monster," supernatural in its powers — even if its strength derives from insanity — and "evil" at its core.

2. A "house," meaning an enclosed space that can include a family unit, an entire town, or "the world."

3. A "sin." Someone is guilty of bringing the monster in the house... a transgression that can include ignorance.

The following breakdowns show the variety of Monster-in-the-House tales and the repeating elements all MITHs have.

ALIEN (1979)

I remember when this film premiered and even the slow appearance of the letters in the title sequence was eerie — and unforgettable. Many consider the sequel, *Aliens*, the superior film, but for me you can't beat director Ridley Scott — or this movie.

Alien is set on a spaceship named *The Nostromo*, a reference to the Joseph Conrad novel about greed. And greed is not good when it comes to monsters. Just look at other "Pure Monster" movies like *Jurassic Park* and *Jaws* to see how a lesson about that particular sin unfolds.

The "monster" is allowed into this isolated "house" after an argument between Sigourney Weaver as Ripley and a cyborg named Ash (Ian Holm). Sigourney will become the hero by stepping up to the challenge this mistake represents — and by growing. She'll go from someone who won't let John Hurt (and a pal) onboard without quarantine, to one who risks her life to save a cat.

It may take place in the future, but what we find in *Alien* is a story that's been re-told for centuries — one with an enclosed space, a beast that won't quit, and a group that realizes too late that life is short.

MITH Type: Pure Monster

MITH Cousins: *Jaws, Tremors, The Thing, Jurassic Park, Anaconda, Deep Blue Sea, Godzilla, Independence Day, Men in Black, Lake Placid*

ALIEN

Screenplay by Dan O'Bannon
Story by Dan O'Bannon & Ronald Shusett

Opening Image: A space cruiser rumbles through the void. Egg-like sleep chambers open and the crew stirs from a state of suspended animation. A computer named "Mother" has given birth to these early risers. There are seven members of the team; there will be a lot fewer by the end of the picture.

Theme Stated: The crew gathers around the breakfast table and amid the banter of camaraderie, Parker (Yaphet Kotto) turns to Kane (John Hurt) and says: "Anybody ever tell you that you look dead?" What is it to be alive — and human? That's our theme.

Set-Up: The world of The *Nostromo* is stratified; each person on-board represents a different class of this society. It is overseen by "Science Officer" Ash (Ian Holm) and a bearded Dallas (Tom Skerritt) as the sensitive '70s leader (aka alien food). And on the periphery, observing, is Ripley (Sigourney Weaver). She stands apart from the others, and is kind of a loner. By Minute 10 we've met everyone in the A story — and know exactly who they are! We also learn something is up with Tom. He goes to a little computer room only he as "the leader" can access. We don't see what it is, but Tom and "Mother" have a secret.

Catalyst: Tom tells the crew they're not "home" yet; they've been called to a strange planet by a distress signal. The underclass complains. But when they're informed that they'll lose their "shares" if they don't go on the rescue, they comply.

Debate: What is this thing the crew has been called to deal with? Sigourney begins to emerge as the "smart one." She investigates the signal and can't determine if it's an SOS or a warning to stay away. And yet, the less cautious members of the crew (i.e., the guy with the beard) press on and decide to land on the forbidden planet anyway.

Break into Two: When the crew disembarks to venture onto the weird world, we have broached the monster's lair. And when John Hurt sticks his face over a hatching alien egg in a cave on this alien planet, a strange beast gloms onto his space helmet. From here on all bets are off, and we are forced to make a new rule: Never stick your face over an alien egg in a cave on an alien planet. Agreed? By the time John is allowed back onboard — after an argument between Sigourney and Ian — we've entered Act Two.

B Story: The B story is usually the love story and is, kind of, in this film too. It is between Sigourney and Ian Holm. Their fight sets this "love story" into motion. And though they won't actually kiss, Ian will make an odd attempt to have "sex" with Sigourney. It is with this "Half Man" she will discuss the theme of being human — and grow as one.

Fun and Games: A classic example of "Fun and Games" is seen in the crew's interactions with the alien intruder. If the "Thesis" world of Act One is normal, the "Anti-thesis" world of Act Two is the "funhouse-mirror" version — all due to the title character: a strange-looking crab that plays "hide and seek" in the lab and bleeds acid that eats through the ship's hull. But when this monster drops off John's face and dies, John appears to be fine.

Midpoint: The "stakes are raised" at Minute 56 when, as the crew eats dinner, the creature explodes out of John's chest and skates away like a big, ugly baby — exactly at the place where Yaphet told John he "looked dead." Now he is. The "fun" is over. A and B stories cross as Sigourney looks to Ian for an explanation.

Bad Guys Close In: One by one the creature kills off the crew, and tension builds. I use the term **Turn, Turn, Turn** to describe how a movie plot must not only go forward, it must change and intensify to be successful — and the way the monster morphs throughout this film is a great example. The crew is always one step behind this supernatural beast, and the stress begins to show. Harry Dean gets it next, and then so does Tom in a really scary "Monster in the Air Duct" sequence. This beat, the male "hero" dying, was a surprise when the film premiered. Without "the leader," both the crew — and we in the audience — see how unstoppable the alien is.

All Is Lost: Finally in charge, Sigourney learns the truth from "Mother": The company knew the alien was a killer, but sent *The Nostromo* to retrieve it because of its value; the "sin" of the company is exposed. Sigourney also discovers Ian is a robot — and a sex-crazed one at that. He even claims to "admire" the alien, that rat! In a battle with Ian, Sigourney is rescued by Yaphet, who clubs the cyborg. The "whiff of death" includes A and B stories crossing as the Half Man tells Sigourney she won't survive.

Dark Night of the Soul: The crew knows they're going to die. Their despair is even greater thanks to their isolation.

Break into Three: But wait, there's hope! Sigourney has a plan: Destroy the ship and the alien, and flee in an escape pod.

Finale: Foolishly Yaphet and another crew member die, leaving Sigourney and Jones, the cat. Sigourney shows Act Three Synthesis by combining her "loner" qualities with wisdom to emerge as the hero. By going back to "save the cat," she proves she's grown — and even though she lets the monster slip into her escape pod unnoticed, she shows ultimate strength when she pushes it out the door to die.

Final Image: One survivor... plus cat... asleep at last.

FATAL ATTRACTION (1987)

Much has been written about the metaphor this STD-era movie represents, but one thing is certain: It's the best cautionary tale about fooling around at the office ever made.

That Glenn Close! She is one scary lady. And while the real bad guy is Michael Douglas for beginning this affair in the first place, the magic trick director Adrian Lyne pulls off is making Michael seem like a victim — because it is *his* sin, infidelity, that brings the monster to his door.

Fatal Attraction represents a special brand of MITH, the "Domestic Monster," as seen in films like *Single White Female* and *One Hour Photo*. Even comic versions of this tale, e.g., *The Cable Guy*, owe a great debt to *Fatal Attraction* — and to Glenn. It is Glenn Close's amazing performance — almost reasonable one minute, boiling bunnies the next — that lets the adulterous Michael off the hook, and makes even a ringing telephone seem scary.

The lesson for writers wishing to add to this branch of MITH movie is clear. One word: primal. From the protection of family, to the "sin" which risks his family's safety, to the pet Michael buys his little girl — a rabbit! — this is a tale about the risks and re-sponsibilities of sex, told in a way that would be clear even to a caveman.

MITH Type: Domestic Monster

MITH Cousins: *Play Misty for Me, The Hand That Rocks the Cradle, Pacific Heights, Poison Ivy, The Fan, Single White Female, The Crush, Swimfan, The Cable Guy, One Hour Photo*

FATAL ATTRACTION
Original Screenplay by James Dearden

Opening Image: Portrait of a happy family. Meet the Gallaghers — Dan (Michael Douglas) and, in the next room, his wife Beth (Anne Archer) and their androgynous child, Ellen (Ellen Latzen).

Theme Stated: Anne gets territorial when her daughter plays with her lipstick. "Ellen, I don't want you messing with my makeup. I told you a million times," Anne warns. Trespassing into places we don't belong will be the running theme.

Set-Up: A big city party for Michael's law firm where, if you look Close, you'll see Alex Forrest (Glenn Close) lurking near the hors d'oeuvres. Michael has it all — a stunning wife and sweet child, a good job, friends. Yet he flirts with Glenn.

Catalyst: Anne takes their daughter and leaves Michael for the weekend. Alone in the city due to a business meeting, Michael bumps into Glenn. Their flirtation can continue.

Debate: Can Michael be discreet? From the moment Michael agrees to have a glass of wine with Glenn, he has already strayed. I know this because I've asked women, one of whom, while watching this film, kept referring to Michael as "You bastard!" The name-calling begins with this innocent-seeming lunch. The debate question seems to argue trespassing is okay — if we're careful. Can two adults have a no-fault affair? For a time, as they lock hips in the elevator of Glenn's edge-o'-hell building and against the sink in her messy kitchen, the answer seems to be: maybe.

Break into Two: Michael returns home after catting around, manages a "make nice" call to Anne in the country, and all seems swell... until the phone rings. Glenn has his home number. When he agrees to meet her again, Michael plunges into the "upside-down world" of Act Two and an affair that is now a relationship.

B Story: The B story is the secret "love story" between Glenn and Michael. And though it isn't love, Michael will get the lesson of a lifetime and learn he really did have it all. By frolicking in the park with Glenn, and later at her place listening to opera, he opens himself up to her. We also learn of a possible root cause of Glenn's fanatical clinging — the sudden death of her father when she was a girl. Does Glenn have abandonment issues or is she just nuttier than a Hickory Farms Pecan Sampler?

Fun and Games: In this tense Fun and Games section, the "promise of the premise" shows what happens when being discreet begins to unravel. And yet for now, Michael is still in control. Sure Glenn cuts her wrists to make Michael stay the night with her. Yeah, she shows up at his job unexpectedly with tickets to *Madame Butterfly*. But so far it's more like a bad date. This is why we signed up to see this movie, to squirm uncomfortably in our seats thinking: "I better call that girl in Accounting and tell her I was kidding when I said we should have coffee sometime."

Midpoint: The "bad date" scenario ends, and the A and B stories cross, when Glenn announces she's pregnant. This news "raises the stakes" and is a great example of an alarming "midpoint bump." Michael is officially in over his head DNA-wise; the consequences of spreading his seed hits home. And while he handles this news with "compassion," offering to pay for the abortion — what a guy! — this is not how Glenn wants to handle the situation.

Bad Guys Close In: Now the "Fun and Games" of a date gone wrong get serious. Both at home with his internal "team" of wife and daughter, and externally, as Michael learns of the "Half Man" in his office (who had an affair and paid the price), the amping up of the trespassing by Glenn gets scarier — and the vice that has Michael in its grip begins to tighten. Posing as a buyer for the home Michael's now trying to sell, Glenn shows up while he's out, and later throws acid on his car. Even at work, Michael's promotion is jeopardized by his stalker.

All Is Lost: The tension finally explodes when Glenn follows Michael to his new home, kills his daughter's bunny, and plops it in a pot of boiling water for Anne to find. (Talk about "whiff of death"!) Symbolically, Glenn is leaving Anne a message: Guess what, the rabbit died — the old school way of proving a pregnancy.

Dark Night of the Soul: With his wife and daughter traumatized by this event, Michael must now admit his sin. He's been putting it off, but this is how he will cleanse himself.

Break into Three: Michael confesses. Anne's reaction to Michael's pitiful tale is reasonable until he tells her Glenn's pregnant — possibly with his baby. The invasion of their home now includes child support. With Anne's back-up, Michael gets on the phone and warns Glenn that his wife knows and she is to stay away.

Finale: But she can't. After kidnapping his daughter and causing his wife to get in an auto accident, Glenn is attacked by Michael in her cave as A and B stories cross for the last time. It's a violent reprise of their earlier sex scene. Then, in one of the great film finishes, a knife-welding Glenn invades Anne and Michael's country home and, in a moment of Synthesis, the couple works together to fight back. But it's Anne who kills the intruder. Glenn was "messing" where she didn't belong.

Final Image: As Michael and Anne bid goodbye to the police, we linger on a photo of Michael, Anne, and daughter — and we know things have changed. The monster is dead! Let the therapy begin!

SCREAM (1996)

Ah, the "dead teenager" movie. Where would our chat about monster flicks be without it? The squirmy, uncertain, acne-plagued years are the perfect time of life to thrust a knife-wielding killer. But by the early '90s, the "dead teenager" movie was day-old toast. "Jason" and "Michael Meyers" were on hiatus and Wes Craven, who would go on to direct *Scream*, was too. Then in a single weekend — or so the apocryphal story goes — Kevin Williamson sat down and wrote the spec screenplay he titled *Scary Movie*, and the teen slasher flick was re-born — tongue firmly planted in cheek.

Movies like *Scream*, and others starring teenagers, are bald in their intent — and aimed about as pointedly as one can at the target market. They are part of a larger category called "Serial Monster," stories starring a human fiend made hyper-powerful by insanity and preying on the citizens of an entire town or group with a common bond or secret (*I Know What You Did Last Summer*). Whatever prompts these monsters to kill — like the twisted form of revenge it is here — is fueled by evil. Though the "Half Man," Jamie Kennedy, won't be knocked off until *Scream 2*, he *sorta* dies in this film — and just where he's supposed to! And his function remains the same: Tell the rules of what it takes for teenagers to survive when a monster is in the house.

MITH Type: Serial Monster

MITH Cousins: *Psycho, Prom Night, Halloween, Texas Chainsaw Massacre, Friday the 13th, I Know What You Did Last Summer, Urban Legend, Red Dragon, Hannibal, Hostel*

SCREAM
Written by Kevin Williamson

Opening Image: A ringing phone. An isolated house. A buxom Drew Barrymore making popcorn. Like the starting point of many a teen horror movie, this initial image is ripe with clichés.

Theme Stated: The caller asks Drew a key question: "Do you like scary movies?" Scary movies, like those they discuss, are the thematic basis of this film.

Set-Up: The "sin" Drew commits is denying she has a boyfriend so she can flirt with her mystery caller. The punishment is death. Both her jock boyfriend and Drew are sliced up like honey-baked hams by someone in a ghost mask and a black hood, and left for Drew's parents to find. This 12-minute sequence "sets the table" for what follows. We next meet our heroine, the virginal Sidney Prescott (Neve Campbell) who, with her single Dad, is getting over the murder of Sidney's Mom one year ago. Neve is joined in her room by the killer (I warned ya!), Billy Loomis (Skeet Ulrich). But for now he's just her James Dean-lite boyfriend who wants to take their relationship from PG to R.

Catalyst: Next day at school, Neve and gal pal Tatum Riley (Rose McGowan) learn of the murder the night before. TV News babe Gale Weathers (Courteney Cox) is on hand with Deputy "Dewey" Riley (David Arquette). The school is shocked by Drew's death and Neve is even questioned by Principal Himbry (Henry Winkler).

Debate: Neve and Rose have a coterie of ADD boyfriends, including Randy Meeks (Jamie Kennedy) — the video store clerk who's seen every scary movie ever made, Stuart Macher (Matthew Lillard), and Skeet. Their debate is who the likely murderer is. Principal Himbry has warned the students to walk in twos and threes for safety, but when Neve is dropped off at her house — where she'll be alone since Dad left (!) — she decides to take a nap. The TV reports are now telling about the anniversary of her Mother's murder and the man Neve fingered as the killer (Liev Schreiber). Maybe last night's murder and her Mom's are related?

Break into Two: At Minute 25, the mysterious caller wakes Neve, drawing her into the "upside-down world" of Act Two. Neve is cool at first. Not knowing the method of the previous night's murder, she assumes it's Jamie playing a joke — but soon discovers this is no laughing matter. When the ghost-masked killer appears, knife in hand, Neve does what she says only dumb girls in these movies do: Run up the stairs instead of sprinting out the front door. Neve is "saved" by Skeet, who pops in her window claiming he heard the ruckus. Neve fears Skeet (smart girl!) as Deputy David arrives to arrest him. This is a world in which Neve can trust no one.

B Story: The "love" story concerns Neve and her dead Mom, and is spurred on by the terrier-like Courteney. As the current murder and her Mom's entwine, Neve will learn about Mom — and herself.

Fun and Games: With the whole town aware that Neve is the prime target of the killer, she is both star and pariah. Did Neve send the wrong guy to jail? Neve crosses paths with Courteney who, ever the info-ette, wants an exclusive. Neve refuses, and even slugs her. But the question remains: Is her Mom's murderer still out there? The ghost-mask slasher shows up again along with icons of scary movies past, including Linda Blair (star of *The Exorcist*) and a janitor (Craven) who looks like Freddy from *A Nightmare on Elm Street*. We get some real danger as Neve eludes the killer in the bathroom at school — and a few red herrings, including teens dressed like the slasher, and even Henry Winkler — who goes a little over the top in the Emoting Department.

Midpoint: The Fun and Games culminate with the death of the overacting Mr. Winkler — and just in time! Cornered in his office, the principal is stabbed by the real ghost-masked killer, which definitely "raises the stakes" of this mystery — not to mention knock one more person off the suspect list. Meanwhile at the video store, Jamie tells us the score, saying to both Skeet and Matthew (ironically enough) that at this point in these movies everyone's a suspect. The kids decide to do what teens in all horror films do: Even with a killer loose who targets their demographic, they will lock themselves in a house and party!

Bad Guys Close In: The "house" is sealed tight, a curfew imposed, and the kids gather for a beer bash while suspects circle in our minds. Chief on the list is Neve's Dad, who's missing. Courteney and her cameraman close in on the story — and on Deputy David, for whom she has the hots. First offed at the party is Rose when she goes for beer. Tension mounts as the killer closes in.

All Is Lost: Neve agrees to have sex with Skeet, a "whiff of death" that includes the death of her innocence. When news comes that Principal Himbry is dead, the kids leave to check it out.

Dark Night of the Soul: The house is abandoned and Neve is alone.

Break into Three: By choosing to break the "have sex and die" rule of these movies, Neve now brings Synthesis to both her story and her Mother's, and enters the monster's secret world.

Finale: Matthew and Skeet reveal themselves as the killers, seeking revenge against both Neve and her Mom, whose "hidden sin" of sleeping with Skeet's father ruined Skeet's life. The twin killers' supercharged powers come not just from insanity, but from being able to be in two places at once. A and B stories cross as Neve and Courteney work together to kill the killers.

Final Image: Courteney wraps up the tale of Neve's Mom and the recent murders, saying: "It's like something out of a scary movie," which brings this postmodern thriller full circle.

THE RING (2002)

Here is a tale seemingly about modern technology and the evils of watching too much TV, but the success of *The Ring* is due to its being grounded in a more primal concern. Much like in *The Exorcist*, from which this film inherits many similarities, career woman Naomi Watts will go from self-involved single mother to one who wants to save her child above all else. The responsibility of parenthood is what this particular MITH tale is about. And its lesson is one Naomi will learn from a video ghost — also a mother — who is the dark mirror image of herself.

Based on the novel, *Ringu*, by Koji Suzuki, and the Japanese film directed by Hiroshi Takahashi, director Gore Verbinski's version is superbly structured. It's an example of MITH I call the "Supra-natural Monster" which, to me, is the most frightening — no matter in what form it comes. Be it devil (*The Exorcist*), ghost (*What Lies Beneath*), or what occurs when we mess with the comforts of sanity (*Gothika*), these monsters can strike anywhere, haunt our dreams, and alter our world until we can't tell what's real — and what isn't.

This classification of MITH movie is the most disturbing because it deals directly with a "sin" of a past life or another dimension, and made more serious by the fear of losing our souls.

MITH Type: Supra-natural Monster

MITH Cousins: *The Exorcist, The Legend of Hell House, The Shining, Poltergeist, Amityville Horror, A Nightmare on Elm Street, Child's Play, What Lies Beneath, House on Haunted Hill, The Exorcism of Emily Rose*

THE RING

Screenplay by Ehren Kruger
Based on the novel RINGU by Koji Suzuki
and the film RINGU by Hiroshi Takahashi

Opening Image: A house in the 'burbs. Inside, a familiar Friday night scene: Two teenage girls are watching videos.

Theme Stated: "I hate television," says one girl. (Don't we all?) TV and its use by parents as a babysitter give a hint as to what the movie is about: the responsibilities of parenthood.

Set-Up: We hear the legend of the videotape that kills you. You watch it, the phone rings, then seven days later you die. One of the girls announces that she viewed the killer VHS a week ago. Tonight her time is up, and lo! She dies just as foretold. We next meet our heroine in a perfect intro scene. Enter bitching while on her cell phone, busy reporter Rachel Keller (Naomi Watts) arrives late to pick up son Aidan (David Dorfman) from daycare. Yes, Naomi wins the coveted Bad Mother Award. But she will do a 180 thanks to this tale. Deep down she's aware of her "sin," and only by re-embracing her love for her child will she save him and herself.

Catalyst: Turns out this dead teenager is Naomi's niece and little David's favorite relative. Naomi, being a reporter and all, is asked to look into this mysterious death. She soon discovers it has something to do with a spooky VHS.

Debate: Is it true? Is it possible that the supra-natural deaths of several teens are linked to a videotape? Naomi hears about a motel the teens visited the week before they died. She checks in, steals the tape from the "Seven Day Rental" section in the front office, and goes to cabin #12 (for those of you who like numerology). Should Naomi look at the tape? Hint: If she doesn't, there is no plot!

Break into Two: Naomi, and we, now see the weird videotape everyone is talking about. On it are various scary images, some the most disturbing since the brainwash scene in *The Parallax View*. Then the phone rings. Naomi has officially entered the Dark World. She has exactly seven days to live.

B Story: A partial answer to why Naomi is a single parent is offered when we meet her child's father, Noah Clay (Martin Henderson). In need of a shave — and a nicer apartment — Martin mostly needs to "grow up." Being a videographer, he can help explain the tape. Martin watches it, blithely ignoring the warning. Now Naomi and Martin are linked as more than parents.

Fun and Games: Separately, Naomi and Martin look into the tape and discover its bizarre properties. The "fun" includes being able to pluck a fly out of the picture while watching it. We learn about the girl on the tape — that her mother died mysteriously, and that a lemming-like plunge by some prize thoroughbreds at their farm once made headlines. Naomi is also beginning to experience bloody noses and an image-bending effect when someone takes her photo. The curse of watching the tape is turning real, yet this adventure is still in its discovery phase.

Midpoint: The "stakes are raised" when Naomi's son watches the tape. Now he too is at risk. Though the kid has special powers, apparently his skills were on "PAUSE" when he popped the tape in. Naomi discovers her son did this as A and B stories cross: Martin calls to say photos of him turned weird — he is cursed as well.

Bad Guys Close In: An actual ticking clock is heard as Naomi and Martin bid goodbye to David and hit the road to continue their investigation. Time is running out. The two learn more about the little girl responsible for the spooky VHS. In addition to a bad case of split ends, she could project bizarre images from her brain onto videotapes and photographs. Her parents committed her to an asylum and we feel sorry for her — even sorrier for Naomi, who is beginning to have the same effect on horses the girl had.

All Is Lost: Naomi confronts a member of the family at the farm where the girl was raised. The Dad, Richard Morgan (Brian Cox), may have survived physically but is warped by the experience with his psychically powerful daughter. This "Half Man" realizes the curse won't end and kills himself by electrocution in a bathtub (water is another motif). All hope dead, Naomi appears to be out of luck. No one is left to help her solve the mystery.

Dark Night of the Soul: Naomi and Martin find the room in the barn where Brian and his wife kept the little girl. The decor includes every parent's favorite pacifier: a TV set.

Break into Three: Martin sees something hidden behind the wallpaper of the little girl's room: a clue! Thus, A and B stories intersect once more and propel us into Act Three.

Finale: The clue leads the pair back to cabin #12. It's the place the teens first watched the video. Naomi and Martin realize the cabin sits atop an old well where the "sin" was committed — the girl was dropped in to die. They uncover the well and Naomi promptly falls in. Naomi is reunited with the girl's spectral self and the curse ends. The girl's body is given proper burial. But the curse is not over. David realizes the joke's on Mom: The girl is evil and Naomi released her! Unaware of this, Martin meets his end when the girl crawls out of his TV and attacks him. Naomi finds Martin's body.

Final Image: The only way to break the curse is to pass it on. Naomi makes copies of the VHS to save herself and her son. This guarantees not only their safety — but a sequel!

SAW (2004)

Who says you can't make a hit movie for $500,000? That's report-edly the cost of this James Wan-directed indie, the first in this franchise. The film proves that when creativity is in play, financial restriction can be as much an inspiration as a handicap. Beyond the producer's delight at having to pay for only one set — and the bonus of putting the co-screenwriter (Leigh Whanell) to work as the co-star — at core you still need a story. It must be one that resonates for a jaded horror audience that has seen it all, and needs a reason beyond "have sex and die" as the "sin" that scares. How can you shock the unshockable? How can you use sin as a means to terrify in a world where sin is relative?

You create the "Nihilist Monster."

You create Jigsaw.

Jigsaw seeks out his victims who have no awareness of what they've done to deserve their fate, and pits one against another in games of life and death. Few survive to tell the tale of what they learned, but by the end each is highly aware of why they were chosen. When Cary Elwes comes to in his basement prison wondering not only how he got there, but *why*, he begins to review his life looking for what he did wrong. Is he a bad father, a bad husband, a bad doctor? We soon discover we have more in common with Cary than we think. We too have to examine our lives, 'cause if we don't, Jigsaw will!

MITH category: Nihilist Monster

MITH cousins: *Peeping Tom*, *American Psycho*, *Cabin Fever*, *Audition*, *The Others*, *Lost Highway*, *The Village*, *The Grudge*, *Identity*, *The Host*

SAW

Written by Leigh Whannell
Story by James Wan *and* Leigh Whannell

Opening Image: As lights come up, we are in the monster's "house" — the basement prison that will be our setting. Lawrence Gordon (Cary Elwes) and another man, Adam (screenwriter Leigh Whannell), are in a bad situation. Each is chained by the leg in an opposite corner. Lying between them — a body. Great start!

Theme Stated: Cary says: "We need to start thinking about why we're here." Cary's on to the "Nihilist Monster" theme: the sin of ignorance, and an even bigger theme: Why are we here, in this life?

Set-Up: Cary, a doctor, introduces himself to his cellmate. Neither recognizes the "dead" man. They note the clock on the wall and a tape recorder. Working together, they snag it and push "PLAY." Meet the third component, the voice of "Jigsaw," a killer who plays games with his victims and turns one against the other.

Catalyst: At Minute 12, the puzzle that sets this dance with death into motion is presented to Cary. He has till six on the clock to kill Leigh, or his wife and kid will die.

Debate: So what should Cary and Leigh do? They notice they've each been given a hacksaw, the idea being that there is one way out of this: They each could saw off a foot and escape... but you'd have to be crazy to do that, right? At Minute 16, Cary adds a piece of the puzzle: "I think I know who's done this to us." In a flashback, we see a series of headlines about the Jigsaw killer and the murders he committed. All are deadly games where the victim is given a "lady or the tiger" choice. We also see Cary interact with an odd custodian at his hospital — "Zep" (Michael Emerson), who will figure into the ending. When Cary's fingerprints are connected to the murder, at Minute 22, he becomes a suspect. The cop investigating is Detective David Tapp (Danny Glover).

Break into Two: Back in the basement at Minute 29, both men know what the killer is after. This is about "sin," and figuring out theirs will be how they solve the mystery and survive. Cary says: "I've been thinking about the last thing I said to my daughter." In further flashbacks (a technique which, given the set-up, leaves the filmmakers no other choice), Cary does not seem to be a great Dad... but he's not horrible either. Is *this* his sin? When Cary plays "This Little Piggy" with his daughter, it foreshadows what will happen to his own little footie.

Fun and Games: The "promise of the premise" starts to unfold. This is a game and they follow the clues that have been left for them. Back in the basement, Leigh asks to see a photo of Cary's family and Cary tosses his wallet to him. Inside the wallet is a photo of Cary's wife (Monica Potter) and child, bound and gagged, but Leigh keeps this info to himself. In flashback we see what happened: A stranger who was hiding in Cary's house kidnaps his daughter and Monica. We also see someone observing this event — it's Danny Glover!

B Story: Danny is the cop who tracked down Cary and suspects him. The B story is how Danny becomes the damaged and obsessed "Half Man" of this saga. In yet another flashback, Danny and his partner (Ken Leung) discover Jigsaw's lair. There, they find a scale model of the basement Cary and Leigh are in — and another victim. The cops get the drop on Jigsaw, but he gets away, slashing Danny's throat and killing the others.

Midpoint: The "stakes are raised" at 1 Hour when Cary begins to suspect Leigh. And when Leigh shows Cary the photos of his kidnapped wife, the urgency to escape intensifies. Cary begins his slide to insanity; he realizes the "time clock" isn't just about *his* life but his family's. He's still got to figure out "why he's here."

Bad Guys Close In: Cary tries to get clever and trick the man who is observing them through a closed-circuit monitor. He pretends to "kill" Leigh by poisoning him, but Jigsaw isn't buying and electrocutes the screenwriter/actor. Stunned but alive, Leigh reveals he knows a lot more. He is a photographer, assigned to catch Cary in the act of adultery. We now replay the events of the night before and see that Cary was about to meet an assignation at a sleazy motel. *A-ha!* Finally his sin will be revealed! But at the last minute, Cary changes his mind. This sequence also explains Leigh's connection to the mystery: Danny hired Leigh to spy on Cary.

All Is Lost: Cary knows what his "sin" is: not appreciating his life. But it looks like it's too late to change his ways.

Dark Night of the Soul: Cary laments his mistakes: "How did I get here? I had everything in order."

Break into Three: Suddenly Cary has an idea about who's behind all this: Zep, the custodian at the hospital. When the phone rings and Cary speaks to his desperate wife and daughter, he knows he must save them. His insanity grows when he hears gunshots. A and B stories cross as Danny catches the "kidnapper," but Zep gets away — and Danny pursues.

Finale: As a frantic and very bizarre climax unfolds, we see Zep is not the killer, but a victim — and just a part of the game, assigned by Jigsaw to kill Cary's family in order to live. Danny is killed. So is Zep. And, completely insane, Cary begins to saw off his own foot to save his family. By the time he hobbles away, only Leigh is left. But the filmmakers have a last surprise.

Final Image: The "dead" man on the floor isn't. The "monster" is alive, and as Leigh watches, Jigsaw rises to go. "Game over," he says, closing the door and entombing Leigh in his "house" forever.

 Tom Hanks and company go "on the road" in Saving Private Ryan. *And just like the story of Jason and the Argonauts, it's not about the "Golden Fleece" — it's how those who go on the journey are transformed.*

2 GOLDEN FLEECE

Talk to any cavemen about what tale they'd like to hear around the ol' campfire and three out of five Neanderthals agree: More road stories!

There's something about recounting what occurs when we leave home to go foraging for food — or look for a better cave. What happens "out there" fires our imaginations, and gives us pointers about what to expect. The bottom line of what makes up the story type I call the "Golden Fleece" is this truism: It's not the destination that matters... it's what we learn about ourselves along the way.

The term "Golden Fleece" comes from the Greek myth about Jason and the Argonauts. In that tale, the fleece is the thing Jason has been sent to retrieve in order to become king. To do so, Jason collects a team, including Hercules — the Vin Diesel of his era — and off they go, leading to many adventures until Jason finally confronts himself and gets his reward. The "Fleece" is the object of the hunt, the goal of the journey, and like many stories in this genre largely a "McGuffin," a thing that sets the quest into motion, but has less meaning once achieved. And it's an oft-told tale. From Greek myth we get not only the story of Jason, but also Homer's *Odyssey*; from Chaucer, the *Canterbury Tales*; and from modern literature, James Joyce's *Ulysses* and William Faulkner's *As I Lay Dying*. This story tradition has carried over to movies, of course, and includes some journeys that may surprise you.

Whenever we screenwriters pitch a "road picture," that story almost always falls into the GF category, but there are many types. A "Buddy Fleece" is often lighter in tone and includes *Planes, Trains and Automobiles*; *Road Trip*; and *Little Miss Sunshine*; while the "Epic

Fleece" is more like its Greek antecedent, as *Saving Private Ryan* and *Star Wars* show. There is also the "Solo Fleece," where a single participant goes on the trip, as seen in *About Schmidt* and *Garden State*, and some biographical films where the road that is one's life reveals the risk and reward of the passage, e.g., *Capote* and *Ray*.

And since there's gold in that-there Golden Fleece, this category also includes "Sports Fleece" movies like *The Bad News Bears*, *Hoosiers*, and *Slap Shot* — where the gold is a trophy, and the "Caper Fleece" like *Ocean's Eleven* — where the gold is an actual treasure kept in a locked room. In these, the team is a variety pack of oddballs who have characteristics the leader lacks, but needs to be whole, and to win.

What's great about a Golden Fleece is the adventure of being away from home, the lift of participating in a team effort with meaning beyond just us. And what a good time at the movies when it's done well!

Like Monster in the House, a Golden Fleece is about three essentials: (1) a "road," (2) a "team," and (3) a "prize."

So let's go "on the road" and take a look.

The "road" is that thing we venture out onto, going away from home and perhaps coming back, but it need not be actual blacktop. It can also be metaphor. The road can be someone's life, a trip across oceans or across the street — so long as the meaning of that journey is life-changing. And as *The Lord of the Rings* and *Three Kings* prove, the road can cross whole universes, planetary systems, war zones, and dimensions of time and space.

The test of whether or not you are writing a Golden Fleece comes when you ask: Are my heroes going somewhere definite, and can I chart their journey? That demarcation can be seen in the rungs up the ladder of a "Sports Fleece," for instance. Think of that stock shot in *Major League* as the Cleveland Indians climb out of the cellar, or in *Dodgeball: A True Underdog Story* when Vince Vaughn's team of Average Joes start knocking off the competition — you can see that whatever path the heroes of these tales are on, these notches let us know how they're progressing on the way to the prize. Whether the road is large, small, or imaginary, it's how the heroes of these tales grow that makes the trip worth taking.

As far as the "team" goes, especially in a "Buddy Fleece" movie like *Planes, Trains and Automobiles*, the story is often about friendship, and whom one picks as one's teammate(s) — or has thrust upon him — is almost as important as the prize itself, whether it's one buddy or a lot of them. The hero in a typical Fleece is an underdog, or iconoclast, and his team often represents other qualities such as "heart" or "brains" or "soul" that will be integrated into the hero's character by the end.

The hero is the centrifugal center of the team, and often the "dull" one. Of all the characters in filmdom, isn't Luke Skywalker the dullest? But that's why he needs to be surrounded by Han Solo, a walking shag rug named Chewbacca, and a couple of snarky droids — each with his own unique voice. Luke shares with Jason the thing that makes him a hero: He is *us* on our best, Type-A day — eager, bright-eyed, and plain as vanilla.

In films with larger teams, the introduction of each member can incorporate a goodly chunk of the set-up and a brilliant entrance for each individual is almost required. Masterful versions of this can be seen in heist films like *The Hot Rock* and *Ocean's Eleven*, in which we establish character and skill set with amazing economy. And check out *Dodgeball* for the comic version of how to intro a team, each with a unique "Limp and Eyepatch" — and in the case of the "Steve the Pirate" character of that film, an actual eyepatch!

When we get to the end of the road, the "prize" doesn't have to be an actual thing to qualify — and your heroes may not even win it! The "Caper Fleece" includes prison sagas like *Papillon* and *Escape from Alcatraz* where the prize is freedom. And even when the prize is money — as in most heist movies — the good ones are those in which there is a primal reason for taking it: revenge, love, or in the case of *Ocean's Eleven*, manhood.

Yet when it comes to winning, there's often a monkey wrench. The **road apple** pops up in a lot of GFs, and is defined as that thing that kyboshes the plan just when victory is in sight, as when Tom Hanks' team rescues Private Ryan — who promptly says "no thanks," and Walter Matthau realizes his "Bad News Bears" can never win. Part of what makes a GF work is our heroes learning that the gold they seek doesn't even matter, and pales in comparison to the real gold of friendship. Just like in *Rocky*, starring my close personal friend Sylvester Stallone, Rocky Balboa need not beat Apollo Creed to learn who his friends are — and it's certainly a great way to set up *Rocky 2*!

If you are assaying a true road picture, however, keep in mind that these are not as easy to write as you might think. Just sending someone out on the road and assuming the adventure will be great is why I read so many bad "lesbians cross America in a car" scripts (that, sadly, all end up winning Honorable Mention at Sundance). The trick of any story where we send our heroes on the road to find something is making each stop along the way count. Each signpost must have a reason, really mean something, and can't just be included because it's "funny" or you've always wanted to shoot a scene that takes place at the site of the World's Biggest Ball of String in Yuma, Arizona. Nope. That may be interesting eye candy, but it really has to have a point to be included.

The journey story is one of the oldest we have in our quiver, but one of the hardest to do well. So take note of what the good ones do right.

And do likewise.

IS YOUR GOLDEN IDEA A GOLDEN FLEECE?

If your screenplay shares any of the following (and I bet it does!), then these are the telltale signs you've got an itch for the broad highway — and a passel of GF movies to watch:

1. A "road" spanning oceans, time, or across the street — so long as it demarcates growth. It often includes a "road apple" that stops the trip cold.

2. A "team" or a buddy the hero needs to guide him along the way. Usually, it's those who represent the things the hero doesn't have: skill, experience, or attitude.

3. A "prize" that's sought and is something primal: going home, securing a treasure, or re-gaining a birthright.

The Golden Fleece tale reveals the amazing range of the genre, each with a unique goal, hero, lesson — and a host of meaningful pit stops!

THE BAD NEWS BEARS (1976)

Some movies are icons. *Die Hard* is one. *Jaws* another. And *The Bad News Bears* certainly qualifies. Not only is it a great example of the "Sports Fleece," it spawned a series of movies that can be pitched with the phrase: "It's *Bad News Bears* with _____" in which the blank can be any sport (e.g., hockey in *The Mighty Ducks*, bobsledding in *Cool Runnings*). Of many "Sports Fleece" films that show a quest for athletic gold, *The Bad News Bears* is the champ.

As this story's down-and-out Jason, an ex-Greek hero with sciatica and a hangover, Walter Matthau is superb; it is to my mind one of his better roles in a long, distinguished career. And with the Bears, that foul-mouthed group of pint-sized Argonauts, director Michael Ritchie treats us to some of the finest sketches of pre-teen suburban dysfunction ever put on film.

To compete for the Little League trophy, Walter and the gang must fight over-involved parents, small minds, and big time Cyclopes, including Vic Morrow as the opposing coach — whom I *still* have nightmares about! And yet the quest these no-names are on is as noble and real as any ancient mythmaker ever put to papyrus: the search for dignity. In the end, the Bears will learn it's not the trophy, it's the journey that makes us heroes. Walter and his peewee players will discover that love and friendship of the team trumps gold every time.

GF Type: Sports Fleece

GF Cousins: *The Longest Yard, Slap Shot, Rocky, Major League, Hoosiers, A League of Their Own, Cool Runnings, The Mighty Ducks, Remember the Titans, Dodgeball: A True Underdog Story*

THE BAD NEWS BEARS
Screenplay by Bill Lancaster

Opening Image: A baseball field watered in preparation for the new season. Morris Buttermaker (Walter Matthau) arrives in a beat-up Cadillac. Walter looks tired; he grabs a beer and spikes it with something stronger, as Kelly Leak (Jackie Earle Haley) watches. Jackie Earle will be key later, but for now he's a stranger who lights Walter's cigar. A child shall lead them — or at least have a handy Zippo.

Theme Stated: Walter meets with the parent hiring him to coach the team. A politician, the man says: "I think we're doing a really fine thing." Are we? We'll find out.

Set-Up: The team Walter is guiding has sued to be included. As their coach, Walter gets the brunt of the disdain from the parents who run the league. Of these, Roy Turner (Vic Morrow) is the draconian Yankees' head, and Joyce Van Patten is the power-mad "Cleveland." Walter is tossed the rule book and meets his team. They are a collection of misfits, each with a peculiar "Limp and Eyepatch," each less talented than the last — and each with an unusual "skill" Walter doesn't have. Tanner is "the mouth" whose racial epithets are hair-curling; Engleberg is "the gut" who can't stop eating; Ogilvie is "the brain" who knows baseball statistics but can't play for beans; and Lupus is "the heart" who — though a "booger-eating spaz" according to Tanner — will be worth protecting.

Catalyst: The season starts. At the league kickoff dinner at the local Pizza Hut, Walter is told he better get on the stick. He needs to get the kids' uniforms. Walter rues the day he agreed to take the job, but now it's too late to turn back.

Debate: Or is it? Walter half-heartedly "coaches" the team, but mostly he drinks and has the boys cleaning pools for him. On opening day the results are clear: The Bears' game against the

Yankees is a disaster. Yankees' coach Vic emerges as the bad guy — and dark opposite of Walter. In the overall scheme of things, it's just a game, but the tragic look on Walter's face while the Bears are embarrassed reveals more. As a metaphor for his life, the loss is a reflection of longtime failure. The humiliation is so bad, one of his team, a Hank Aaron wannabe, Ahmad, runs off the field, strips out of his uniform, and climbs a tall tree (ironically, the exact same reaction I had the day *Stop! Or My Mom Will Shoot* came out).

Break into Two: In the aftermath of the game, Walter realizes what he's done, but does he have the guts to take responsibility? He's given an out when he's "fired," but he won't give up. This "quitting thing" is a hard habit to break, he tells the boys, then yells at them. Walter is coming alive.

B Story: We meet Amanda Whurlitzer (Tatum O'Neal). The long-lost girl phenom with the great curve ball is selling maps to the star's homes. She is the daughter of a woman Walter used to date and clearly hurt by his departure. Whiskey-voiced Tatum is poised between childhood and young ladyhood, but Walter needs her, and offers Tatum a bribe to get her to join the boys.

Fun and Games: As the quest unfolds, we see how difficult the Bears' challenge will be. The "fun" is in watching them come together as a team. If there were ever underdogs worth rooting for, these are them. They become the "Bad News Bears." As Tatum joins the misfits, the "upside-down version of the world" now includes girls. And when Walter recruits Jackie Earle, we know they're going to get somewhere. He may be a juvenile delinquent, but he's the best athlete in town. The team bonds further when Lupus is bullied and Tanner defends him. Being a Bear, even if a "booger-eating spaz," now trumps everything. The Bears start to show promise; the "road" is now open and the "prize" may be attainable.

Midpoint: At Minute 58 the Bears win their first game, but it is a "false victory" that keeps getting falser. Will they become soulless weenies like the Yankees? The possibility exists, especially as Walter's relationship with his charges becomes colder in the guise of being "professional." When a player gets hurt, Walter is less concerned with the kid and more concerned with beating Vic. Walter has peaked and the "fun" has turned serious.

Bad Guys Close In: Walter has caught Little League fever and wants victory no matter what. He tells Jackie Earle to handle the ball — even if it means cutting out the other players.

All Is Lost: On the eve of the championship, Tatum begs Walter to have dinner with her and her mother after the game. Walter gets angry. He throws beer at Tatum and she cries.

Dark Night of the Soul: The result of going for gold is a "road apple": Jackie Earle is ostracized by his teammates, and Tatum's pitching arm is hurt.

Break into Three: After arguing, the Bears decide to play anyway.

Finale: The final game is a bookend of the first. Egged on by Vic, Walter wants to win at any cost. Having learned the Little League way, Walter has become one of them — and it isn't pretty. But when Vic slaps his own son during a tense moment of the game, the truth of "doing a really fine thing" becomes apparent. Walter goes back to the old way, letting all the Bears play. Despite this, fate almost smiles on them; in the final play, they nearly win. But no. Afterward, in a great Synthesis moment, Walter gives the boys beer. Tanner throws their 2nd place trophy back at the Yankees, and all celebrate.

Final Image: As we pull back from the ball field, the American flag waves, dissolving into the Bears' team photo. They've secured the prize — it just isn't the one they expected.

PLANES, TRAINS AND AUTOMOBILES (1987)

Between creating teen touchstones like *The Breakfast Club* and kid classics like *Home Alone*, writer-director John Hughes made one for adults. And though the hi-jinks of this "Buddy Fleece" are light, the quest Steve Martin is on is one of the most meaningful: to go home. Two days before Thanksgiving, Steve must get from New York to Chicago, and the only thing in his way is a snarled transportation system — and John Candy.

As a frozen-in-time moment before the handy use of cell phones and the Internet, Chicagoan Hughes paints an enduring portrait of mid-America. He dips again into icons like the wood-paneled lime green rent-a-car (from his first script, *National Lampoon's Vacation*), chipper airport employees discussing the little marshmallows in the Thanksgiving "Ambrosia," and the strange lives of desperate men.

As marketing man Neal Page, Steve is out of touch with this America at the start. His dainty shoes, lush cashmere coat, and snappy fedora will be taken away and replaced with a general store deerstalker and boots. With a chill in the air, and frost on the ground urging him home for the holidays, Steve will discover how much of his family life he's taken for granted. And as his guide, John Candy will offer an even bigger lesson: the importance of one stranger helping another.

GF Type: Buddy Fleece

GF Cousins: *Easy Rider; National Lampoon's Vacation; Stranger than Paradise; Fandango; Thelma & Louise; Finding Nemo; Road Trip; O Brother, Where Art Thou?; Little Miss Sunshine; Wild Hogs*

PLANES, TRAINS AND AUTOMOBILES
Written by John Hughes

Opening Image: A NYC skyscraper, with the sounds of train whistles, bus motors, and jet engines. "Two days before Thanksgiving" reads the legend. Neal Page (Steve Martin) is in a meeting, waiting for the client to okay his campaign.

Set-Up: Steve has tickets for the flight to Chicago. A co-worker warns: "You'll never make it." Will he? Competition in traveling starts when Steve tries to hail a cab. His foe: Six Degrees of Kevin Bacon. Steve loses, thanks to nearly breaking his neck when he trips over a trunk. "You're messing with the wrong guy," Steve yells. We briefly see the trunk's owner, John Candy. When Steve gets to JFK, his flight's delayed. Steve calls home where his wife and kids are waiting. By minute 10, we've met everyone in the A story.

Catalyst: Steve is bumped from first class and forced to sit in coach right next to you-know-who. John is Del Griffith, shower curtain-ring salesman and boor. The flight begins and Steve is beset by John's foot odor ("My dogs are really barking today!") and dull stories. Late in the flight, the wiser John turns to Steve and tells him: "We're not landing in Chicago." O'Hare is snowed in. Their flight is diverted.

Theme Stated: In Wichita, Steve calls home again. His wife is irritated, and a tad suspicious. John sees Steve react. John tells Steve his motto: "Like your work, love your wife." Home is a place Steve needs to get to out of duty, but his lesson will be learning to appreciate it — and our theme.

Debate: What will Steve do now? John offers to find Steve lodging for the night. Should Steve join him? That is the question.

Break into Two: Steve and John ride with Wolf, whose "Taxiola" is part jukebox and part opium den. Steve has entered the "upside-down world" of Del Griffith and he won't be the same again. When they arrive at the motel, John is welcomed by the owner — as he will be all along the road. John is crass but lovable. Steve, uptight and effete. What better way to find out *how* effete than by forcing Steve to share a small room and an even smaller bed with John? Messy shower, reading in bed, cracking knuckles, draining sinuses — all lead to a fight. Steve lists his complaints about John; John listens and takes it.

B Story: The "love story" is between these two men. We will also begin to hear the mystery of John's wife, for John has his own arc that Steve will help him with. "I like me. My wife likes me," John claims during their fight. He also carries her picture.

Fun and Games: Cheery music announces Fun and Games. "I'm Back in Baby's Arms" is heard as the men wake, cuddled together, John's hand between two pillows. "Those aren't pillows!" Steve cries and they leap out of bed. John suggests that the only way to get to Chicago is by train, and now the "promise of the premise" is unveiled: By any means possible, using all manner of transport, and paid for by credit card, they will reach Chicago. After a ride from a strange pal of John's, the two board the Amtrak. Soon they pass scenes of America and families heading home for the holidays, moments marketing man Steve needs to experience. When the train breaks down, the two board a bus where snob Steve tries to lead passengers in a rousing chorus of "Three Coins in the Fountain" until John gets them really singing with the "Theme from The Flintstones."

Midpoint: Steve's been trying to dump John. At a diner, after the "false victory" of John selling his shower curtain rings to raise cash for food, Steve suggests they split up. A and B stories cross as John mentions he's been away from home, and his wife, for too long. Now without John, Steve doesn't do so well, and after his airport rental car turns up missing, he loses his cool. His expensive shoes are ruined, his hat blows away; he's being stripped bit by bit of his dignity. Steve confronts the marvelous Edie McClurg as the perky rent-a-car gal, and drops the f-bomb an estimated 18 times in two minutes. Desperate, Steve is about to hire a cab when John pulls up in the rent-a-car that was Steve's.

Bad Guys Close In: As they drive home, the insults now go both ways as John lists Steve's faults. John knows who he is. Steve does not. And the conflict is starting to eat at both men. They can't wait for this trip to be over.

All Is Lost: When John almost gets into a wreck and then heads the wrong way on the highway, both have a near-death experience. Until now it's been difficult, but not dangerous. In the "whiff of death" moment right before they cheat the reaper, Steve turns and imagines John as a cackling Devil. Some post-accident bonding ends when the car catches fire and Steve laughs... until he learns John used *his* credit card to rent it.

Dark Night of the Soul: Hating each other, they check in to the El Rancho Motel. Steve takes the room and leaves John out in the cold. John laments his suffocating personality and Steve ponders the mystery of why he hooked up with John in the first place. Finally, he relents and lets John in. A and B stories cross again as the two men drink mini-bar cocktails and toast their wives.

Break into Three: Having learned from each other and bonded as a team, the two men escape for the final part of their trip. In a great moment of Synthesis, they finally find a song they can sing together: "Blue Moon Of Kentucky." Though their car is impounded, they make the last leg in the back of a truck.

Finale: On the train platform in Chicago, they bid goodbye. "I'm a little wiser," Steve admits. On the final El ride, while reviewing the trip, the lesson of the B story kicks Steve into a revelation: The wife John talks about so much is dead. Going back to save John, Steve shows how much he's grown.

Final Image: Steve and John haul John's trunk to Steve's door. Home for Thanksgiving, Steve introduces John to his wife, who smiles warmly. John is now part of Steve's family.

SAVING PRIVATE RYAN (1998)

Be it an historic backdrop, such as war, or an imaginary one set a long time ago and far, far away, the "Epic Fleece" uses a vast canvas, a mission of daring, and a squad of heroes to tell its tale. At the end of many a journey in this sub-genre, what the journeyers find is something they did not expect. Nowhere is the terrible beauty of this lesson more in evidence than in director Steven Spielberg's *Saving Private Ryan*.

When the movie premiered, many talked about the violence of its D-Day opening. The bar was raised for portraying the ugly realism of the battlefront. Based on several accounts of the event by, among others, historian Stephen Ambrose (who served as a consultant for the film), and the oral histories of the soldiers themselves of the shocking, banal, and surreal moments of panicked combat, it was indeed something new for audiences. But at the heart of this story is much more: a lesson in how a soldier's role may appear small, but is in fact a part of a greater whole.

Tom Hanks stars as the unassuming leader of men with a mission. His team, like all typical Epic teams, is a mix of skills, temperaments, and experience in the field. They are assigned to retrieve a special soldier caught behind enemy lines. But at the end of the journey, a surprise: The one they were really sent to save... is us.

GF Type: Epic Fleece

GF Cousins: *The Guns of Navarone, The Dirty Dozen, The Professionals, Star Wars, Apocalypse Now, Glory, Three Kings, Master and Commander: The Far Side of the World, National Treasure, The Lord of the Rings*

SAVING PRIVATE RYAN
Written by Robert Rodat

Opening Image: A battlefield cemetery. An old man and his family. He served in World War Two and finds the gravesite of a fallen comrade. We will learn just who this brave man is by story's end.

Set-Up: The opening gives way to flashback. D-Day. June 6, 1944. The landing at Omaha Beach is bloody. Captain John Miller (Tom Hanks) shows courage and saves lives as his unit helps secure the objective. This sequence sets up the world of hellish war and Tom's leadership skills. Tom's men are a highly functional team.

Theme Stated: As the dead of the invasion are accounted for, one has special meaning. His last name is Ryan, one of four brothers — three now dead. Back at home, General George Marshall (Harve Presnell) cites a letter written by Abraham Lincoln and orders the fourth brother, lost in post-D-Day France, brought home. "That boy is alive. We are gonna send somebody to find him and we are going to get him the hell out of there." One man counts. That's our theme.

Catalyst: Tom is given the mission and we now meet a new member of the squad, a wet-behind-the-ears translator, Corporal Upham (Jeremy Davies). Tom will be the leader, but Jeremy will act as the interpreter of both French and German — and of events.

Debate: Should the squad go? Jeremy's nervousness shows the nature and risks of the journey. Like us, he is a novice.

Break into Two: Tom accepts the mission and we meet the rest of his squad: Sergeant Mike Horvath (Tom Sizemore), "the muscle," enforces Tom's orders. Pvt. Stanley Mellish (Adam Goldberg), "the conscience," has a special hatred of Nazis. Pvt. Daniel Jackson (Barry

Pepper), "the soul," possesses sniper skills enhanced by God. And Pvt. Richard Reiben (Edward Burns) is "the heart." Each has a unique way of speaking, point of view, and experience to share. And we're all guessing: Who's gonna get it first?

B Story: The B story is the question: Who is Captain Miller? Tom's background is a mystery; apart from a shaky hand and a firm grip on leadership, little is known of him. Tying in to the "Theme Stated" idea of one man counts, Tom exemplifies the value of individual sacrifice for the benefit and protection of others.

Fun and Games: Marching through the hedgerow country of France, coming upon the surprises and adventures of war, is the "promise of the premise." We are on the road, each signpost ahead another chance for a revealing look at, and growth of, each character. It is a journey echoing that of Jason and other men of battle who strike out on a special mission. There is a lift the men have been given from surviving D-Day. No time to think about anything more than the next detail, so off they go. This is why we came to see this movie: to learn up close about men at war and its light and dark sides. As dangerous as battle is, there's a sense we're on a lark, an adventure. The friendship, easygoing patter, and even the secret language they share (FUBAR becomes one of the code words) — are all taken in through Jeremy's POV.

Midpoint: After a run-in with a French family, a shootout with a squad of Germans, and a midnight talk (A and B stories cross) that continues the debate over the importance of the individual, the squad seems to have come to an impasse when they find a downed glider and dozens of dead and wounded paratroopers. This marks one of the mistakes of the D-Day invasion, a screw-up where good men died needlessly and a typical "false defeat." Most midpoints are a "false victory" where events peak. This is the opposite, a down, compounded when the squad searches through the dogtags of the dead and thinks they'll never find Ryan. Then a soldier who lost his hearing says he knows Ryan's location. Buoyed, the squad moves on.

Bad Guys Close In: This particular journey is marked by the steady disintegration of the team, both in number as they die one by one, and also by the doubts about the mission that chip away at camaraderie and faith. Infighting grows when Tom decides to take the squad off course to knock out a German machine-gun nest. The men want to avoid the fight, but Tom insists. They lose another of their comrades though they capture a German prisoner. His fate is hotly debated and the team is ready to mutiny. Tom stops the argument by sacrificing his identity, revealing he's a schoolteacher — and that they must band together. They agree, and let the Nazi go.

All Is Lost: The squad finally finds Private Ryan — blonde, blue-eyed Matt Damon. The surprise comes when Matt refuses to go home. Matt doesn't want to leave his own team in the lurch, and the "road apple" is: death of the mission.

Dark Night of the Soul: With Matt refusing to be saved, Tom and the survivors of the trek to find him wonder what to do.

Break into Three: Tom decides to dig in and defend the bridge where Matt and his squad wait for a Nazi attack. A and B stories cross as Tom chooses individual sacrifice for the larger goal of saving others and bringing the war to an end as soon as possible.

Finale: The big battle as Tom and Matt and the rest defend the bridge. In a final irony, the Nazi soldier they freed returns to kill. Man by man, many die — including Tom. But one survives.

Final Image: Back at the gravesite, a bookend. All along we've had the feeling (*I* did anyway) that the old man at the gravesite was Tom Hanks. We now see it's Matt Damon. Private Ryan survived. He was given his life back by the soldiers who rescued him. We realize that Private Ryan is us. Just as Tom's "team" saved Private Ryan on the battlefield, Tom — and men like him — saved us at home. And we must thank them for their sacrifice. It's a powerful coda and a heartfelt salute to those who serve.

OCEAN'S ELEVEN (2001)

Every once in a while the remake turns out better than the original. In the millennium upgrade of *Ocean's Eleven*, director Steven Soderbergh and star George Clooney had an advantage — the 1961 film starring Frank and Dean and Sammy was fun, but no masterpiece. What Team Clooney crafts here goes beyond its namesake and is a great example of the "Caper Fleece," especially in its lineup of supporting players. We also see an example of a B story that starts late — but is no less powerful for doing so.

Clooney plays con man Danny Ocean, whose mission — on the surface — is one of avarice. But in collecting his team, plotting the impossible heist, and executing it with hairsbreadth timing, we learn his mission is about something more. It's about a girl. In this case: Julia Roberts. And it's about getting her back from the guy who took her: Andy Garcia. The other themes are "performance" and "disguise," and nowhere does show biz meet crime biz better than when Carl Reiner and Elliott Gould steal scenes from younger stars Matt Damon, Scott Caan, and Casey Affleck — for topping one another and proving one's stripes is what this story is about. The Fleece in this mission, it turns out, is "manhood," and with that as each character's primal stake... we must go along.

GF Type: Caper Fleece

GF Cousins: *Rififi, Topkapi, The Great St. Louis Bank Robbery, The Hot Rock, Papillon, Escape from Alcatraz, Quick Change, Sneakers, The Usual Suspects, The Italian Job*

OCEAN'S ELEVEN
Screenplay by Ted Griffin
Based on a Screenplay by Harry Brown *and* Charles Lederer
And a Story by George Clayton Johnson & Jack Golden Russell

Opening Image: Prison. "Man walking," yells a guard. Enter Danny Ocean (George Clooney). It's a parole hearing and he's on his best behavior. A caged lion, he looks unnatural behind bars.

Set-Up: We hear George had a wife who left him. Asked "What do you think you would do if released?" George says nothing. When he's processed out of prison, he gets the personal effects he came in with: a tuxedo and a wedding ring. What would a "man" do? We'll see. George shows up in Hollywood where Rusty Ryan (Brad Pitt), his long-time partner in crime, is teaching poker to movie stars. Brad has gone to seed; he's bored and ready for adventure. And despite the result of their last caper, which landed George in prison, seeing George reinvigorates Brad.

Catalyst: George lays out the plan for Brad: a casino heist in Las Vegas — not just any heist, the king magilla raid of all time. It's crazy but Brad is intrigued. And yes, for those who look for such things, the blueprint of the casino they'll rob *does* resemble a penis.

Theme Stated: Brad has to know why George wants to pull off this caper. George gives a fast answer: "The house always wins... unless, when that perfect hand comes along you bet big and then take the house." Brad isn't quite buying, but agrees to go along.

Debate: Can they do it? Elliott Gould as Las Vegas kingpin Reuben Tishkoff tells them — and us — how crazy it is to rob a casino. No one has *ever* done it. Then he hears who the target is: owner Terry Benedict (Andy Garcia). Like George, Elliott had his manhood stolen by Andy, who tears down old casinos to build new ones that make gobs of money. He took Elliott's hotel along the way. Backed by Elliott, George and Brad set about to collect the rest of the team, each with a different skill required to pull off this amazing feat. It helps that when we meet Ocean's Eleven, theirs are the best heist film intro scenes since *The Hot Rock*: Saul Bloom (Carl Reiner) has hung up his con man shoes; he is old school hoping he still has game. Others like Linus Caldwell (Matt Damon) are young up-and-comers in the heist biz; Matt has to prove himself to his father, also a crook.

Break into Two: At Minute 30, all are gathered at Elliott's place. "You're Bobby Caldwell's kid from Chicago," Elliott says to Matt. "Yeah," Matt blinks. "That's wonderful," Elliott replies. "Get in the goddamn house." There's no more debating. They're all in.

Fun and Games: Now the plan is unveiled — yet we will know only a part of it. The "fun" of any heist movie is based on three things: (1) showing how the team plans on robbing the bank, (2) showing how the plan gets screwed up and, (3) keeping some of the caper's details hidden from the audience. This part of the movie also includes demonstrations of the team's skills. Bernie Mac is hilarious as he turns a conversation about skin care into the purchase of some vans the gang needs; likewise, diminutive Shaobo Qin shows acrobatic pluck. As the surveillance wiz, Livingston Dell (Eddie Jemison) is their nervous techie. This is why we came to see this movie: the thrill of watching these diverse characters circle the bank.

Midpoint: The "stakes are raised" and the Fun and Games end when we meet Andy Garcia and learn that casino owner Terry Benedict is robotic, ruthless, and feared by all. And if that weren't enough, we now have the complication of... The Girl.

B Story: We thought up till now that this was only about money. Then Tess (Julia Roberts) walks in. And though Julia's actual walk is a little clunky, her entrance raises the degree of difficulty of the heist. We learn Julia is dating Andy; she left George while he was in prison and found a new guy — *this* guy. When Brad discovers that Julia is involved, George admits there is more than money at stake. Now the real theme is revealed in a reprise of their earlier conversation; George admits why he's doing this. "I lost something," he tells Brad. Was it something shaped like a *penis*?! Well, yes, that too. But now they're stealing gold *and* a girl. Which will George choose if forced?

Bad Guys Close In: Whether connected to Julia or not, "road apples" start popping up everywhere. The electric whammy that "Basher" (Don Cheadle) was planning to use is kaput. On top of that, because George can't stop running into Julia at the casino buffet, the hotel has "red-flagged" him. Meanwhile, Carl is looking none too good. Is his heart scare linked to the scam? And is Andy the sucker, or are we?

All Is Lost: As the heist unfolds, there are more near misses. When Carl has an apparent heart attack, we think he's dead. Good heist film that this is, the "whiff of death" is fake: Carl's condition is part of the plan, as is George's zooming Julia.

Dark Night of the Soul: Literally a dark night as all the lights go out in Las Vegas, thanks to Don — and not only is the town in the dark, so are we. What is going on?

Break into Three: When Brad calls Andy and lets him know the casino's being robbed, we enter Act Three. Julia is now included in the plan. By going along, she guarantees the heist and lets us know she may be part of the prize. A and B stories cross nicely.

Finale: Under Andy's watchful eye, the gang disguised as SWAT cops exits the vault with the loot. In a final irony, Andy chooses money over Julia. By picking gold, he loses both. George is arrested and the guys take a last look at the hotel they robbed: phallic imagery erect once more in the fountain of the Bellagio.

Final Image: Out of prison, George reunites with Julia. They now have two rings of gold — and George is a man once more.

MARIA FULL OF GRACE (2004)

Sometimes the journey is one the hero must take alone. In many biographical movies, such as *Ray* and *Capote*, and personal quests, like *About Schmidt*, *Garden State*, and *Cast Away*, he may have allies, and even find friends along the way, but at the heart of the trip is a lesson he can only learn by himself.

One of the better examples of the GF sub-genre called the "Solo Fleece" is writer-director Joshua Marston's *Maria Full of Grace*. A foreign language Sundance winner, it is a textbook demonstration of the BS2 and of the importance of "primal." It tells the story of a Colombian girl, pregnant and unemployed, who takes a job as a drug mule. Maria will leave her small town and dying hopes, and take a chance on escape by ingesting pellets of heroin and smuggling them on a treacherous journey to America.

When we talk about "primal," this is one of the more practical demonstrations of why thinking stories through on this basic level is so vital: On a low budget like this — with no money for special effects, chase scenes, and big stars — what is most compelling is identifying with the immediate needs of a hero we can root for. It is a lesson the studios might take into account when running the numbers on the next *Lara Croft* sequel they're considering. And as an example of a "Golden Fleece," none is more riveting than this simple but highly charged indie.

GF Type: Solo Fleece

GF Cousins: *Barry Lyndon, Coal Miner's Daughter, About Schmidt, Capote, Garden State, Cast Away, Ray, Walk the Line, Vanity Fair, Cold Mountain*

MARIA FULL OF GRACE
Written by Joshua Marston

Opening Image: Maria (Catalina Sandino Moreno) and her friend Blanca (Yenny Paola Vega) wait for the early bus to go to work. We're in a small town in Colombia, but the routine of family and job is universally understood.

Theme Stated: After work, Maria makes out with her dullard boyfriend, Juan (Wilson Guerrero). Maria sees the roof of the building they're kissing beneath and says she wants to go "up there." "You can come down the way you went up," Juan says. "Alone." Maria yearns for more. Will she get it?

Set-Up: Maria works in a flower factory, stripping the thorns off long-stemmed roses. She and her friend Blanca survive by trading gossip about the cute boys who work there. We meet one of these, Felipe (Charles Albert Patiño), who will become important. At home, Maria's sister is raising a baby alone, the father long gone. The family survives thanks to Maria's contribution of her pay. How do you say "Save the Cat!" in Spanish? Maria's common sense worldview, sacrificing for her family, and inner drive for more makes us root for her. When Maria gets sick at work, her boss yells at her; her family does too when she tells them she's quitting. All around her, the future is clear and it's a dead end. This is a definitive Stasis = Death moment in which we sense the hero must risk change — or "die."

Catalyst: Maria goes to a party and sees Felipe. They dance in front of Juan. It's clear there's a problem with her low-wattage lover. The next day Maria breaks the news to him that she's pregnant. Juan offers to marry her. She refuses.

Debate: What will she do? The fear of turning out like her sister, with an illegitimate baby and a stolid life, offers very little for Maria. And we know she wants better.

Break into Two: Felipe takes Maria on his motorcycle to the city Bogotá, where his Boss offers her a job as a drug mule. It's illegal and dangerous. By taking the money the Boss offers, she accepts the mission and enters Act Two.

B Story: While waiting for the mission to begin, Maria meets Lucy (Guilied Lopez), another drug mule she saw when she met the Boss. Lucy is a pretty and sophisticated city girl. A classic B story character, she is the "funhouse-mirror" version of Maria's own sister and her opposite in every way. Lucy will be Maria's guide to this new world. This is also the "love story" where the theme of the movie will be discussed. Maria's yearning for more will be raised to yet higher planes through Lucy.

Fun and Games: Maria's training begins. Lucy coaches Maria on the art of swallowing grapes whole, a skill she will need to ingest the heroin pellets. Lucy has done this before and can show Maria many tricks. Maria can't tell anyone. Then Blanca breaks the news she's a mule, too. The day arrives when Maria must ingest the heroin pellets and be readied for her trip to the US. Maria hears a last warning from the Boss: If any of the pellets go missing, Maria's family may be harmed. Maria gets on the plane. Not only are Lucy and Blanca onboard, but a fourth woman too. The flight is perilous; Lucy is ill, and Maria loses some of the pellets she must re-swallow. This is the crux of a movie about drug running: the fear, danger, and grim details of the journey.

Midpoint: The midpoint is a "false victory." After being pulled aside by US customs agents, Maria is spared being x-rayed because she is pregnant, and thus can't be exposed as a drug smuggler and arrested. Unlike the fourth woman, who is detained, Maria's free to go. Now Maria, Blanca, and Lucy are met by their drug handlers. Lucy is very sick as both A and B stories' "stakes are raised."

Bad Guys Close In: With the drug run over, real problems start. Kept in a dive motel until they defecate the heroin pellets, the women are guarded by thugs. In the middle of the night, the men take Lucy away. Maria and Blanca find blood in the bathroom. Scared, they steal the drugs and run. Now real bad guys are pursuing the two women, who are out of their element in a foreign land. Maria takes refuge with Lucy's sister, Carla (Patricia Rae). She will be Maria's new mentor. Carla puts Maria up and introduces her to Don Fernando (Orlando Tobón), a stateside troubleshooter for illegal immigrants needing assistance.

All Is Lost: Don Fernando offers to help Maria find work: Can she sew? Maria sees a man stripping roses on the street and realizes the US is just like Colombia: the problems of job, family, and paying rent are the same. And when Maria learns Lucy was murdered and the pellets cut out of her stomach, the "whiff of death" hits her.

Dark Night of the Soul: After seeing a sonogram of her baby, Maria talks with Carla about her life in America. Like Maria, Carla is pregnant, but she has a hardworking husband and dreams of a bright future. What will Maria do?

Break into Three: When Carla learns Lucy is dead, and Maria was involved, A and B stories cross as she kicks the girls out of her house. Maria and Blanca decide to confront the bad guys.

Finale: Maria and Blanca surrender the drug pellets to the thugs and Maria bravely insists they get their pay. Maria covers the cost of Lucy's funeral, makes amends to Carla, and both she and Blanca go to the airport to get on a plane home.

Final Image: Blanca boards the plane, but Maria decides to take her chances in the US. She wants more for her child and will stay. A true Golden Fleece end, it isn't the outcome Maria wanted, but it's the one that changes her life. In a final image, a now proud and independent woman walks toward a new future. Synthesis! The hero has transformed her world.

🐾 *Eddie Murphy realizes he's had one too many Krispy Kremes in* The Nutty Professor. *His dream of being thin is nigh, as is the lesson of every "Out of the Bottle" tale: The real "magic" is being yourself.*

3 OUT OF THE BOTTLE

Magic. *That's* what movies are made of! And movies that specialize in magic are among the most popular of all time.

There is something dream-like about these tales that immediately resonates for us. Perhaps that's why the genre I've named "Out of the Bottle" indulges our fantasies and offers the most delightful of escapes.

This grouping gets its moniker from the legend of Aladdin, in which a genie is summoned "out of the bottle" and all manner of wishes are granted with one fell poof! Stories using magic are found in every culture, across the ages. And whether they're about flying carpets, magic beans, or witch's spells, all share this recurring warning that is the real lesson:

Be careful what you wish for!

Deep in the human psyche is both the fantasy of being able to, say, fly — and the deeper-seated knowledge that we can't.

Not yet.

We long to be better than human to overcome what holds us back, but secretly know that being human is a pretty good thing.

Inevitably, in these films is an Act Three beat in which the hero rejects the magic that's been loaned to him, and solves his problems without assistance — which gives us a clue why the OOTB genre resonates. Life is good, these stories tell us... the real magic comes from enjoying what is already ours.

The variety of "Bottles" — and the many kinds of magic that spill out from them — is amazing! Take a look at the "Body Switch Bottle," stories where gender, age, or species are swapped to give each participant a lesson in gratitude — as seen in *Big*, *13 Going on 30*, and *The Shaggy Dog*. Also note the "Thing Bottle" where elixirs, formulas, or totems bring about a desired transformation in one's life, such as the wish to be attractive to the opposite sex (as in *Love Potion #9*), to be slim and sexy (*The Nutty Professor*), or to have a magic remote control that can speed up your life (*Click*).

In addition, the OOTB family includes the "Angel Bottle," those tales of special beings that magically appear, such as *Oh, God!* and its twin *Bruce Almighty*, *Cocoon*, and *The Love Bug* series (for which I co-wrote, with partner Colby Carr, the first draft of the most recent *Herbie* incarnation). There is also the "Curse Bottle," films such as *What Women Want* and *Liar Liar*, whereby the hero suddenly finds himself saddled with magic he may not have asked for, but that comes with a lesson he soon learns he needs. And finally we get the "Surreal Bottle," films with those OOTB *premisi* that change the world by other kinds of magic like a time warp or pseudo-science, where the hero becomes part of a parallel universe — seen in films like *Groundhog Day*, *Pleasantville*, and *The Butterfly Effect*.

In all OOTB films, the "magic" is simply acquired and the "how" quickly forgotten. These include such magic-gaining faves as: knocks on the head (*Peggy Sue Got Married*), enchanted vending machines (*Big*), Nordic visors with Tex Avery-like powers (*The Mask*), and even requests by little boys so their fathers won't fib anymore (*Liar Liar*). The audience excuses the simplicity of the way these powers are dished out because filmmakers suspend our disbelief once, and thereafter stick to the logic of how the magic is granted that — if we screenwriters make clear from the start — will let us get away with one "leap of faith" per movie.

All OOTB tales, as in the previous genres we've discussed, have three handy elements that put them in this category. These include: (1) a "wish," (2) a "spell," and (3) a "lesson."

Shall we take a look at these?

Your wish is my command!

Making the hero deserve the magic that is bestowed on him is what makes the "wish" in any OOTB story more plausible. There is a school of thought that there are only two kinds of stories: an "empowerment tale" about an underdog who needs help, and a "comeuppance tale" about a bigshot who needs a lesson. Nowhere is this bifurcation (a $45 word) more clear. Whether the hero of an OOTB is a Cinderella type who makes the wish himself — as seen in movies like *13 Going on 30* and *Big* — or some un-evolved, smart-aleck deserving a lesson in humility who has the wish thrust upon him in a "comeuppance tale" (like *Liar Liar*, *Shallow Hal*, and *What Women Want*), the dynamics are the same: The hero dearly needs to be the recipient of whatever magic he will be granted.

The actual "spell" that's cast — no matter how it's bestowed — must be unique, offering a take on the OOTB we've never seen before, and also have limits. So when we screenwriters come up with magic, we need to create a set of boundaries called **The Rules**. Together, the magic and its limits are a one-two punch. In *Bruce Almighty*, Morgan Freeman says it right up front when he awards Jim Carrey his godly powers: "Let me explain the rules."

Being careful with The Rules is a tough task — but great stuff happens when we stick to them. Look at *Love Potion #9*, where two scientists (one is Sandra Bullock) invent a formula that makes them catnip for the opposite sex. Not only is there a time limit for each dose of the potion, the dose-ee has to speak to the person he or she wants to enchant. Once set up, screenwriter-director Dale Launer holds to this rule, and gives us situations where it's a handicap. To not take The Rules seriously is sloppy screenwriting. It lets studio executives get out their red pens and start making "notes." So let's not give 'em the chance, eh?

Making sure our audience buys into the magic is key. We're asking them to trust the spell is possible, so if we break our contract with the audience by bending The Rules, we run the risk of losing them. This is a little menace I call **Double Mumbo Jumbo**, which piles one empowerment on top of another and makes the story fuzzy. *13 Going on 30* is an example of DMJ by using two bits of magic: (1) sending a 13-year-old into the future, and (2) turning that tween into a 30-year-old. Once done, the writers must deal with two sets of "jokes": (1) 1980 person sent to 2004 jokes, and (2) 13-year-old in a 30-year-old body jokes. But piling on the magic does not make "*Big* with a girl" twice as good.

The most important part of this whole caboodle is the same as it is for any story that we tell: How is the hero transformed by this adventure? In the case of movies that use magic, the "lesson" the hero learns is the realization that what he had at the beginning of the story is what he's wanted all along. Coming full circle is what most OOTB films are really about. Like existential homing pigeons, heroes of magic tales return to base with their eyes opened. But had it not been for this flight of fantasy, that life-affirming change would never have occurred.

A big part of learning the lesson, and one you will now see in every OOTB movie, is the Act Three beat where the hero **learns to do it without the magic** — a key phrase in my box of tools whenever I develop an OOTB. It's Dumbo without the feather! In *Bruce Almighty*, it's only *after* Jim Carrey (as weatherman Bruce Nolan) loses his girlfriend, gets his archrival fired, and quits his job at the end of Act Two that he becomes willing to change. The part of his godly powers he hasn't picked up on yet is helping others without getting anything in return. When Jim finally understands that, he receives everything he always wanted — the same things he had all along!

Many Out-of-the-Bottle movies feature a character called the **Confidant**, an ally whom the hero can trust with his secret. There is a practical screenwriting reason for this: The hero has to tell *someone* — and us — what's happening. Yet the Confidant can only watch the hero have fun, often held back by a lack of faith in the "magic." He might even use his knowledge of it to gain an unfair advantage or harm the hero at a crucial moment. Those deserving of the benefits of the magic are the only ones who can learn from it and, in the end, that's what all OOTB tales are about: the power of believing in yourself.

WHAT'S MAGIC ABOUT YOUR BOTTLE?

Whether your hero is a comeuppance character who needs a lesson, or a Cinderella type for whom magic is a blessing, the model OOTB film must have the following elements:

1. A "wish" asked for by the hero or granted by another, and the clearly seen need to be delivered from the ordinary.

2. A "spell" which, in setting up this illogical *thang*, we must make logical by upholding "The Rules," no matter how tempting it may be to use "Double Mumbo Jumbo."

3. A "lesson": Be careful what you wish for! It's the running theme in all OOTBs. Life is good as it is.

The following films are all about magic. And where OOTB flicks are concerned... there's always a wish for more!

FREAKY FRIDAY (1976)

Ask any woman of a certain age and the secret will spill out: The movie that got them through adolescence, the film that touched them more than any other, the late-night-popcorn-in-bed-DVD-in-the-player comfort flick of all time is the Jodie Foster version of *Freaky Friday*.

I don't know why.

I think it has something to do with that special time in life when mother and teen daughter realize the unique tension between them. Daughter feels like an ugly duckling; Mother feels under-appreciated. Little wonder this was also a successful remake directed by Mark Waters and starring Lindsay Lohan and Jamie Lee Curtis in 2003.

We revisit the early version not only because it is a nostalgic touchstone, but also to see how far we have come in the technology of introducing "magic." If you think *Liar Liar*'s "spell" is thin, you won't believe how the Mumbo Jumbo transpires here. But it reveals an OOTB truism: If we're rooting for the participants, we don't care how the magic happens.

The Walt Disney Production of director Gary Nelson's *Freaky Friday* is one of several successful films of the "Body Switch Bottle," including *Big* and *13 Going on 30*. It works, still, for a simple reason — because the lesson is primal.

OOTB Type: Body Switch Bottle

OOTB Cousins: *Vice Versa, Like Father Like Son, 18 Again!, Big, Dream a Little Dream, 13 Going on 30, All of Me, Switch, The Hot Chick, The Shaggy Dog*

FREAKY FRIDAY
Screenplay by Mary Rodgers
Based on the book by Mary Rodgers

Opening Image: Young Jodie Foster asleep in bed. It's 7:30 a.m. on Friday the 13th. In an hour things will get "freaky."

Set-Up: As 13-year-old Annabel Andrews, Jodie has braces and no bustline, a goody-goody brother who shows her up, and a Mom who constantly rags on her. Barbara Harris (who is outstanding in this role) is a neglected housewife whose husband (John Astin) is a well-meaning male chauvinist. The set-up includes Dad needing both Mom and Jodie to help at a business event later. (NOTE: It's always good to have "a big event" in the offing to make the magic extra inconvenient.) Barbara's under-appreciated life is spent cleaning up after everyone, and ground zero is Jodie's messy room. What's wrong with that girl? Well, Jodie's at an age where she has a life beyond her home. She is captain of her field hockey team, a water skier, and has a crush on Boris, the boy next door and perhaps a distant relative of Napoleon Dynamite. Mom and daughter are at a transition stage. It is that point in many OOTB tales — and in life — when, for all of us: Stasis = Death.

Catalyst: The actual body switch occurs in a rudimentary way that may appall Ingmar Bergman fans. At the same moment, while complaining about each other, Jodie at a local diner and Barbara at home say: "I wish I could switch places with her for just one day." Via split screen and with some psychedelic light show flashes, they do.

Debate: How will they deal with this? Realizing that Jodie is in Mom's body and Barbara is in Jodie's, the acceptance of this condition is a tad quick. There is no "denial." It's the premise, so they go with it — a process that has become more "realistic" in subsequent OOTB movies. Some of the ways both accept the transformation are a bit strange. Jodie, in Barbara's body, has boobs — and likes it. Barbara, in Jodie's body, calls home and asks for "Bill," her "husband," beginning the odd sexual tension that permeates the whole film. Primal? Like a car crash. Jodie tries to tell her friends about the switch but they only laugh at her.

Theme Stated: Exiting the diner for school, Jodie's friends say: "Our goony mothers couldn't even get through a day like we put in." What's harder, Mom's life or Jodie's? We shall see.

Break into Two: By accepting how this happened, Jodie and Barbara decide to go with the magic and see how the other half lives.

Fun and Games: For now we're just working the concept. Let's see, what fun can we have here as Mom and teen daughter swap lives, what **set pieces** and **riffs** can we use to exploit this puppy? At school, Jodie (really Mom) acts prudish, wrecks a photography class, and goofs up her typing test. At home, Barbara (really teen daughter) tries on make-up, makes a mess of the laundry, and deals badly with a Marx Brothers-like invasion of repairmen, chatty neighbors, and drapery installers. Barbara's body language and telling reactions to the adult world make the "promise of the premise" come to life.

Midpoint: The "stakes are raised" by Dad at work. The big account is riding on both his wife and daughter. The former must show up to be at his side like a dutiful spouse; the latter must star in the water-ski aquacade to wow his client.

B Story: Barbara (Jodie) decides to work her magic on Boris. She plans on making a pitch for herself while in disguise as her beautiful mother. In what will probably be a therapy-inducing sequence for Boris later in life, Barbara flirts with the underage minor. Boris likes Mom, pleased that an adult has time for him, but also cottoning to the underlying sexual implications. Barbara is at her best here as she negotiates this fine line. And plot-wise, other changes occur as daughter begins to realize... her room *is* a mess!

Bad Guys Close In: The Rules are now restrictive and getting worse for both parties: Jodie (really Mom) is alienating her friends by acing History class, and lets them down in field hockey. At home, Barbara (Jodie) learns her brother admires her, and later confronts the school principal and discovers she has a high IQ. Meanwhile Jodie (Mom) drops in on Dad and his sexy secretary. Though in Jodie's body, Mom gets Jodie's braces off, has her hair done, and looks at her daughter in the mirror in a way that makes us believe change really has occurred. The death of old ideas is at hand as each of the women now defends the other.

All Is Lost: But the true "death" moments deal with the amping up of danger. As the climax nears, the "whiff of death" is a threat of physical harm as Jodie (Mom) straps on water skis and Mom (Jodie) races to save her.

Break into Three: As the chase continues, the women reverse the spell. "I wish I had my own body!" they both say. And poof! They do. But there's a new wrinkle to the magic — this time they also switch places!

Finale: Now Jodie, who can't drive, and Barbara, who can't water ski, wow the world. Dad's clients are charmed. And mother and daughter are reunited... never to argue again.

Final Image: In a coda, Barbara and Jodie are now friends. A Synthesis moment occurs as both say "thanks" when Dad compliments Jodie. Jodie has won Boris and is nice to her brother. The world has definitely changed for the better — thanks to magic.

COCOON (1985)

Whether asked for or not, a magical being comes into a unique world with a unique cast of characters and bestows a wish on those deserving of it. This is the definition of an "Angel Bottle" tale, and in most of these stories the one getting the gift is young (e.g., Cinderella) with his or her whole life ahead. It's ironic that in director Ron Howard's *Cocoon* the only young person is Steve Guttenberg (of *Police Academy* fame) and the ones who receive the gift these "angels" are offering are all over 65.

In many an "Angel Bottle," we start with a unique (often professional) setting, the underdogs who inhabit it, and a problem that needs fixing. In *The Love Bug*, it's about racecars, in *Angels in the Outfield*, baseball — both featuring teams that are looking to reverse their fortunes and needing a miracle to do it. In *Cocoon*, we establish the world of the retirement home, and meet its residents (Jessica Tandy, Hume Cronyn, Don Ameche, Wilford Brimley, and Maureen Stapleton) facing "golden years" that aren't so golden. Death, regret, and depression loom. Then Brian Dennehy and Tahnee Welch arrive, put some strange rocks in a nearby swimming pool, and create a "Fountain of Youth." By the time the Fun and Games peak, and the real issues are dealt with, there's a choice: Stay on Earth and die the old-fashioned way... or choose "magic" and live forever.

OOTB Type: Angel Bottle

OOTB Cousins: *Mary Poppins; The Love Bug; Oh, God!; *batteries not included; Short Circuit; Angels in the Outfield; Aladdin; Meet Joe Black; Bruce Almighty; Nanny McPhee*

COCOON
Screenplay by Tom Benedek
Story by David Saperstein

Opening Image: A telescope pointed at the stars. A little boy gazes at the moon. The boy is our bookend character.

Set-Up: A retirement home in Florida. The old folks who live here are in various states of decline; some suffer in silence, others live it up in dance class. Arthur Selwyn (Don Ameche) is the Sun City Casanova. Benjamin Luckett (Wilford Brimley), his ornery sidekick. Alma (Jessica Tandy) and Joseph Finley (Hume Cronyn) are happy lovebirds. Hume, we find out, just got bad news from a doctor. As the three men strike out to sneak into the estate next door and go swimming, their lives are pretty much at an end. Wilford's only other bright spot is his grandson, David, the telescope owner we met up front. And seemingly unrelated to this world, we also meet Jack Bonner (Steve Guttenberg), a commercial boat operator. His business is bad and won't soon change.

Catalyst: Into the lives of both Steve and the old folks come Walter (Brian Dennehy) and Kitty (Tahnee Welch). Though they appear "normal," there's something odd about them. They hire Steve's boat and lease the house next door where the old men have been swimming, now off-limits to trespassers.

Debate: What are these strangers up to? Steve takes them out to sea to retrieve some strange rocks; despite Tahnee's weird demeanor, Steve is intrigued. And what should the old men do about the restriction to their afternoon swim? After Wilford loses his license at the DMV due to poor eyesight, the guys decide to trespass and go swimming like always, saying...

Theme Stated: ..."I can't remember the last time I took a risk." Our theme: Is it too late to take a chance in life?

Break into Two: At the pool, the three old dudes see several big rocks at the bottom of the deep end. They jump in anyway, splash around, and cavort like children. Soon they feel younger, more energetic. The pool is regenerating them.

B Story: While the B story is in many ways the love story between Steve and Tahnee, it's also about another retirement resident, Bernard Lefkowitz (Jack Gilford). Jack is friends with the other men; his wife has Alzheimer's. Yet he refuses to risk changing his life. Jack is a Confidant with mortal fears. His debate with the others is where the theme of this story is discussed... whereas Steve and Tahnee's sex romp is there to bring a younger demographic into the movie theater!

Fun and Games: As the old men find a new lease on life, the "promise of the premise" is revealed as basically an updated Fountain of Youth story. We now get the ironic notion of picking Florida for the setting of this film, the site of Ponce de Leon's fabled attempt to discover just such a tourist attraction. The Fun and Games is textbook as the silver foxes become Viagra superstars. Hume's threatening disease goes into remission, and word of the rejuvenating pool quietly spreads. We learn why the pool has powers when Steve stumbles upon Tahnee's secret. Both she and Brian are aliens! The rocks they are retrieving from the ocean and keeping in the pool are "cocoons" containing their brethren. The spacemen become friends with the old folks, frolicking in the pool with them and even playing cards.

Midpoint: At mid-movie, we have a "false victory" and the beginning of the downward slide toward "All Is Lost." In a great revenge scene, Wilford returns to the DMV and aces the eye test. The Preparation H Squad celebrate out on the town in Wilford's car and show the "kids" a thing or two at the local break-dance club. By now the old dears are getting a tad irritating. The magic is curdling. It's the perfect time to discover Hume is seeing another woman in town. His "feeling good" has a downside: He's risked losing Jessica's love — and their marriage.

Bad Guys Close In: Hume and Jessica separate. "I'm happy you're going to live Joe, but I've got to live too," she says. Jack's refusal to go swimming with the others and heal his wife has become a sticking point. His loud public revelation of the pool's magic leads to a gray stampede as the residents rush to jump in.

All Is Lost: Brian discovers the old folks' invasion of the pool house has cracked one of the cocoons. The alien inside has died and the life force has been drained from the water. When Jack finds his wife dead later that night and tries to revive her in the magic pool, it's too late.

Dark Night of the Soul: Jack's wife is taken away in an ambulance. And the cocoons have only hours to survive.

Break into Three: The only hope is to get the cocoons back in the ocean. A and B stories cross as Steve and the old folks join forces in a moment of Synthesis to help return the cocoons to the sea. As thanks, Brian offers everyone eternal life. All the humans have to do is come with him to outer space... forever.

Finale: What a dilemma! Stay or go? Wilford shares his plans with David, who takes the news hard. The race to escape includes David agreeing to let Wilford go. The alien craft lifts off with the risk-takers, as B story characters Jack and Steve stay behind.

Final Image: A "funeral" for Wilford. Bookend character David looks toward heaven. Grandpa's up there, happy at last.

THE NUTTY PROFESSOR (1996)

"*Now* a warning?!"

This line from *Death Becomes Her* is one of my favorites. It's spoken by Meryl Streep, subsequent to her swallowing a potion to make her forever young and told The Rules too late. It's a hilarious beat and reinforces an OOTB truism: The curse becomes apparent only *after* we get what we most desire. This is also one of the signatures of the "Thing Bottle," those tales where magic is delivered to us by totem (*Like Mike, The Mask*) or elixir (*Love Potion #9*). One of the best is director Tom Shadyac's CGI tour de farce, *The Nutty Professor*.

Like the original Jerry Lewis masterwork, the Eddie Murphy reprise is a Jekyll and Hyde story. Instead of just being about a meek scientist who turns egomaniac by use of a potion, the new version adds obsession with weight loss. As tubby Sherman Klump, Eddie is sweet and brilliant. But his bulk is stopping him from getting ahead. Only after he invents a fat-reducing potion and becomes Buddy Love (an homage found in the name of another genre we'll soon discuss!) does his inner egotist come out — and the battle between his two halves begins. Being Buddy may get him places, but it stops Sherman from finding happiness. The lesson of "doing it without the magic" is nigh. Every wish is a curse, turns out, even when we get everything we *think* we really want.

OOTB Type: Thing Bottle

OOTB Cousins: *Electric Dreams, Love Potion #9, The Mask, Jumanji, Flubber, Death Becomes Her, Like Mike, Clockstoppers, Click, The Last Mimsy*

THE NUTTY PROFESSOR

Screenplay by David Sheffield & Barry W. Blaustein
And Tom Shadyac & Steve Oedekerk
Based on the motion picture
Written by Jerry Lewis *and* Bill Richmond

Opening Image: Eddie Murphy plays many roles in this film. First up is Richard Simmons clone, Lance Perkins, leading an aerobics class on TV. In the foreground, a tubby man gets ready for his day.

Set-Up: Meet Sherman Klump (Eddie in a fat suit), a college professor working on a weight-reduction formula. We get a "Save the Lab Rat" moment as he protects his guinea pig from more tests. We admire Sherman, as does his assistant (John Ales). But the college's Dean Richmond (Larry Miller) does not. Calling him on the carpet, Larry reveals Sherman's weakness: He alienates donors to the school. We also meet Miss Purty (Jada Pinkett Smith), who'll be Sherman's love interest. Sherman is too shy to ask her out. Instead he goes home where we meet the rest of the Klumps at a scatological family dinner. Through the magic of make-up, Eddie brilliantly portrays all the Klump adults. All XL.

Theme Stated: You're always going to be fat, Sherman is told by his Mom (also Eddie) in a Stasis = Death moment, but adds: "All you got to do is believe in yourself and you can do anything."

Catalyst: Inspired by his Mom, Sherman asks Jada out to a hip club, The Scream — but will Sherman get in shape in time?

Debate: Love or food? The battle between Sherman's appetite and his need to be "normal" is primal. Sherman has a nightmare that includes a take-off of *From Here to Eternity* as Sherman crushes Jada in the surf. But by the night of his date, he's ready. Sherman and Jada go to The Scream and all goes well until an insult comic (that's Dave Chappelle!) wallops Sherman with fat jokes. Sherman takes it, but the pain is palpable. After the show, Sherman drops Jada at her place and sadly heads home to stuff his face in front of the TV.

Break into Two: Later that night, he has another dream in which he imagines himself as Fatzilla. Fed up (in more ways than one), Sherman goes to the lab and creates the magic potion that will transform his life. It is a fat-reducing formula that messes with DNA and testosterone levels. Taking the potion, he now becomes, well, Eddie Murphy: confident, obnoxious... and thin!

B Story: Eddie meets Jada in Sherman's lab at school and gets stuck for an ID. He tells Jada his name is Buddy Love, a nod to the original film. We now see the Jekyll and Hyde element. Buddy asks Jada out and she agrees. But the true B story is between Sherman and Buddy. It's where the theme will be discussed. Which of his "selves" is the real Sherman?

Fun and Games: A hilarious Fun and Games montage in which Buddy discovers "Spandex!" is followed by a reprise of his date with Jada at The Scream, this time as Buddy. Extroverted Buddy seems to have been honed by Eddie himself and, like Jerry Lewis before him, there is a hint of self-revelation in his performance that adds to this amazing character. As Buddy, he is ready and bests the comic who nailed him the night before. But The Rules include the hitch that after a certain time, the effects of the potion reverse. At the club, Sherman's assistant suspects Buddy and follows him out. Discovering that Buddy is Sherman, he now becomes the Confidant.

Midpoint: With the "false victory" of the successful date, Sherman rushes to class the next day and finds the Dean waiting. Larry threatens to kill Sherman — *really*. He also sets a "time clock" in motion, and tells of an upcoming dinner that a big donor will attend. Either Sherman bags him or Larry will kill Sherman — *really*.

Bad Guys Close In: Sherman does the unthinkable and asks Jada to his family's house for dinner — and more scatology. As Sherman he can't get anywhere with Jada, yet neither can Buddy. The pressure is building. Sherman becomes Buddy to meet and woo the college donor (James Coburn) and takes Jada with him. It goes well. Too well. Egotist Buddy dumps Jada for three party girls.

All Is Lost: Jada stops by Sherman's house the next day and, since the potion has worn off, discovers *him* with the three women! Now Sherman loses Jada, too. He also gets evicted and finds his name being removed from his door at school: He is fired. A perfect "All Is Lost" moment, Sherman is "worse off than when this movie started" — all compliments of the bad mojo.

Dark Night of the Soul: Gorging with food, Sherman watches an exercise video — interrupted when Buddy appears in a spot he recorded the night before. "You can't beat me," taunts Buddy.

Break into Three: "Yes I can," says Sherman. Determined, he pours out the potion. "If I'm going to change my life, it's not going to come from some magic drink!" But Buddy tricked him; he dosed Sherman's diet-shakes with the formula. Sherman drinks one, and becomes Buddy again. Buddy now reveals his plan to "kill" Sherman with a super dose of the potion — and be Buddy forever! A and B stories cross as Buddy takes control. Knocking out his assistant, who tries to stop him, Buddy races to the big donor dinner.

Finale: Obnoxious Buddy arrives. Jumping onstage, he admits he is Sherman, exposing himself as fat then reducing instantaneously by using the formula as the audience looks on. But something goes awry. The danger of the formula is revealed as the two sides of his personality fight it out. In the end, Sherman dispatches Buddy, re-embraces his true body type, and admits his mistakes to all.

Final Image: Sherman leaves in shame. Jada runs after him. "I'm gonna be big no matter what I do," he tells her. His bulk doesn't matter to Jada or the donor. Sherman gets the girl — and the grant. Mom was right. By believing in himself, Sherman has triumphed! As we fade out, he and Jada share an awkward but loving slow dance.

WHAT WOMEN WANT (2000)

In creating a hero, it's best to start with one who has the longest journey. The protag with the furthest to go to change his ways offers the biggest bang for the peso on the premise. So when it comes to choosing someone to get the power to be able to hear *What Women Want*, who better than Mel Gibson as Nick Marshall, the ultimate ladies' man?

Director Nancy Meyers' first effort after her split with long-time partner Charles Shyer was a solid choice — for when done well these stories are favorites. And for a movie using "magic," it is one of the most thoughtful in the "Curse Bottle" category — those OOTB movies about magic the hero did not ask for, or is cursed by — but needs in order to grow. With a romantic co-starring role for Helen Hunt, and cameos by Valerie Perrine, Delta Burke, and Bette Midler, the film is a prime example of smart moviemaking. It works because it answers the question filmmakers assaying the OOTB genre must confront: What would happen if this amazing thing occurred in real life?

OOTB films might seem silly on the surface, but a good one is "about something" — and the substance of *What Women Want* is in its theme, which explores the female mind through the one guy who can benefit from the magic more than any other. What starts as an empowerment becomes a powerful example of "be careful what you wish for." It might just lead to change.

OOTB Type: Curse Bottle

OOTB Cousins: *Witchboard, The Craft, Liar Liar, The Devil's Advocate, Ella Enchanted, Bedazzled, Practical Magic, The Animal, Shallow Hal, The Ant Bully*

WHAT WOMEN WANT
Screenplay by Josh Goldsmith & Cathy Yuspa
Story by Josh Goldsmith & Cathy Yuspa *and* Diane Drake

Opening Image: "You know the expression 'a man's man?'" asks a female voice. A lot of women are talking about Nick Marshall (Mel Gibson): his ex-wife, his daughter, and the female employees at the ad agency where he works. All agree: He's a rogue. We meet Mel waking in bed, a lipstick kiss on his cheek from yet another date. Mel smiles with satisfaction, not realizing Stasis = Death.

Set-Up: Mel is a successful ad exec who lives in a luxury NYC apartment. We set up a day in Mel's life that includes chatting with his maid; his female doorman; flirting with Lola (Marisa Tomei), the girl at his building coffee shop; and being top dog at work — even if it means ignoring an office worker, Erin (Judy Greer). Mel is up for a promotion and seems sure to get it.

Theme Stated: At Minute 11, Mel's boss (Alan Alda) tells Mel: "If we don't evolve and think beyond our natural ability, we're gonna go down." Alan's talking about the agency's need to change with the times, but we know he's talking about Mel — and the theme!

Catalyst: Alan gives Mel the bad news: Mel not only lost the promotion, he lost to a woman.

Debate: Will Mel accept this affront or fight it? Mel goes to his ex-wife's wedding and learns he's getting his daughter, Alex (Ashley Johnson), for two weeks — a complication. Women are suddenly a problem for the man's man. The new boss arrives and Mel meets Darcy McGuire (Helen Hunt). Mel's first look at her in the conference room is an admiring view of her legs. This is still Mel's mindset, but we sense it's about to be challenged. New boss Helen's mantra is female-driven advertising. To get her team up to speed, she gives everyone in the meeting a pink box filled with women's products. Mel receives the totem not knowing it contains part of the "magic" he will need to transform.

Break into Two: We've come a long way since *Freaky Friday*. We know why we're seeing this movie: the magic of Mel hearing women's thoughts. But how will he acquire this power? We delay the in- evitable as Mel gets drunk and puts on nail polish and eye liner to feel in synch with the woman consumer. Director Meyers is doing a modified "Pope in the Pool" here, obscuring what we know *must* happen with fun. This includes Mel's daughter and her boyfriend surprising Mel while he's wearing pantyhose. Mel shoos them away, then gets his stockings in a twist and falls into the bathtub filled with women's products. As a magic-inducing final touch, a plugged- in hair dryer plops in, too. Mel is shocked and falls unconscious. When he wakes, we reprise Mel's "day in the life" — a common trick to show change has occurred. And it has. Mel can hear what females are thinking — even female poodles. (Double Mumbo Jumbo alert!) Welcome to Act Two, Mel.

Fun and Games: We put the B story on hold for a while to revel in the "promise of the premise." It's a fun movie idea, and part of that fun is seeing Mel deal with the magic in a "realistic" way. In director Meyers' hands, it's textbook. Step 1: Denial. Mel can't believe it, but every- where he goes, he hears women's secret thoughts. Step 2: Horror. At work, he not only hears what his female co-workers think, but what they think about him! Step 3: Sharing. The Confidant (Mark Feuerstein), a male co-worker of Mel's, doesn't believe him. Step 4: Testing. Mel overhears cries for help, too — and the one that will become most important comes from office worker Erin. Just in time for Step 5: Rejection. Mel goes home and tries to get rid of the powers by re-enacting the magic. Unable to do so, Mel visits his ex-therapist, Bette Midler. Bette tells Mel what we've known all along: He can *use* his powers! "If you know what women want, the world can be yours," she says. Step 6: Work it! Mel runs amuck using fem-telepathy to get a date with Marisa, outthink his boss Helen, and get in good with his daughter's female friends. Having the power is now amazing — and profitable — and Mel exploits it to the max.

Midpoint: Yet Mel is still not happy. As a metaphor for growth, he's failed to get the lesson — and by midpoint he knows it. A "time clock" is now in place: Mel has two weeks to learn "what women want" to win the Nike Woman account and best Helen. But after sex with Marisa — when he wows her with his insight into her thoughts — Mel starts to sense the "false victory."

B Story: Mel's real catalyst for "evolving" is Helen. In short, Mel's in love. It is through Helen that he will learn and grow.

Bad Guys Close In: Mel wins the Nike account, dazzles his daughter when they shop for a prom dress, and kisses Helen — but his powers make this a cheat. We are "closing in" on the fact that Mel is hopelessly self-centered and still resists change.

All Is Lost: Helen is fired and Mel gets her job — and he sees how wrong he's been. Ironically, by getting everything he wanted, he is "worse off than when this movie started." The "whiff of death" includes overhearing Erin, who is considering suicide.

Dark Night of the Soul: Mel runs through rain to save Erin from killing herself. On the way, a lightning strike reverses the magic and takes his powers away. Has Mel learned his lesson?

Break into Three: Mel now tries to negotiate the world of women without hearing their thoughts. A and B stories cross as Mel tells Alan that Helen should be boss. And when he gets a call from his daughter, who's being pressured for sex by her boyfriend at the prom, he rushes there and shows love — just by listening.

Finale: Mel has yet to win Helen. In a showdown, he seeks her out to tell her he got her job back — and confesses he stole her ideas. Helen fires Mel, but still loves him. Mel calls Helen "my hero" for helping him evolve (an echo of *Pretty Woman*'s ending).

Final Image: Helen and Mel kiss and Mel can now begin anew. No longer "a man's man," Mel has become... Synthesis Man! He has transformed his world by changing his attitude about it.

ETERNAL SUNSHINE OF THE SPOTLESS MIND (2004)

Sometimes the magic is like an acid trip. But just because the word "trip" is involved doesn't mean you went anywhere. In director Michel Gondry's *Eternal Sunshine of the Spotless Mind*, the tale is less journey than psychedelic brain-scrub in the OOTB sub-genre "Surreal Bottle." In this category — whether it's playing with time in *The Butterfly Effect* or changing the rules of fate like in *Groundhog Day* — the movies all feel like "a dream." But each ends with the hero learning what all heroes of the OOTB movie discover: that things were pretty good back in "real" life.

Featuring a toned-down Jim Carrey, an amped-up Kate Winslet, and written by Charlie Kaufman (*Adaptation*), who is best known as a screenwriting iconoclast, the film asks the question: Can you erase the memory of love and defy fate? Thanks to the sci-fi-ish Lacuna Inc. ("lacuna" defined by Webster's as "a gap or place where something is missing"), Jim will try to do just that, and x out the memory of a relationship gone wrong. Midway through the process Jim regrets his decision, and together he and Kate will try to save their love. What follows is a mad dash across the mindscape that purportedly abandons the boring old three-act screenplay structure.

But does it?

You decide.

OOTB Type: Surreal Bottle

OOTB Cousins: *It's a Wonderful Life, Heaven Can Wait, Field of Dreams, Scrooged, Groundhog Day, Pleasantville, The Butterfly Effect, Primer, Sliding Doors, The Family Man*

ETERNAL SUNSHINE OF THE SPOTLESS MIND
Screenplay by Charlie Kaufman
Story by Charlie Kaufman & Michel Gondry & Pierre Bismuth

Opening Image: Joel Barish (Jim Carrey) wakes, not sure where he is. He goes out to his car and finds it dented. It's Valentine's Day. ("A day designed to make people feel like crap.") Jim skips work and gets on a train to Montauk. He finds pages ripped out of his sketchbook: "It appears this is my first entry in two years."

Theme Stated: On the way back, Jim meets Clementine (Kate Winslet). She says: "I can't tell from one minute to the next what I'm going to like, but right now I'm glad you're here." That is our theme: the battle between the ideal and the real.

Set-Up: Turns out Jim and Kate were lovers. What we are seeing is the day *after* Jim had his memory of her erased. Now he gives Kate a ride home, and, as strangers, they fall in love all over again. Only after dropping Kate off does Jim sense trouble. A stranger (Elijah Wood) appears asking: "Can I help you with something?"

Catalyst: We now go back to the day that Jim headed home to begin the Lacuna Inc. process. He'll take a sleeping pill, lie down in bed, and await the Lacuna team to come in and erase his memory of Kate. A neighbor Jim meets in his mailroom mentions that Valentine's Day is getting close.

Debate: What's going on? As Jim re-lives that mailroom scene, we flash back to how he learned of this amazing process. A friend (David Cross) tells Jim that Lacuna Inc. erased Kate's memory of him. Jim storms into the ramshackle office, meets perky office assistant Mary (Kirsten Dunst) and the inventor of the Lacuna procedure, Dr. Mierzwiak (Tom Wilkinson). Jim demands an explanation and learns that Kate wanted him gone.

Break into Two: At Minute 27, Jim decides to do likewise and is told to collect everything connected to Kate so they can destroy all evidence of her. This explains why his sketchbook is missing two years of entries — the length of their relationship. Now, with Jim asleep, Stan (Mark Ruffalo) and the mysterious stranger we'll know as Patrick (Elijah Wood) arrive to oversee the brain scrub. More flashbacks as we learn how Jim and Kate met for the first time: in Montauk at a beach party with friends. We also see how their initial happiness devolved into alcohol-soaked co-dependence. Time begins to cut out; is Jim conscious or not? Hearing the name Patrick makes Jim resist the memory erase. It was the name Jim heard when he visited a post-scrub Kate at work.

B Story: There are multiple B stories, all dealing with love. Elijah is the Confidant; he was present when Kate underwent her procedure and is using what he learned about her life with Jim to woo her. We also see Mark and Kirsten flirt when she drops by — and Elijah ducks out to have a Valentine's date with Kate. But the main B story is Kirsten's crush on Dr. Mierzwiak. The fallout of their relationship will kick the A story into Act Three, where the theme is clarified.

Fun and Games: We have two worlds at play now. Up top, in "real" life, Kate and Elijah go out for Valentine's Day. But in his mind, Jim is having second thoughts about the erasure. Having sensed something is not kosher with this Patrick character, Jim chases Kate in his imaginary world to convince her to come back to him, and to keep his memories of her intact. But even in his mind, she's still mad at him and eludes him as scenes of their relationship vanish. This is the "promise of the premise" as Jim runs through his imagination, from memory to memory, trying to understand The Rules in order to stop Kate from being expunged.

Midpoint: At Minute 54, Jim yells, "I want to call this off!" In "real" life, Elijah takes Kate out and repeats a line Jim used; Kate realizes something's wrong, but doesn't know what. This is the "false victory" turn, as back in Jim's mind, his memory version of Kate agrees to help him. Their only hope is to look for spots in Jim's mind where the erasure process won't find her.

Bad Guys Close In: Flashback to Jim's childhood, as Kate and Jim don many guises. Bad guys (in this case the Lacuna process) search and destroy Jim's memories. There is conflict too as Mark and Kirsten discover Jim's brain erase is off track. Dr. Mierzwiak is called to Jim's house to fix the problem.

All Is Lost: Looking for a place in his memory to hide her, Jim and Kate find a day as a boy when he killed a bird ("whiff of death"). As two little kids, like narrators observing this incident, they know they can't hang onto their love for long.

Dark Night of the Soul: Left alone with Dr. Mierzwiak, Kirsten quotes the Alexander Pope poem from which the title of the movie stems. Kirsten tries to kiss Dr. Mierzwiak, who resists her as Mark watches through the window. Then Dr. Mierzwiak's wife shows up and spills the beans: Kirsten and the Doc had an affair. Even though Kirsten had her memory of the affair erased, she is doomed to keep repeating her behavior. The Lacuna process does not work.

Break into Three: Jim and Kate relive the day they met. "I wish I'd stayed," he says. "I wish I'd done a lot of things." Before she vanishes, Kate whispers: "Meet me in Montauk." A and B stories cross as a spurned Kirsten steals Jim's and Kate's files.

Finale: We return to the beginning with Jim waking, memory erased. He gets up, goes to Montauk, and meets Kate. But they now get a real second chance: Kirsten has sent files to all Mierzwiak's

clients. Hearing tapes of themselves describing their past relationship, the brain-scrubbed Kate and Jim realize they already met
and failed at love. Should they consider it again?

Final Image: Jim and Kate recommit. Synthesis! What they had
adds to what they learned. Eyes opened, they will try once more.

🐾 *Let's get chummy! The first fin is spotted at Minute 31 of the indie gem* Open Water, *and the "life or death" struggle that ensues is pure "Dude with a Problem."*

4 DUDE WITH A PROBLEM

When fellow screenwriter Mike Cheda and I were sitting around one day trying to figure out what to name a certain type of movie, we kept calling each other "dude." We are 40-year-old adults at this point, seasoned movie veterans wary of the fads Hollywood is prone to — even fads of language. And yet there we were:

"Dude, listen you're wrong…"

"No, dude, you don't get it…"

So when it came to coining a term for the genre of movie that pits an "ordinary man" against "extraordinary circumstances"… the "D word" just naturally crept in.

And "Dude with a Problem" was born.

In trying to categorize the kind of story in which the hero finds himself in way over his head, there seemed to be no better way to phrase it. For this is the story type typified by *The Wrong Man* with Henry Fonda, *North by Northwest* starring Cary Grant, and *Die Hard* with Bruce Willis. Average schmos, minding their own bee's-dust, who, through no fault of their own, suddenly have a dragnet closing in on them — and a hot blonde offering her train compartment for the night because she is the only person who "believes."

The roots of these movies are found in any story about survival. From the Bible, Daniel in the Lion's Den and Noah and his flood dilemma come to mind. We could also look to author Jack London and his Arctic adventures as a source of what it means to endure the challenges of nature. These are tales of the "lone man," "lone woman," or "lone group" that find themselves facing incredible odds — and whose survival often includes a struggle with sanity.

The best DWAP stories remind us we're not only *not* average, but have hidden strength. Like the heros of many a DWAP movie, we are looking for a chance to prove ourselves. There is also the sense of something special happening, an electric feeling in the air that the whole world is suddenly consumed with the hero and, by proxy, *us*! The survival instinct this story sharpens makes us feel alive — and may be why there are so many variations.

There is the "Spy Problem" as seen in *North by Northwest* and *Enemy of the State*, where a lone man or woman runs afoul of secret agents. There's the "Law Enforcement Problem" (*Die Hard, Breakdown*) where a hero must go it alone by skating between the bad guys *and* the police. There's the "Domestic Problem" like *Sleeping with the Enemy* and *Wait Until Dark* — stories in which the hero finds his home is not as safe as he thought! There are also "acts of God" that send us into a world of hurt I call the "Nature Problem," stories that show how alone we can feel when facing disease (*Lorenzo's Oil, Champions*), wild animals (*The Edge, Open Water*), and survival outdoors (*Alive*). And since the end of the world is a disaster for lots of dudes, we get the "Epic Problem" to see how the many survive (*Armageddon, Outbreak*).

As you can tell, the situations are endless, but the rules are the same: (1) an "innocent hero" thrust into trouble without asking for it; (2) a "sudden event" that draws him in with no warning; and (3) a "test of survival" — it's life or death, and whether the hero endures will try his every fiber.

One of the reasons we identify with the "dude," or "dudette," as the case may be, is: We are dudes, too. Yup, we're just like Jimmy Stewart in *The Man Who Knew Too Much*, well-meaning *dufi* on vacation in Iraq — or some such place — just dippy-doodling along when wham! An international plot drops in our lap. Like Jimmy, we aren't looking for trouble. And though this kinda thing doesn't often occur — it might!

Did Bruce Willis do anything to cause euro-baddies to take over his wife's building in *Die Hard*? No. Did the human race cause a meteor to zero in on the eastern seaboard in *Deep Impact*? Did not. But because these are tales of survival, and not punishment for a sin we committed, what the hero did to get into this dilemma is not what the movie's about.

Another key factor in the traditional DWAP set-up is the "suddenness" of the event that puts the hero in over his head. These catalysts come from nowhere and force the hero(es) to come to grips with what's happening ASAP. As in *Breakdown*, when Kurt Russell finds his wife gone, and even in *Sleeping with the Enemy* when Julia Roberts is violently struck by her husband, it's clear the heroes must make a choice — and that includes taking action quickly.

What is the "problem" a dude must confront? Hopefully, it's big. It must be "life or death." The true test of whether or not the script you're working on falls into the DWAP category is when you pitch it, describing the situation you've put your hero(es) in, the listener has only one reaction: "Dude! *That's a PROBLEM!!*" And hopefully what the pitchee thinks next is: What would *I* do in that situation?

If so, you know you have a winner!

Many of the movies in this category star men, but whether it's a dude or a dudette who's the hero of your story, often that hero's love interest is the only person who believes — and the one who offers solace. The stellar example is Eva Marie Saint in *North by Northwest*. It's been a wild ride up till then for star and DWAP poster boy Cary Grant, with no respite until *she* comes along. And though Eva is a spy working for the other side, at the moment it feels like just the relief Cary needs.

This is a common beat in the DWAP adventure: When our hero is tossed into many a maelstrom, there is often that **eye of the storm** moment — and a partner who is the one friendly ally in a sea of trouble. It doesn't have to be a love interest offering a romantic interlude — although it helps! This character not only provides a place to discuss what's happening, but gives the screenwriter a break from the A story. In *Die Hard* it's a cop, Reginald VelJohnson; in *Deep Impact* it's Tea Leoni's mother, Vanessa Redgrave. And in *Open Water*, when the couple treading water have no "other" to turn to, it is the moment when they play down their situation and find escape in a game of movie trivia.

Most DWAP movies are of the "triumph of the spirit" variety and most end with that beat — the rugged individual has survived! It would be a pure downer if after going through this adventure, the hero's efforts add up to nothing. Yet movies like *Open Water* and *The Perfect Storm* prove that surviving the saga isn't in the cards for everybody. This is a benefit of the group adventure. With more than one "dude," you can kill off a few, save others, and show the valuable lesson of what each did to deserve his fate. *Alive*, *The Flight of the Phoenix*, and *The Edge* show us the various ways to survive the saga with our nobility intact — or not.

One thing is certain: A good Dude with a Problem story is immediate and as primal as a bear attack, for like Monster in the House, this is the kind of tale we like to hear when our fellow cave dwellers come home bruised and battered and we ask:

"Geez, Og, what happened?!"

THE TELLTALE SIGNS YOU HAVE A PROBLEM, DUDE

Here's a fast test to see if the idea you're circling is of the Dude variety and if Eva Marie Saint is in your future:

1. An "innocent hero" is dragged into this mess without asking for it — or even aware of how he got involved.

2. A "sudden event" that thrusts our innocent(s) into the world of hurt is definite — and comes without warning.

3. A "life or death" battle is at stake — and the continued existence of an individual, family, group, or society is in question.

The wide variety of problems and life-or-death situations that follow show just how much trouble we get into when we dudes aren't looking.

THREE DAYS OF THE CONDOR (1975)

A direct descendant of *North by Northwest* and uncle to recent offerings like *Enemy of the State* and *The Bourne Identity*, this smart, Sydney Pollack-directed, Robert Redford vehicle is a notable DWAP stepping stone and a great example of the "Spy Problem."

In the midst of the Watergate era and its can't-trust-anyone zeitgeist, films like this one, *The Parallax View*, and *Marathon Man* are mid-'70s paranoid classics. It also offers truisms seen in any DWAP story in which the group turns against the individual, and what we thought of as safe becomes uncertain — and even dangerous. Friends are suddenly suspect, all because — by accident or design — the hero appears to have gone over to the other side. Now the network that clothed and fed the hero becomes his adversary, and the lesson learned includes how he joined up with this group in the first place.

And since all stories are about transformation, Bob starts as a mild-mannered reader for the CIA and ends up a man of conviction toppling a nefarious plot from the inside. Only by being "on the run" can he get to the bottom of it — but will he? With the help of Faye Dunaway as a reluctant "eye of the storm," Cliff Robertson as the spy who knows too much, and the ever-fabulous John Houseman as... John Houseman, the movie is prescient in ways other spy sagas of its era are not.

DWAP Type: Spy Problem

DWAP Cousins: *North by Northwest, The Man Who Knew Too Much, The Long Kiss Goodnight, The Net, Enemy of the State, The Bourne Identity, Paycheck, The Bourne Supremacy, Nowhere to Run, Shooter*

THREE DAYS OF THE CONDOR
Screenplay by Lorenzo Semple, Jr. *and* David Rayfiel
Based on the novel SIX DAYS OF THE CONDOR
by James Grady

Opening Image: Information being processed by a primordial computer. We're in the American Literary Historical Society — a CIA front. Everyone is at work but one. Joseph Turner (Robert Redford) is riding his moped through NYC traffic, late again.

Theme Stated: At work, Bob (I call him Bob) talks to his boss about his job as a CIA reader. The boss is critical of Bob's ability to be secretive. "I actually trust a few people," Bob replies. Who can Bob trust? And who can we?

Set-Up: Across the street, G. Joubert (Max von Sydow) checks off everyone arriving at ALHS. We suspect something bad is about to happen. Bob and his workplace girlfriend talk of their plans for the evening.

Catalyst: Bob ducks out the back under the radar to pick up lunch as Max and his hit men enter. All in the ALHS, including Bob's girlfriend, are assassinated.

Debate: Bob returns and finds the group wiped out. But why? Bob grabs the receptionist's handgun and exits fast. Now everyone seems suspicious. At a phone booth, Bob calls CIA headquarters. Though the spy tech and lingo are creaky, the "Limp and an Eyepatch" bits include "The Major," a wheelchair-bound agency operator who's always on duty, and the suave CIA chief, J. Higgins (Cliff Robertson). Cliff advises Bob not to go home. He is reminded of his code name: Condor. Typical rebel, Bob disobeys and visits a co-worker, finding him dead. What is going on?

Break into Two: Bob is to be "brought in" by his section chief Wicks (Michael Kane) and a friend, Sam (Walter McGinn). But when Bob arrives in the dark NYC alley and begins to come in from the cold, gunplay. Sam is killed, and Wicks is wounded when Bob makes a lucky shot. *Run, Bob, Run!* Dude, we're thinking, you have *so* got a problem! But this is what happens when you work for the CIA.

B Story: Seeking an "eye of the storm," Bob kidnaps Kathy Hale (Faye Dunaway) and takes her to her apartment at gunpoint. "I need some safe quiet time to pull things together," he tells her. Faye is a photographer whose work reflects her loneliness. It's through this "love story" that Bob will learn about "trust" and grow as a man... and a spy.

Fun and Games: The "promise of the premise" is the lone man on the run. Adding to the intrigue, when Cliff meets with CIA higher-ups, they speculate about who Condor really is. We now meet Wabash (John Houseman). Other than his role in *The Paper Chase*, this is one of his most Houseman-y performances. In discussing Condor, the CIA agents repeat the set-up of what makes this character so compelling: "He reads everything." Can Bob's skills as a catholic bookworm make him a super spy? We shall see. Reminiscent of *North by Northwest*, the CIA is willing to let Condor draw fire to see how this intrigue pans out.

Midpoint: Spurred by a TV news report that whitewashes the murder in the alley, Bob decides to risk leaving Faye tied up, and visits his murdered friend's wife. When Bob gets to the apartment building, he interacts with Max and barely escapes. In and out of the lion's mouth, it is a "false victory," but he's met his foe — a key dramatic convention in these stories (see *Die Hard*). Despite Bob's efforts to escape unnoticed, Max spots the license plate of Faye's car. Returning home, Bob unties Faye and indulges in a cheesy love scene — even for the fondue '70s. A and B stories cross as two lonely people find each other.

Bad Guys Close In: The next morning, head cleared by his nude wrestle with Ms. Dunaway, Bob has a chance to re-think events. Just as he's figuring it out, one of Max's hit-man buddies appears at Faye's door. This is one of the best close contact fight scenes ever, one that surely influenced a similar clash in *The Bourne Identity* with Matt Damon as another Dude with a Problem. Fighting off "The Mailman," Bob barely kills the killer as Faye cries out in fear. Having doubted his story, she finally believes him. Faye and Bob now work together to kidnap Cliff from the Twin Towers where he works — ironic, no? Something's rotten in the company, Cliff tells Bob. Even more so when Bob learns...

All Is Lost: ... Wicks died. Someone snuck into the hospital where he was recuperating and finished the job. The "whiff of death" includes the death of hope to solve this mystery.

Dark Night of the Soul: Bob is nowhere, neither in the agency nor out of it. "Maybe there's another CIA inside the CIA?" he asks.

Break into Three: Bob tries Synthesis to solve the mystery. Using the knowledge he gained as a reader, plus the new skills — suspicion and deception — he has acquired while on the run, he taps Max's phone and turns the tables on his CIA bosses.

Finale: After saying goodbye to Faye, and returning to the B story theme of "trust" by making her promise she won't talk, Bob heads off to confront a CIA heavy at the heart of the mystery in Washington DC. In a showdown, Bob confronts the man and learns what the conspiracy is about. At ALHS, Bob had unwittingly turned up a secret plot to invade the Middle East for its oil. *Hmmmmm*. Before Bob can learn more, Max enters and kills the man, saving Bob from the task and bringing the episode full circle. In a much-parodied coda, Max tells Bob how the end will come for him, then gives his gun back. "For that day," he tells the man he now respects.

Final Image: Bob takes Cliff to *The New York Times*, revealing he told them everything. In a bookend image, information is being processed again, this time by "the people" — but will anyone believe Bob? As Bob ducks into the crowd, Cliff wonders — and so do we. In light of recent events, it's a haunting finale.

DIE HARD (1988)

"Yippie-ki-yay!" gets a postmodern patina when concrete cowboy Bruce Willis brings *High Noon* to Century City as "Law Enforcement Problem" über-dude, John McClane. Director John McTiernan's action classic is one of those iconic movies that has been re-set in many situations, and with many stars, but from *Under Siege* (*Die Hard* on a boat) and *Speed* (*Die Hard* on a bus) to the more recent *Red Eye* and *Flightplan* (both pitched and sold as *Die Hard* on a plane), all pale by comparison.

What makes the original unique is its primal-ness. The logline includes the fact that Bruce and his wife (Bonnie Bedelia) are separated when the movie starts. She is pursuing her career, and average Joes like Bruce aren't needed in a world of expense accounts and Lear jets. Part of what makes Bruce stick to the task of ridding his wife's building of pesky German terrorists (led by a never-better Alan Rickman) is to prove average Joes have worth.

The confrontation is also an example of how good guy and bad guy are a perfect fit. If Bruce were a civilian, it would stretch believability; a retired CIA agent, too cliché. The balance of one street cop, one muscle T, and one .45 is just right against ponytails and accents. But as the sex objects and bullets fly by, we're clear on what's really at stake: When a man loves a woman... no Uzi can stop him.

DWAP Type: Law Enforcement Problem

DWAP Cousins: *Outland, Breakdown, Under Siege, The Fugitive, Speed, Air Force One, Flightplan, Red Eye, Firewall, Man on Fire*

DIE HARD
Screenplay by Jeb Stuart *and* Steven E. de Souza
Based on the novel NOTHING LASTS FOREVER
by Roderick Thorp

Opening Image: A plane lands at LAX. On board, a businessman advises "how to survive" traveling. The advisee is John McClane (Bruce Willis). Pre-9/11 Bruce carries a gun. He's a NYC cop.

Theme Stated: "Survival" is our theme — and Bruce's mission.

Set-Up: Atop Century City, Mr. Takagi (James Shigeta), the boss here at Nakatomi Plaza, wishes Merry Xmas to his employees, including Holly Gennero McClane (Bonnie Bedelia) and coke-head co-worker, Harry Ellis (Hart Bochner). I often use the term "on the verge of" to set up the heroes of a movie, and here Bruce and Bonnie are "on the verge of" divorce. As Bruce explains to his friendly limo driver, his wife had "a good job that turned into a great career" and now they are unhappily bi-coastal. From her office, Bonnie calls home to say hi to her kids (more stakes) as Bruce arrives and sees Bonnie is using her maiden name. But as Bruce washes up and gets into a fight with Bonnie, there is more trouble than the marriage. At Minute 14, a mystery truck arrives.

Catalyst: The truck signals an invasion as "suddenly" a dozen robbers posing as terrorists enter, kill the lobby guard, lock down the building, and storm the party. Meet Alan Rickman as their ringleader, Hans Grüber, and his henchman of few words, Karl (Alexander Godunov).

Debate: Alerted to the commotion, Bruce grabs his gun and begins to assess the situation. Bruce's low-tech approach, like noting the names the robbers call each other and where they're located in the building, will help defeat them. And speaking of *da feet*, Bruce is handicapped by being barefoot – nice touch! Corralling the hostages and Bonnie, Alan gets down to business. He wants the millions in the vault and demands the combination. When Takagi refuses, he is killed, and Bruce is spotted. What is Bruce to do?

Break into Two: "Think, think," Bruce says to himself. His running patter, and the "lone defender of the fort" odds, are what humanize him and what is original about this character. He's not superman, he's a street cop, and a smart one. The action is divided into three phases: (1) Bruce trying to get the cops to help; (2) Bruce working with the cops to stop the baddies; and (3) Bruce realizing he has to stop the baddies alone. Phase 1 begins at Minute 31 when Bruce pulls the fire alarm, hoping to bring the LAFD. Bruce has now entered the "upside-down world" of Act Two.

Fun and Games: The LAFD thinks the alarm is a hoax, and one of the baddies is sent after Bruce. At Minute 38, Bruce fights with the guy and rolls down the stairs, breaking the man's neck. Now Bruce ups the ante. He takes the baddie's machine gun and (seemingly unnecessary) lighter, and sends the body in an elevator car to Alan with a message: "Ho-Ho-Ho." Alan is perturbed. But Alexander is pissed: The dead man was his bruddah! Alexander goes after Bruce on the rooftop and Bruce fires back. Despite the gunplay, the cops are still MIA. Bruce is chased into the elevator shaft where, using the lighter to see, he has a memorable line: "Come out to the *coast*! We'll get *together*, have a few *laughs*!"

B Story: LAPD Sergeant Powell (Reginald VelJohnson) arrives to check on the fire alarm. Freed from his air duct, and having killed two henchmen, Bruce throws one body through the window to get the cop's attention and make Reginald the "eye of the storm." Finally, the cops are on their way, and it's all due to Bruce.

Midpoint: "False victory" his, Bruce now "raises the stakes" for himself. Using the bad guy's walkie-talkie, Bruce contacts Alan, letting him know he killed three of his men, brought the LAPD, and has his detonators. Alan cites Bruce for being a cowboy and Bruce replies with his famous Roy Rogers epithet. Alan is worried and asks his men how much longer the safe-cracking will take.

Bad Guys Close In: Pressure builds with this new "time clock" and Bruce has an ally in Reginald, but Reginald's boss (Paul Gleason) thinks Bruce is one of the bad guys. At 1 Hour 15 Minutes, Bruce sees the cops try to storm the building, not realizing Alan's planned for this. With an LAPD vehicle under fire, Phase 2 (Bruce trying to help the cops) begins as Bruce sends a bomb down the elevator shaft and kills two more of Alan's men. All Bruce needs to do is wait it out. But then one of the "internal team" members, Hart, does a dumb thing. Coked up, he decides to negotiate with Alan, and is killed. The baddies now know Bruce's name — and so do the cops. But it doesn't matter: The FBI has arrived on the scene.

All Is Lost: As the FBI take over the operation, Alan bumps into Bruce while searching the building, and pretends to be a civilian. This is a very nice moment — and vital — for without a mano-a-mano with Alan before the climax, the ending would not be nearly as effective. Alan also learns of Bruce's handicap: his bare feet. "Shoot the glass," he yells at Alexander. Bruce escapes but his feet are bloody and the detonators are back in Alan's hands.

Dark Night of the Soul: Bruce has done all he can. A and B stories cross as he laments via walkie-talkie with Reginald, who reveals he accidentally shot a kid while on duty several years earlier. Reginald too has a personal issue to overcome.

Break into Three: Baddies open the vault and, with the detonators back, get ready to escape. But when Bonnie is exposed on the news as Bruce's wife, Alan takes her as his own personal hostage. With his wife in jeopardy, Phase 3 kicks in: Bruce must save her, with or without the cops.

Finale: With the bad guys about to escape with the bearer bonds (that's what all worthwhile crooks stole in the '80s), Bruce jumps into action. We get some great set pieces as Bruce "kills" Alexander and barefoots it to the roof to save the hostages. Then a returned-from-hell Bruce makes an appearance with back lighting to rescue his wife. "Hi honey," he deadpans. In the shootout with Alan, Bruce outsmarts and kills him. "Happy trails, Hans." Bruce and Bonnie kiss.

Final Image: Bruce meets Reginald and they hug. Alexander makes a last appearance and is killed by Reginald who, by doing so, gets over the shooting incident that's haunted him. Together again, Bruce takes Bonnie home in the limo to the tune of "Let It Snow."

SLEEPING WITH THE ENEMY (1991)

Trouble abounds out there in the world, but when you cross paths with CIA agents and bank robbers posing as terrorists, what, pray tell, do you expect? All the more surprising that the sub-genre of DWAP movie called the "Domestic Problem" offers so many variations of survival issues that happen right in your own home — or very close to the home front. None is more indicative than the Ronald Bass-scripted, Joseph Ruben-directed variation on the "woman in jeopardy" flick that secured Julia Roberts' fame immediately after *Pretty Woman*.

The problem here is that Julia has married the wrong guy, and though I too like my kitchen counters to be nice and clean, I don't need 'em *that* clean — but Mr. Obsessive-Compulsive, Patrick Bergin, does. He also, in his own weird way, "loves" Julia, which is why he controls her every second of every day — until Julia decides to fake her death and make a run for it. And if you thought the guy was mad before, he is super-duper p.o.'d now — especially when he discovers Julia's ruse in one of the great horrific moments in movie history.

As Julia tries to make a new start with an "eye of the storm" romance (Kevin Anderson), the bad guy closes in, and we realize a life-or-death finale of the "Dude" kind is in the offing.

DWAP Type: Domestic Problem

DWAP Cousins: *Sorry, Wrong Number; Wait Until Dark; When a Stranger Calls; Blink; Cape Fear; Misery; Suicide Kings; A Perfect Murder; Hostage; Enough*

SLEEPING WITH THE ENEMY

Screenplay by Ronald Bass
Based on the novel by Nancy Price

Opening Image: A lone woman, Laura Burney (Julia Roberts), walks along the shore digging for clams; she appears to be content. Then an equally attractive man, Martin Burney (Patrick Bergin), joins her. He is wearing a suit and when she brushes up against him, getting sand on him, she apologizes. "Don't worry, I have time to change," he says. Something's odd, but what?

Set-Up: The brilliance of this set-up is we are being shown a "happy couple," but the tension between them is hypnotic and draws us in. When they go to a party that night, he insists she wear a different dress than the one she picked out, and at the party, he watches her. Is he in love or obsessed? The next day when he calls Julia into the bathroom to berate her for not having the towels hanging... just... so... we know. The guy has OCD. Like, really bad. He then talks to a neighbor with a boat and reveals Julia is afraid of water.

Catalyst: At Minute 10, jealous that Julia may have talked to the neighbor, he hits her without warning. Though we know it isn't the first time, this "sudden event" forces our hero to take action. Like real stories of domestic violence, this is life or death. Dudette, you have so got a problem.

Debate: Does she have a plan? We watch Julia knock out the lights along the shore in front of their beach house, and though she's afraid of water, the couple goes for a midnight sail.

Theme Stated: "We can't conquer our fears by running away," Patrick says. He thinks he's talking about Julia's fear of water.

Break into Two: They set off on their sailing trip and it begins to rain. During a tense moment, Julia drops off the back of the boat, seeming to drown at sea. By Minute 25, Patrick arrives back home and throws their honeymoon statue through the window and screams "Loora!" (translation: Laura!) Let the "upside-down world" of Act Two begin. In flashback, we now see the real story, and hear her voice-over: "That was the night that I died..." Though afraid of water, she forced herself to learn to swim. The broken lights in front of the house were so she could ID a landmark from the water that night. Her well-planned escape includes cutting her hair, flushing her wedding ring down the toilet, and donning a wig. She relates all this to a lady on the bus and reveals a DWAP truism: When Julia married Patrick, she was unaware of his problems. Julia lands in a new town, rents a house, and at Minute 35, she's moved in and started a new life. Meanwhile back home, Patrick discovers the broken glass of the light bulbs.

B Story: Julia now meets Ben Woodward (Kevin Anderson). He is a drama teacher at the local college. He seems a little creepy at first, but maybe that's just because Julia, and we, are still weirded out about her trusting any man again. He will help Julia "conquer" her fears.

Fun and Games: Being on the road, moving into a new place, and setting up her new identity is the fun of this premise. The idea that we can re-invent our lives is a fantasy many entertain, and how we would do it if we could get away with it is the "poster" of this movie. We also sense that Patrick is not giving up so fast. Back home, he is bereft and wondering what he did wrong — while scouring things and keeping the towels nice and straight.

Midpoint: A and B stories cross as Julia starts to cotton to Kevin and her confidence returns. He lives next door and stops by a lot and, after awhile, we can see that this might go somewhere. But this "false victory" is short. Patrick learns Julia took swimming lessons at the Y. And at Minute 46, he finds her wedding ring in the commode. She is alive! The "stakes are raised."

Bad Guys Close In: Having wondered why Julia seems to have been bruised, Kevin now learns the truth about Julia's condition and her name: "Sarah Waters" is thematic but fake. Julia doesn't want to share and he walks away — something new in her experience with men. Patrick hires detectives to track down Julia's mother, who lives in an old folks home and is blind. We get the sense that Patrick is capable of anything now.

All Is Lost: After a star-driven montage in which Julia tries on costumes for Kevin at the drama department — to the feel-good crooning of Van Morrison's "Brown Eyed Girl" — Kevin tries to make love to her, but she can't. Julia is "worse off than when this movie started." She had thought by escaping she might live again. Now she knows more change must occur.

Dark Night of the Soul: Julia is in a nether world; she can neither go back nor move forward.

Break into Three: In a great bit of Synthesis, Julia takes action and disguises herself as a man to visit her blind Mom. "You have yourself," Mom tells her. Julia doesn't realize that Patrick is also there. In an eerie scene after Julie leaves, Patrick pretends to be a cop; when he can't get Julia's address from her Mother, he is about to smother her when a nurse interrupts.

Finale: Tracking down Julia, Patrick now zeroes in. And the show-down is great. It's night. She's in the bathtub and senses something's wrong. The towels are straight, and, when she goes into the kitchen, the cans of tuna are stacked just so. She knows. And so do we. A and B stories cross again as Kevin comes to the rescue but is knocked cold. See, this is the part Julia has to do herself to conquer her fear.

Final Image: Shooting Patrick, Julia watches as he reaches out for her wedding band that's fallen from his grip. She ends the reunion with a last blast. Julia is finally free.

DEEP IMPACT (1998)

And then there is a problem for the many. Like any DWAP, this time a multitude of dudes is going about their business when a news flash comes: Sorry, folks, the end of the world is… now!

Be it the raining down of nuclear warheads (*The Day After*), a pestilence loosed on the land (*Outbreak*), a bad wire that causes a holocaust in your *Towering Inferno*, or a change in weather that freezes the planet (*The Day After Tomorrow*), the "upside-down version of the world" now includes a *bunch* of you trying to survive. Better known as the "Disaster Movie," the "Epic Problem" gives us a chance to bid farewell to our big, blue marble — and lets us enjoy getting a free run of the place!

One of two "comet hits the Earth" movies in 1998, along with *Armageddon*, director Mimi Leder's *Deep Impact* is a thoughtful meditation on what "the end" might look like. But with the comet not hitting until Act Three, the lack of urgency could lead to a **Watch out for that glacier!** feeling — the peril of *nothing* happening while we wait for the end to come. It may explain why, when you veer from the rules of this or any story type, you do so at your own risk. How do we fill up the middle? Let's see how two of our most admired screenwriters, Bruce Joel Rubin (*Ghost*) and Michael Tolkin (*The Player*), met the challenge.

DWAP type: Epic Problem

DWAP cousins: *The Towering Inferno, The Poseidon Adventure, Earthquake, Meteor, The Day After, Volcano, Dante's Peak, Outbreak, The Day After Tomorrow, Armageddon*

DEEP IMPACT
Written by Bruce Joel Rubin *and* Michael Tolkin

Opening Image: Telescopes point at the sky. Teenager Leo Beiderman (Elijah Wood) flirts with Sarah (Leelee Sobieksi), then sees some kind of astral anomaly; Frodo snaps a phodo.

Set-Up: A nerdy astronomer (Charles Martin Smith) examines Elijah's pictures and guess what: It's a humongeroid heading right for us. Alarmed, Charles jumps in a jeep with the evidence and is killed in a crash. At Minute 7: "One year later." Meet Jenny Lerner (Tea Leoni), ambitious reporter. Tea wants to be news anchor but her boss (Laura Innes), the mother of a little girl, is holding her back. Tea meets her mom (Vanessa Redgrave) and talks about the coming re-marriage of Tea's dad in a Stasis = Death beat. Back at work, Tea gets a tip about a government official who resigned under a cloud because of "Ellie."

Catalyst: Tea chases down the official (James Cromwell), thinking the tip's about an affair. But no. When she asks him about "Ellie" he says: "It's the biggest story in history."

Theme Stated: At Minute 14, James adds: "What differences does anything make anymore? I wanted to be with my family. Can you understand that?" In a roundabout way, James has touched on our theme: What are our priorities, and how should we live life?

Debate: If "Ellie" isn't a girl, what is it? At Minute 16, Tea is grabbed by the FBI and taken to a secret location to meet the President (Morgan Freeman). Sit on the story for two days, Morgan bargains, and Tea will get a front row seat at the press conference. Still in the dark, Tea says yes. At Minute 20, Tea uses Google (in what has replaced the microfiche-at-the-library scene) and discovers "Ellie" is "E.L.E." an "Extinction Level Event." Shaken, Tea meets her father (Maximilian Schell) and his new bride and is rude to both.

Break into Two: At the White House, Tea outshines her boss and is placed front row center as Morgan announces a giant asteroid is heading toward Earth. All are scared, but calmed somewhat by Morgan's announcement that he has a plan. At Minute 29...

B Story: ...Morgan introduces the US/Russian astronaut team of the *Messiah* spacecraft. Led by Captain Spurgeon "Fish" Tanner (Robert Duvall), they will fly up there and blast the thing with nuclear warheads. Also watching at Minute 33 is Elijah, who learns it's the comet he discovered and is named for him!

Fun and Games: Believe it or not, there is fun attached to this cataclysmic situation. Elijah is put on the cover of *Newsweek* and becomes a heartthrob, but all he really wants is Leelee. *Messiah* launches as Tea is at last chosen to be news anchor. The spacecraft lands on the asteroid and despite losing a guy in the take-off, the team plants the nuclear depth charges. The nukes are detonated and *Messiah* is buffeted.

Midpoint: At 1 Hour, A and B stories cross as Morgan goes on TV and says: "*Messiah* has failed." We kind of knew, but the "raising of the stakes" has a scary wrinkle: The back-up plan is for 1,000,000 US citizens to be sheltered in the limestone caves beneath Missouri until the crash dust clears. Those who get saved will be chosen by lottery — and no one over 50 is on the list. Everyone else (including my gray-haired editor, BJ Markel) will perish.

Bad Guys Close In: Internal conflict galore. Both Tea and Elijah have been selected because of their fame, but can only take their immediate families. On *Messiah*, the crew argues about what to do next. And on TV, Tea reports the chaos. She got her wish — she's the anchor — but it's a hollow victory. Martial Law is in effect and troops guard "The Ark," the name for the underground city, as it's prepped with every kind of animal and plant. It's a little "glacial" in this section, and why BGCI is the toughest part of any script. Elijah even marries Leelee so her family can be saved. But at 1 Hour 18

Minutes, the bus comes to pick up both families — and Leelee's isn't on the list. Elijah must go on without her.

All Is Lost: Elijah has lost the only girl he ever loved. And now Tea's mother dies. Lots of "whiff of death" here. The whole world is about to end, and everyone — even onboard *Messiah* — is helpless.

Dark Night of the Soul: Tea sits in the rain when her dad drives up. We learn his bride left to be with her mother. Now they're both alone. "I feel like an orphan," Tea tells Maximilian.

Break into Three: Elijah arrives at The Ark with his parents, but leaves to find Leelee. Earth gets a last chance as Titan missiles are shot at the comet, but only succeed in chipping off a piece. Morgan goes on TV to describe how the small part of the asteroid will hit first just off the east coast, causing massive tidal waves for 600 miles inland, before the big chunk wipes out humanity. Onboard *Messiah*, A and B stories cross as Robert has an idea: a suicide mission that will destroy the big chunk!

Finale: The aster-ette is about to hit — the moment we've all been waiting for! Elijah gets home and grabs a cool motorcycle to go find Leelee. Tea gives her safe passage to her boss and child; Tea has grown, and now drives to a beach house to face the end with her dad. Elijah finds Leelee and her baby sister and races to higher ground. The little comet lands in the Atlantic and a huge tidal wave builds. As *Messiah* begins its run at the bigger comet, the tidal wave swamps Tea and her father and everyone else in the lowlands. But in the end, the earth is saved from greater ruin: The big comet is destroyed. *Yay!*

Final Image: Against the backdrop of the capital building, which is being rebuilt, Morgan leads a prayer: "Let us begin."

OPEN WATER (2004)

The pitch for this first-rate indie DWAP is *"The Blair Witch Project meets Jaws."* Shot by director/writer Chris Kentis, a lot of it with a handheld camera (as was the breakthrough *Blair Witch*), the story concerns a 30-something couple that goes skin-diving while on vacation in Mexico and promptly gets left in the middle of the ocean. Soon they are in *Jaws*-land, swarmed by an ever-circling "Nature Problem."

Like other films that pit an ordinary man against nature or a life-threatening illness, the interesting thing about this supposed "free-form" movie is that it follows the BS2 almost beat for beat. It proves again that whether planned or not, a satisfying story demands structure. Here you will see the "Fun and Games," the "All Is Lost," and especially the "Dark Night of the Soul." But what makes this film so gripping is the up close view of real live sharks — and the raw fear of what it must feel like to know your fate is sealed.

The success of the movie, however, comes with the slow reveal of its protagonists. Are they just your average modern urbanites — or something more iconic? There is an odd blankness in this couple. They blame themselves for their plight, and will battle each other as much as the sharks at times, but their isolation from life began long before they got on a plane to Mexico.

DWAP Type: Nature Problem

DWAP Cousins: *The Flight of the Phoenix; Champions; Lorenzo's Oil; The Edge; Alive; Apollo 13; Twister; Six Days, Seven Nights; Into Thin Air: Death on Everest; The Perfect Storm*

OPEN WATER
Written by Chris Kentis

Opening Image: Water. A vast horizon. Looking out to sea, it's peaceful... and ominous. A man (Daniel Travis) packs for vacation. He's on his cell phone making plans for when he gets back. We meet her (Blanchard Ryan), also on her cell.

Theme Stated: They take a breath before they start. "This is supposed to be a vacation," he says. Separated by their busy lives, they are about to see if a vacation can reunite them.

Set-Up: There is an odd chemistry to this pair, and we're never sure of their marriage status. As they leave civilization behind, they begin to unwind. Arriving in Mexico, the couple joins other tourists buying gewgaws, getting their photo snapped inside the jaws of a plastic shark, and trying to relax. It doesn't solve their ennui. They are bored and boring. The night before they're to go diving, they lie naked in bed. When he broaches sex, she stops him. "So how are you?" asks he. "Fine," says she. It's Stasis = Death for this couple and they don't even know it.

Catalyst: The two get on a tourist boat to go deep-sea diving. They join the others, little knowing what awaits.

Debate: "You don't have to worry about sharks," says the boat owner. Is this true? A rude diver interrupts the safety talk; he forgot his swim mask, a mistake that will affect our couple.

Break into Two: The dive begins and the couple joins others in the water, drifting far from the safety of the boat. The rude diver insists on borrowing a mask, grabs a buddy to jump in the sea, and is inadvertently counted twice when he gets back onboard. The boat owners pull up anchor and leave. Our couple has been left behind. When they come up from their dive, they quickly realize what's happened. They have emerged into the "upside-down world" of Act Two, far from cell phones, easy communication, and civilization — just the two of them. Thanks to their bland personalities, life continues back on shore without them.

B Story: The first fin is spotted in Minute 31, and dude this is *really* a problem. But the real B story is about the couple's isolation. Doing everything apart from the group — and each other — has left them alone in more ways than one.

Fun and Games: The "promise of the premise" is now revealed as the couple treads water, the circling sharks appearing and vanishing. The two try their best to keep up their spirits, finding an "eye of the storm" by recalling favorite films and TV survival tips, but real life keeps interfering. They are attacked by jellyfish and the stinging strike is jarring. Up close in the water, every splash is a cause for panic. This is the "fun" of the concept — and its "poster." For now, we don't know what will happen. After several hours, the woman slowly nods off.

Midpoint: She wakes up floating in the ocean alone. Both fell asleep and drifted apart, and now A and B stories cross as they cry out for each other and swim back together. But something has happened while she slept. She's been bitten; the "stakes are raised." This is serious. No more talk of Shark Week on the Discovery Channel. Putting his mask on and looking under the water, he sees that she has been a victim of a shark attack.

Bad Guys Close In: With the woman bleeding, drifting, and desperate, it's only a matter of time. The "bad guys" are circling. The vice-like grip of this movie begins to include panicked ways to deal with an insane situation. "I don't know what's worse, seeing them or not seeing them," she says. But when he puts his mask on, peers under the ocean surface, and sees a swarm of sharks, we know. The "internal team" begins to fall apart, too. He rages against her — and their vacation: "We wanted an ocean view; boy did we get it!" "Feel better?" she says. He laments the lost opportunity for sex the night before. Arguing in the middle of the ocean, they reveal the true despair of their situation. This is a movie about sharks, but there is something in the torture between this couple rivaling *Who's Afraid of Virginia Woolf?* for raw pain.

All Is Lost: Circling birds overhead indicate the couple's time is running out. Nature has pegged them for chum, yet they still cling to hope. When the two spot a buoy to swim to, and even discover some food in their dive bag, things seem to be getting better. Then without warning he is struck — and bleeds profusely.

Dark Night of the Soul: As night falls, their fate is sealed and they know it. A lightning storm highlights the two adrift, surrounded by sharks. He is attacked again and again.

Break into Three: Next day on shore, the boat operator realizes the two did not return from the dive. In any other story, this is where the rescue boats swing into action, the wife and husband are saved and learn their lesson. But not in this movie. Back at sea, the man's half-eaten body bobs in the chop. A and B stories cross for the last time as she lets him go and watches as sharks finish the job.

Finale: There is only a slim hope that she can be rescued. Then in one of the great climactic surrenders, she allows herself to sink — swallowed by the sea to end the madness.

Final Image: In a coda, a shark is caught. Inside its belly is the couple's camera. You won't find many Kodak moments.

The midpoint "false victory" of Napoleon Dynamite *finds our hero almost in the arms of school crush Deb, but only halfway to his real victory: the solo dance finale of this indie "Rites of Passage."*

5 RITES OF PASSAGE

Whenever we hear that a friend or loved one is "going through something," we innately understand the implication. Be it midlife crisis, adolescence, death of a family member, divorce, or any other "fun" thing like that, we get what's really going on: Our friend, whoever it may be, is sitting squarely in the time-out chair of life. And though we can offer all kinds of advice, there is no way for them to get through the episode, but to learn from it... and grow.

Stories that fall under the "Rites of Passage" label seem, on the surface, the least caveman-like of all the genres, and have the fewest antecedents in myth and legend. While "life change" is universally understood, the luxury of discussing it is a prerogative of the post-Freudian world. Yet this story has shown up in hidden ways throughout time. The trials of the knight errant, forced to choose two seemingly illogical paths, may mimic the very real mysteries of a rites-of-manhood tale. The story of Job might be the ultimate Biblical ROP; while Job's ordeal is about faith, it also involves life problems he did not ask for — but gets by the pantload. And we understand. Though we aren't ancient Biblical figures, we've all had those "Job on the ash heap" kinda days — and wondered if they would ever end!

One thing is sure about the ROP; it is recognized in every culture because we each get our turn. From puberty to midlife to death, these passages await us all. And just like life, only when the hero embraces his true self — warts and all — can the torment end. That is the lesson of every ROP, no matter the type.

10, starring Dudley Moore and directed by Blake Edwards, is about a distressing "Mid-life Passage" in which Dudley turns 40 and thinks his problems will be solved by hooking up with Bo Derek. Divorce, departure, and child-custody battles are part of the "Separation Passage" in *Kramer vs. Kramer* and its comic cousins, *The War of the Roses* and *The Break-Up*. In these, like all ROP stories, the shock of change, or just the changing of routine, is enough to send the principals searching for new ways to cope.

Puberty, growth spurts, and the ordeal of becoming an adult are what make up the "Adolescent Passage" as *16 Candles*, *American Pie*, and *Napoleon Dynamite* show. When it comes to stories of drug and alcohol abuse, the torment is explored in movies labeled "Addiction Passage," from the best — *The Lost Weekend* and *Days of Wine and Roses* — to more recent versions that include drug use like *Clean and Sober*, *When a Man Loves a Woman*, and *28 Days*, starring *Cat!* fave Sandra Bullock. Finally, the "Death Passage" story involves a hero who must come to grips with facing... The End... seen in the only ROP musical I know, *All That Jazz*.

In each of these films, the wallowing in pain seems at first a bit self-centered, but in fact frames the problem in a way that gives us a hero we can root for. "Get over it!" we are likely to say when Michael Keaton goes on yet another bender in *Clean and Sober* — yet until we understand his addiction a little better, we are likely to assume that's all that's needed. While tragedy, like that found in *Ordinary People*, is an ideal starting point for any screenwriter, we must often work harder to set up the protags of these tales with a rooting interest. Even though we are advanced from the caveman, who might not so easily get what all the fuss is about, we must be given a good reason to cheer for someone whose only problem is "getting through it."

The ROP yarn, like the other genres in this book, has three telling indicators: (1) a "life problem," (2) the "wrong way" to fix it, and (3) the solution to the problem: "acceptance."

More will be revealed... if we only take a look!

In every ROP, the "problem" *is* the movie — and its poster. "What's it about?" we ask a writer working on an ROP script, and the answer is: It's about drug addiction, or teen angst, or "a guy who turns 40 who suddenly realizes his life is half over." Your pitch will be just that. And it's a grabber. This is especially true if the solution to the problem, e.g., chasing a perfect 10, is the ironic punch line to your set-up.

Often the "problem" is one that offers no real action to solve. When *Ordinary People* begins, Tim Hutton — remorseful over his dead brother — has just attempted suicide. Now what is there to *do*, per se? Not much. Tim just has to get back on track and feel better. This is tougher than it looks. "I'm okay," a constant response by Tim throughout the movie, is a lie. This denial, in fact, is exactly what makes him ripe for the journey — and its end point. "When the going gets tough... keep going" as they say in the rooms of any well-lit 12 Step meeting, but the sad part — and what makes ROP tales so riveting — is this "easy" answer is never apparent to the hero.

Having sensed the problem, yet not knowing exactly what to do about it, the ROP lead will inevitably flail and grasp at any solution that might help, but is in fact the "wrong way." In *Kramer vs. Kramer*, once Dustin Hoffman is left alone when Meryl Streep abandons him and their child, he tries to organize a routine to help him cope, and even attempts an office romance to make it feel like he's not so alone. But being alone *is* the lesson. Change is the bitch, not Meryl. Until Dustin figures that out, through trial and error, and even with further mistakes in judgment, he is doomed to keep spinning in his hamster wheel.

Many middle sections of ROP flicks show how "the wrong way" seems like a good idea, but is actually just a way of avoiding the inevitable. Sandra Bullock thinks a romance with Viggo Mortensen during her *28 Days* in rehab might fix her. Wrong. Likewise Tim Hutton assumes that acting as a dutiful son, staying on the swim team, and pursuing Elizabeth McGovern will mute his pain. Wrong 2. Nope, these poor saps are experiencing what many an ROP hero wallows in — the compounding of mistakes — and the reason this works so well is... it is so human. Avoiding pain, recoiling from the hot flame, is natural, even logical — yet only the counterintuitive move of embracing pain will help.

Because of this paradox, the solution must often be forced on the hero. It's been coming all along; we know it, and secretly so do they: The only thing that can save the ROP lead is turning the flailing inward and realizing *he* must change, not the world around him. This is the "acceptance" part of every ROP film, that moment of surrender and honesty that we have known about all along, but which the hero of our tale has failed to grasp. In the end, the sad soul finally understands that while some passages may be a pain to get through, life would be a lesser experience without the trial.

If you really want to show your stuff, the ROP script — if done smartly and with a fresh take — can be the greatest calling card a screenwriter has. But to pull off the story of a unique character suffering from a life problem we all understand — executed with gobs of painful torment and a little humor thrown in for balance — is tough to accomplish. If you can get beyond the "sounds like a Movie of the Week" criticism you are likely to hear, and deliver on something that is a cut above, it is the dream sample script and may put you on track to acceptance of your own... acceptance of acclaim! To do so, you must dare to go through the "passage" of facing a *real* trial: 110 blank pages.

HOW TO TELL IF THE PASSAGE IS WORTH RITING

If your script has these painful elements (which you may recognize from your own life), get out your damn handkerchiefs; there's an ROP filmfest playing near you soon.

1. A "life problem"— from puberty to midlife to death, these are the universal passages we all understand.

2. A "wrong way" to attack the mysterious problem, usually a diversion from confronting the pain, and...

3. A solution that involves "acceptance" of a hard truth the hero has been fighting, and the knowledge it's the hero that must change, not the world around him.

The following breakdowns show the many ways the Rites-of-Passage hero can be put back on the happy road to recovery.

10 (1979)

Can growing pains be funny? Why, of course they can! In the hands of director Blake Edwards, Dudley Moore became a star in this late-'70s imprint that mixes slapstick and pathos — set to the sensual urging of "Bolero." The love-making anthem was made fun of by Dudley on the talk show circuit post-*10*, when he complained that while Ravel's classic got louder as it built to its climax, regrettably… it did not get faster.

Beneath the laughs of the film are guideposts for anyone seeking to write a "Mid-Life Passage," for as silly as *10* can be, it mimics the hard truths of the journey. When we begin, Dudley has just turned 40 and can't commit to lover Julie Andrews. Plagued by a fellow mid-lifer who is doing it the "wrong way" across the canyon with a series of '70s-era California orgies, musician Dudley is stuck on a song he's composing with his gay writing partner (Robert Webber) — who's handling his mid-life funk by dallying with a young lover. Sex seems to be the solution. And then Dudley sees… her. Corn-rowed "it" girl Bo Derek forever became a cultural landmark and proof that, as far as sensuality in hair care is concerned, hope is indeed a thing with feathers. But Dudley will find out not even a "10" can stave off the course of aging — and acceptance is ultimately a far more beautiful thing.

ROP Type: Mid-Life Passage

ROP Cousins: *Seconds, Save the Tiger, That's Life!, The Weather Man, Lord of War, On a Clear Day, The Upside of Anger, Lost in Translation, Living Out Loud, I Think I Love My Wife*

10
Written by Blake Edwards

Opening Image: A surprise birthday party for muscian George Webber (Dudley Moore). He is 40. Lover Sam (Julie Andrews) is on hand to balm the pain of aging, but her efforts fail. Dudley feels blue.

Theme Stated: Dudley's friend and composing partner, Hugh (Robert Webber), tells Dud: "After 40 it's patch, patch, patch." Is this true... and what exactly does it mean?

Set-Up: A day in the life as Dudley goes to Robert's house in Malibu to work. The gay, and older, Robert is in a relationship with a young hunk, but the mismatch shows signs of trouble. Driving home afterwards in his yellow Rolls Royce — with its personalized license plate that reads "ASCAP," a salute to the royalty checks of his trade — Dudley ogles girls and shows middle-age pangs. Dud experiences that ol' Stasis = Death feeling, when suddenly...

Catalyst: ...there she is. The perfect "10," the hottie from La Cañada, Bo Derek is Jenny Hanley (as if we care what her character's name is). Bo is a vision in white as she smiles at Dudley from the back of a Mercedes, on the way to her wedding!

Debate: Can Bo be pursued? Trouble starts immediately as Dudley jumps into "the wrong way." Following Bo to the church, he crashes into a cop who tells Dudley his license has expired. After his car is towed, Dudley sneaks into the chapel to watch the wedding... and is stung on the nose by a bee. Smitten, swollen, and Rolls-less, he goes home. Julie visits, and he lies to her about where he's been. Brooding, he uses his telescope to check the middle-aged neighbor across the canyon who's always partying with naked girls. Orgy Guy also has a telescope, but has yet to see anything worth watching at Dudley's pad. Trying to cheer him, Julie offers romance, but Dudley rejects her in a nice adult argument you don't hear at the movies anymore. The next day, he goes to his therapist, who explains that what Dudley really sees in Bo is her virginity. (Yeah, right!)

Break into Two: Dudley makes the choice to pursue Bo. He returns to the church, and on a pretense, talks to the priest who performed the ceremony. Dudley's entered the "upside-down world" of Act Two — and mid-life crisis — and his punishment includes humoring the priest, who fancies himself a great songwriter.

B Story: And speaking of songs, Dud needs to finish work on his, but not without getting some helpful advice from partner Robert, who is experiencing problems with his boyfriend. Can all life be solved with "patch, patch, patch" — or must true change occur? Robert will counsel both Dudley and Julie, and be their guide.

Fun and Games: Dudley learns Bo's dad is a dentist and goes for an office visit. He has six cavities — more evidence he's been letting life go by. But he gets new information: Bo is on her honeymoon in Mexico. The dental work is extensive and includes pain pills. Dudley heads home and when Julie calls is unable to speak; she thinks he's a mumbling burglar and calls the cops. By the time she gets there, a drunken Dudley has traveled to the other side of the canyon to join the orgy and is bare-bottom naked when Julie spies him from the telescope at his own house. Embarrassed, and with nowhere else to go, Dud calls his therapist — then his travel agent. He is flying to Mexico to find Bo.

Midpoint: Having "raised the stakes" by risking the love of Julie, and being bold enough to seek out a perfect 10, Dudley arrives at the Mexican resort, still groggy from his dental work. The resort is a surreal weigh station for mid-life change. Dudley also needs to work on the song he's been writing with Robert.

Bad Guys Close In: The "bad guys" of truth begin to crowd Dudley. Away from LA, he meets Don the bartender (Brian Dennehy) and they discuss how the old songs are best. Later when he can't sleep, Dud bumps into a barfly (Dee Wallace) whom he met at a party years ago and doesn't remember. He picks her up, but can't make love to her. The resort becomes a haunted hotel where Dudley is forced to confront his whole life. In between all this middle-age depression, Bo and her husband (that's *Flash Gordon*'s Sam Jones!), the pretty newlyweds, glide by flaunting their youth.

All Is Lost: Dudley can't stop chasing Bo. The next day, at the beach, he experiences more pain when he attempts to walk barefoot across the hot, hot sand. Finally close enough to Bo to observe her, he begins to fantasize, running toward her on the beach in a hark back to the movies of his youth. Then Dudley gets his chance and rescues Bo's husband, who had drifted out to sea on a surfboard, and becomes a hero by helping Bo's better half avoid the "whiff of death."

Dark Night of the Soul: Thanks to Robert, Julie sees Dudley's heroics on TV. Then in a heartfelt moment at the hotel, Dudley plays the song he composed while Brian and Dee look on. A and B stories cross as Dud's "old-fashioned" and moving tune reveals this mid-age episode has given him deeper appreciation of life. We've also seen Dud's buddy Robert lose his young boyfriend — a warning to Dudley that the same can happen to him with Julie.

Break into Three: Dudley asks Bo to dinner. With Mr. Bo in the hospital, the hour of reckoning is at hand — as is his goal.

Finale: After dinner, Bo takes Dud back to her room. Dudley is surprised that Bo will gladly sleep with him; she is a "modern" girl. Bo introduces Ravel's "Bolero" as the perfect lovemaking song and, after smoking a little grass, they get naked. But Dud now realizes sex isn't the answer — and neither is Bo.

Final Image: Returning to LA, Dud tries Synthesis by combining what he had in Act One with what he learned. To the oboe-wooing of Ravel, he makes love to Julie. Dudley's midlife pain is over.

KRAMER vs. KRAMER (1979)

Ah, the French toast scene! That is how I first became aware of the true impact of *Kramer vs. Kramer*. A commercial for a breakfast cereal of the era referenced the moment between Dustin Hoffman and Justin Henry (the actor who plays his son), dipping bread in a coffee cup full of egg yolks — and shells — to show the awkwardness of a father in over his head on the domestic front. When Meryl Streep up and leaves Dustin on "one of the five best days" of his life, breakfast is the least of his problems. He has entered a world of pain and begun a very real "Separation Passage."

As such, writer-director Robert Benton's adaptation of Avery Corman's novel is about those sudden jolts in life when a brick hits us when we least expect it, hurled by the person we least expect it from. One day he's got a family; the next day he's a single dad.

The side effect for Dustin is his change from a self-centered, status-conscience go-getter in the ad game, to a caring, real, and much more in-touch human being — one who, by movie's end, can make French toast like a master. He didn't know it when he began this life episode, and it certainly doesn't feel good along the way, but by the end he's a better man for his wife's having left him. And ultimately, that is what a good ROP tale is all about.

ROP Type: Separation Passage

ROP Cousins: *Divorce American Style, Blume in Love, An Unmarried Woman, Modern Romance, The War of the Roses, The Break-Up, The First Wives Club, Bye Bye Love, Stepmom, Dinner with Friends*

KRAMER vs. KRAMER
Screenplay by Robert Benton
Based on the novel by Avery Corman

Opening Image: A middle-class apartment in New York City. A sweet domestic moment. Or is it? Joanna Kramer (Meryl Streep) has something on her mind as she tucks her son Billy (Justin Henry) into bed.

Set-Up: Ted Kramer (Dustin Hoffman) is an ad man at work late. The boss gives Dustin the big account. Dustin's thrilled. Mixed in are scenes of Meryl packing. A collision of these two people — one happy at work, one sad at home — is coming fast. Yet the set-up is so universal, we immediately understand the conflict.

Catalyst: Dustin arrives home with his great news, only to be told by Meryl she's leaving him and her son: "He's better off without me." Dustin tries to stop her, but Meryl's out the door.

Theme Stated: With Meryl gone at Minute 9, Dustin whines on the shoulder of neighbor Margaret Phelps (Jane Alexander). "Can't you understand what she's done to me?" he asks. Jane deadpans: "She loused up one of the five best days of your life." The exchange sets the table for Dustin's journey. He will learn that love means being able to put someone else's needs before your own.

Debate: Is Meryl really gone? At Minute 12, Billy wakes up asking where his mother is. Dustin is frantic and a little scary as he tries to cook french toast "just like Mom." At work, Dustin makes the mistake of confiding in his boss, who has second thoughts about his decision to recommend Dustin for the big account. Dustin tells him not to worry. Then at Minute 22, he gets a letter from Meryl, confirming that she isn't coming back.

Break into Two: Dustin sweeps the apartment clean of photos, clothes, and memorabilia of his marriage. Boldly stepping into the "upside-down world" of Act Two, he doesn't yet understand how very different his life will be. We also begin to see Dustin devote less time to work in order to take care of Billy.

B Story: The "love story" between Dustin and Billy is where Dustin will slowly give up his selfish ways and learn to put another's needs ahead of his own. He is helped also by his neighbor, Jane. Divorced after her husband left, she will mentor Dustin as he and Billy make a life for themselves — and help him understand why Meryl was unhappy.

Fun and Games: Dustin and Billy are equally at sea without Meryl. At first Billy is cold. He misses his mom, blames his dad, and misbehaves in every way to test him. But the two Kramers work out a routine of surviving the basic moments of life. They both read at the dinner table — in silence at first — and we get a running joke of the men scampering in and out of the bathroom to pee. Yet there are challenges: Billy throws a fit when Dustin picks him up late from a birthday party, and when Billy defies his dad by eating ice cream without permission, we see how much the lack of a woman in their lives affects them. Dustin seems to be juggling family and business okay, until he brings home a date from work — and Billy catches her naked in the hallway. It's a clear indication that Dustin's selfish behavior is resulting in "the wrong way."

Midpoint: By mid-movie, routine has turned into a pleasant life. Father and son have not only survived, they've gotten closer. With the midpoint "false victory" of Dustin teaching Billy to ride a bike, all's well. Even an accident that sends Billy to the hospital has a "happy" ending. A and B stories cross as Jane tells Dustin he's doing a good job. But as sure as Godzilla heads straight for Tokyo, we know trouble's coming, and at Minute 52, Meryl calls. Thinking she wants to reconcile, Dustin meets her at a cafe. Then she drops the bomb and "raises the stakes." Even though she hasn't seen or talked to Billy since the day she left, she wants custody.

Bad Guys Close In: The titular part of the story, the trial of Kramer vs. Kramer, begins as Dustin's lawyer (Howard Duff) tells him they have to play hardball. This would be the worst time for Dustin to get fired but perfect for the BGCI section of any script, so he's let go by the agency. Without a job, he's at risk of losing Billy for sure — now his first concern. We have a great scene when Dustin looks for work at Christmas time. His "one time only offer" of taking a pay cut gets the attention of a potential boss, even during a Christmas party, and Dustin gets the gig.

All Is Lost: Dustin prepares for court but there is a wrinkle: He learns Meryl has the legal right to see Billy. Will Dustin be "worse off than when this movie started" and lose them both?

Dark Night of the Soul: In Central Park at Minute 71, Dustin lets Billy go. He watches Billy run happily into his mother's arms.

Break into Three: At Minute 72, the trial begins — and it's rough. Meryl is questioned and we learn she has boyfriend. A and B stories cross as Jane takes the stand on Dustin's behalf.

Finale: Finally getting to tell his side, Dustin argues for "men's rights," but really talks about what he's learned in the B story. "I'm not a perfect parent, but I'm there. We've built a life together." Despite this plea, Meryl wins. At home, in a flip of the earlier scene, Dustin and Billy make French toast like pros.

Final Image: Meryl arrives to pick up her son and surprises Dustin, telling him Billy can stay. From page 1 to this touching finale, we've seen an amazing transformation for all the Kramers. But none has changed more that Dustin, who has gone from selfish to selfless and learned the true meaning of family.

ORDINARY PEOPLE (1980)

Here's a great example of a whole movie plot leading to a single dramatic moment. When a bereft Timothy Hutton tracks down therapist Judd Hirsch to unburden his pain, it is the release we've been waiting for, the quivering climax of a wrenching and effectively told "Death Passage."

And I cry like a sorority girl every time I see it.

When we begin director Robert Redford's translation of Judith Guest's best-selling novel, all seems swell. The middle class world Tim's parents, Mary Tyler Moore and Donald Sutherland, inhabit seems immune from pain. Despite the lovely setting and safety of the environs, there is an elephant in the living room — and the pressure of needing to talk about it begins from scene one and builds to its inevitable conclusion.

The pachyderm in question involves an accident that took the life of older brother Buck, the favorite son, a boating tragedy Tim survived. In order to recover, Tim will have to see a much larger truth — and accept it. He will be forced to go from one who believes mothers love all their children, to someone who can forgive his own for being unable to. By doing so, Tim will force others to see the truth, and upend the family forever. My hero, screenwriter Alvin Sargent, won an Oscar® for this script — and no wonder. As Rites of Passage go, none is more powerful than this well-told tale.

ROP Type: Death Passage

ROP Cousins: *All That Jazz, My Life, Dying Young, Wit, The Sweet Herefter, You Can Count on Me, Ponette, The Doctor, The Accidental Tourist, One True Thing*

ORDINARY PEOPLE

Screenplay by Alvin Sargent
Based on the novel by Judith Guest

Opening Image: Beautiful homes, fall leaves. And in a church, a choir sings. Among its members: teenagers Conrad Jarrett (Timothy Hutton) and Jeannine Pratt (Elizabeth McGovern). Tim looks tired.

Set-Up: Meet Tim's upscale parents, Beth (Mary Tyler Moore) and Calvin (Donald Sutherland). Everything *seems* normal. So why is Tim having nightmares? One morning over breakfast, Tim is asked if he called "that doctor" yet and we wonder what the tension is and why Mary is so distant. We are catching a family post-trauma. Though it is not revealed until later, they have recently lost their older son Buck, after which younger son Tim tried to off himself. He has just returned from a psychiatric hospital, agreeing that if he isn't feeling better, he'll seek help.

Theme Stated: "You okay?" Donald asks Tim over pancakes. It is a question that will become a running litmus test, and our theme.

Catalyst: When Tim doesn't eat the pancakes Mom made, Mary takes them away brusquely and dumps them. Her harsh attitude prompts Tim to call the therapist.

Debate: That night, Tim's terrifying dreams reveal a boating accident and a storm. Tim meets the therapist, Dr. Tyrone C. Berger (Judd Hirsch), the next day. Tim tries to be honest: "I don't like this," he tells Judd. Can Tim commit to therapy?

Break into Two: Still resisting, Tim works out a schedule with Judd. At school, Tim is on the swim team, trying to emulate his swim-star brother, and has a crush on Elizabeth. But both routes offer the "wrong way" — at least for now.

B Story: Through Tim's sessions with Judd, he will accept what happened and be healed. Their relationship is the "love story" of the film. Tim can only work with Judd a few hours a week, and must cut into his swim-team practice time to do so, but what he learns in Judd's office will be applied in the world as he gets stronger.

Fun and Games: Though their relationship is awkward at first, Judd gains Tim's trust. "Aren't I supposed to feel better?" Tim asks at one point. "Not necessarily," Judd answers — proof positive that Judd speaks the truth. The "promise of the premise" also includes small moments of the very intense kind: Tim reconnects with Karen (Dinah Manoff) from the hospital; she too tried to kill herself. Dinah did not stay in therapy and, unlike Tim, seems fine. Yet it is the interactions between Tim and his mother that are the most wrenching. When their uncomfortable conversation in the garden after school one day is interrupted by a phone call, Mary is asked what she's doing and responds: "I'm not doing anything." The "Fun and Games" end with the famous Christmas photo scene where Tim loudly refuses to take a picture with Mary. The therapy is working; Tim is at last coming alive — even if his emotion is anger.

Midpoint: Through Judd's encouragement, "false victories" now begin: Tim talks to Elizabeth, quits Buck's swim team without telling his parents, and starts to stand up for himself. And when he is "okay" enough for Elizabeth to agree to go out with him, Tim heads home singing "Hallelujah." But feeling "okay" is about to be challenged. Threatened by how Tim is changing due to his sessions with Judd, Mary confronts Tim about quitting the team, accusing him of lying and embarrassing her — on purpose.

Bad Guys Close In: The crack in the family begins when Tim tells Judd: "I think I just figured something out." The conflict expands as Donald also meets with Judd. When Donald reports this to Mary, looking for approval, she is instead appalled. The truth is starting to dawn on Donald, too. As for Tim, his date with Elizabeth shows how not "okay" he is when they go to McDonalds and Tim can't handle some boisterous kids whom Elizabeth jokes with. Maybe Tim is not getting better, after all. And later after a swim meet, when a pal makes a remark about Elizabeth, Tim overreacts and pummels him. "You're crazy," the friend yells.

All Is Lost: After the fight, Tim calls Dinah and learns she killed herself, even though she was "feeling fine." The "whiff of death" includes Tim thinking he could have saved her from suicide.

Dark Night of the Soul: Instead of following suit, Tim runs through the streets in panic and phones his doctor. Judd, unlike any therapist *we* know, meets Tim at his office. And now it all spills out. In flashback we see the night of the accident, the storm, Buck's death — and the one thing Tim did wrong: He didn't drown. "I hung on. I stayed with the boat," he cries. Tim now realizes his sin was being stronger than his "perfect" brother. A and B stories cross as Tim accepts what happened — thanks to Judd.

Break into Three: Next morning, Tim waits at Elizabeth's house. "Have you eaten?" she asks. In a reversal of the earlier pancake scene, Tim is now ready for nourishment. Elizabeth ushers him inside — and back into the world.

Finale: On vacation, Donald and Mary fight about Tim, with Donald standing up to her. The dynamics are changing. When the couple returns, a reinvigorated Tim hugs his mother, who stiffens — not knowing how to hug back. Later, Mary finds Donald sobbing in the middle of the night. "Do you really love me?" he asks. "I feel the way I've always felt about you," Mary says. Now he has his answer. Donald tells Mary: "I don't know who you are. I don't know what we've been playing at."

Final Image: Mary packs. She's been insulted — or found out — and instead of trying to change, she's leaving. In a bookend of the opening, "Canon in D" by Pachelbel as we pull back from this town. We are wiser about what goes on behind its well cared-for façade.

28 DAYS (2000)

Tales of obsessive drug and alcohol use offer some of the most compelling starting points in modern story craft. From the breakthrough *The Lost Weekend* directed by Billy Wilder, to the best, Blake Edwards' *Days of Wine and Roses*, to funny and surreal indie treatments like *Trainspotting*, the "Addiction Passage" can be heart-breaking... and triumphant.

Director Betty Thomas tackles the subject by focusing on the story of a standard 28-day stay in rehab that has become not only a rite of passage, but also a badge of honor. It is a look inside a world in which people from all walks of life address a universal problem and face an overwhelming challenge: change. With an eclectic cast of characters, and the underpinning of program-based recovery, *28 Days* focuses on those who take their recovery seriously, those who don't, and one person who becomes desperate to "get it."

Sandra Bullock stars as a sophisticated urbanite whose drinking and using is out of control when we begin. She nearly kills herself in a scary opening scene that gives new meaning to the term "wedding crasher." Sandra does not heed the wake-up call and has a way to go to discover that the problem lies inside. As her low-key guidance counselor, Steve Buscemi offers a portrait of someone already on the happy road of recovery, who wants all the company he can get.

ROP Type: Addiction Passage

ROP Cousins: *The Lost Weekend, The Man with the Golden Arm, Days of Wine and Roses, When a Man Loves a Woman, Clean and Sober, Permanent Midnight, Postcards from the Edge, Trainspotting, Barfly, Clean*

28 DAYS
Written by Susannah Grant

Opening Image: Meet Gwen Cummings (Sandra Bullock), drunk and dancing in a club to The Clash's "Should I Stay Or Should I Go?" Weird voices, weird music, and weirder behavior blur. Sandra's boyfriend (Dominic West) takes her home and, while making love, they start a fire. Laughing, they put it out — not realizing they could have died.

Theme Stated: Remembering her sister's wedding the next morning, Sandra and her man race to the train station. He asks: "Are you all right, darling?" and she replies, "I could care less." "Isn't that the whole point?" says Mr. Sensitive. Caring about others, and herself, will be key to Sandra's recovery and our theme.

Set-Up: Arriving at the wedding, Sandra continues to drink to excess and act rudely to guests. During the reception, Sandra — now way drunk and dancing wildly — falls into the wedding cake. As her boyfriend laughs, Sandra teeters out of the reception, hijacks a limousine, drives away on a mission to replace the cake, and careens into a house.

Catalyst: Sentenced to rehab for her crime, Sandra enters the world of recovery. Though this facility is a plush and touchy-feely kind of sober living, it's either here or a jail cell.

Debate: Should she stay or should she go? Despite the threat of prison, Sandra is torn. "They chant here," she complains. But 28 days of rehab is not only the title; it is her punishment. Sandra meets the other patients, each with a different horror story. Even early on, separation from drinking has an effect. Experiencing withdrawal, Sandra has flashbacks — some about her alcoholic mother. Still, Sandra resists joining group therapy, holding hands, and saying the Serenity Prayer. On a break in the woods, she meets Cornell Shaw (Steve Buscemi). She thinks he's a patient, but he's her counselor.

Break into Two: Caught by Steve after she and her boyfriend go on a bender during visitor's day, Sandra is asked to leave. She is told she must go to jail. Desperately, she tries to convince Steve she's not alcoholic. But when she climbs out of a second floor window to retrieve some contraband pills, she falls and injures her leg. It is the moment of clarity she has needed; she knows she must stay.

B Story: Sandra's relationship with everyone in rehab is how she learns to care and begin to heal. We also get a "love story" with handsome Viggo Mortensen as alcoholic major-league pitcher Eddie Boone. But it comes with an ROP curveball.

Fun and Games: Recommitted to the program, Sandra starts to take a look at herself. "I don't want to die," she says to Steve. Recovery begins. This is why we came to this movie: Rehab stories, the grind of cleaning bathrooms, going to group, sharing feelings, being honest, and getting at the root of the problem are the "promise of the premise." There's more fun as the patients are brought to a nearby farm to learn to shoe a horse — a lesson in "letting go." Sandra continues to have flashbacks about her mother's death by alcoholism — set to the groovy sounds of Crosby Stills Nash & Young.

Midpoint: On his second visit with Sandra, her boyfriend proposes. He brings champagne to celebrate. Sandra dumps the champagne out and refuses this "false victory." "Maybe there *is* something wrong with me," she now admits to Steve. Sandra is changing. A and B stories cross as she starts to care about other people when she rescues her Goth roommate (Azura Skye) from cutting herself. And she's starting to like Viggo, too. She learns they both are fans of the same soap opera, which they begin to watch together.

Bad Guys Close In: Pressure mounts on Sandra as both her past and current behavior threaten her recovery. Sandra's sister (Elizabeth Perkins) agrees to show up for family day, and reveals that Sandra mortified her with the rude wedding toast she gave during an alcoholic blackout. And when Sandra seems to be getting closer to Viggo during a game of catch, they're interrupted by her boyfriend, who winds up getting punched out by the pitcher.

All Is Lost: Unable to face the trauma of life on the outside without drugs, Sandra's Goth roommate OD's. Now Sandra has lost her sister, her boyfriend, and this new friend. The final swizzle stick in her heart: She catches Viggo with another girl. Sandra's hoped-for happy ending in rehab seems out of reach.

Dark Night of the Soul: Sandra sits by the river and contemplates her life. Her sister arrives and, in an effort to make up, reminds Sandra that she has always been the special one.

Break into Three: Sandra leaves rehab. A and B stories cross as she gets a send-off from her buddies knowing she might not "make it."

Finale: Sandra resumes her life, but it's different without booze. Her apartment that seemed bohemian by candlelight now looks dirty and cheap. And when Sandra's boyfriend takes her to the club where we began this story, their conversation is dull. While taking a stroll after dinner, she approaches a horse on the street and motions for it to raise its hoof, just like she learned in rehab. The horse complies, which Sandra takes as a sign: Nature or God is ready to help if she asks. Sandra kisses her boyfriend goodbye forever and walks away. Synthesis as Sandra accepts herself for who she is.

Final Image: A last scene has a clean and sober Sandra buying a houseplant — a first step toward "caring" for another. She spots a friend from rehab doing the same. A new life has begun.

NAPOLEON DYNAMITE (2004)

Director Jared Hess' film of the script written by him and wife Jerusha Hess began as a short and expanded to feature length as its hero found fans (and backers). It is an ROP story that seems to defy structure analysis. As Napoleon might say to one attempting the task: "What are you stupid or something?"

The "Adolescent Passage" Napoleon goes through is not only a direct descendent of *Porky's*, *Sixteen Candles*, and *American Pie*, it hits all the beats — both structural and emotional. Napoleon begins this movie under the watchful eye of his grandmother, but when she has an accident and his dim-bulb Uncle Rico takes over as guardian, Napoleon's ROP adventure begins. Frozen in his teen years like a bug in amber, young Master Dynamite experiences a journey of growth through friendship. And while *you* may not have had to deal with a pet llama or a brother who swears by a time machine when you were a teen, you recognize Napoleon's embarrassing plight. His world may not be real; it just *feels* like it is.

In his quest for dignity, Napoleon (the brilliant Jon Heder) will come up against bullies and prom queens, yet ache to belong. And the finale, in which he takes the stage to save his pal Pedro from embarrassment, is one of the most celebrated — and hypnotic — moments in film history.

ROP Type: Adolescent Passage

ROP Cousins: *American Graffiti*, *Breaking Away*, *Risky Business*, *Sixteen Candles*, *Lucas*, *American Pie*, *Porky's*, *Pretty in Pink*, *Dazed and Confused*, *Thirteen*

NAPOLEON DYNAMITE
Written by Jared Hess & Jerusha Hess

Opening Image: Titles are displayed on shag rugs, plates of junk food, high school library cards, Chapstick, and pencil drawings on three-hole-punch binder paper. Then we see our dorky hero, outside his house, waiting for the bus — alone.

Theme Stated: "What are you gonna do today, Napoleon?" the hero is asked by a little kid. "Whatever I feel like I wanna do, gosh!" he yells. The conflict between what Napoleon wants to do, and what he *can* do, is what this ROP is about. He lives in his own world, but will he ever succeed in the real world? We'll see.

Set-Up: Between doing reports on the Loch Ness monster ("our underwater ally") and playing tetherball alone (in a snapshot that will have a bookend in the Final Image), Napoleon invents stories about wolverines and gets beat up at his locker by Don the bully. After a particularly rough day at school — when his brother Kip (Aaron Ruell) refuses to pick him up — Napoleon reaches a Stasis = Death moment.

Catalyst: Napoleon is introduced to the new kid in his school, Pedro (Efren Ramirez). And at Minute 11, a knock at Napoleon's door: School crush Deb (Tina Majorino) is selling her glamour photography services. When Deb leaves her sample case behind and runs, Napoleon's much-repressed quest to win her love begins.

Debate: Will Pedro and Deb be a way out for Napoleon? Will the friendship of these newfound commiserants change his life? To remind us of where he still is, Napoleon meets the local Tae Kwan Do teacher and learns that self-respect is key to winning the girl; Lyle, Napoleon's farmer neighbor, shoots a cow; and Napoleon's grandmother — and surrogate parent — leaves their home to go motorcycling out on "the dunes." Later, over "tots" in the school cafeteria, Napoleon secures Pedro's friendship and is prompted by him to speak to Deb. We also meet prom queen Summer (Haylie Duff). But what lucky girls will the two friends take to the school dance?

Break into Two: At Minute 21, Grandma has a motorcycle accident and calls Napoleon's Uncle Rico (Jon Gries) to watch the two brothers. The sudden loss of this parental authority gives Napoleon an unnerving freedom. There's no real adult in charge as Napoleon steps into a brand new world.

B Story: The "false mentor," Uncle Rico, is a former high school football player, perpetually longing for 1982. At the moment, Rico is selling Tupperware and breast-enlargement cream door-to-door. Despite his emotionally challenged moxie, he is the Sears catalogue version of the best Napoleon can hope for in his family. Rico enlists Kip to help in his schemes, but a wary Napoleon has his number from the get-go.

Fun and Games: Let loose to try new things, Napoleon and Pedro bond as they work together to help Pedro ask Summer to the dance. Napoleon looks on as Kip brings Uncle Rico to Deb's photography service, and we see her trick to relax subjects by imagining they're "floating in the ocean surrounded by thousands of tiny seahorses." When Pedro scoops Napoleon and asks Deb to the dance first, Napoleon must use his "skills" to ask Trisha (Emily Tyndall), a friend of Summer's. A and B stories cross as Rico urges Napoleon to get a job ("Do the chickens have large talons?") and buy a suit for the dance.

Midpoint: Trisha agrees to go with Napoleon, then abandons him at the prom. Napoleon has a "false victory" when he dances with Deb. There are sparks between them, but neither is "there" yet. At the dance, Pedro sees the sign that will change his life: a poster announcing elections for student president. Pedro decides to "raise the stakes" — for himself and for Napoleon.

Bad Guys Close In: The two challenge Summer in a campaign they are sure to lose. The biggest challenge to Napoleon's goal occurs when Pedro shaves his head. Not even Deb's wig stylings can help his chances now. Pressure builds on Napoleon. Uncle Rico is embarrassing him by hawking his breast-enlargement cream to the girls at school. Kip has an Internet girlfriend, LaFawnduh. When she visits, Kip blooms. Why can't Napoleon? Tired of "the wrong way," Napoleon turns inward and, using a dance video he found in a remnant store, begins to learn new moves in the privacy of his bedroom.

All Is Lost: When Uncle Rico speaks to Deb and implies Napoleon wants her to use his breast cream, Napoleon's life crumbles.

Dark Night of the Soul: Deb calls to let Napoleon know she's mad. Napoleon's life is "worse than when this movie started."

Break into Three: Napoleon fights back. He attacks Uncle Rico for ruining things with Deb. And when he sees Uncle Rico video-taping yet another rendition of himself throwing the football, Napoleon realizes his uncle is no role model. A and B stories cross.

Finale: The election campaign requires a speech from Pedro, but when the two friends get to the assembly, they discover they have to put on a "skit," too. Pedro's speech promises students that "all your dreams will come true." The audience expects more, but Pedro has prepared nothing. To save the day, Napoleon takes the stage and begins to dance. He's good! Amazing, actually. And all, including Deb, are impressed. A nerd's fantasy becomes real.

Final Image: Life returns to normal. Grandma is back home, Kip's girl and Rico leave, Pedro is "El Presidente" — and Napoleon has found his true tetherball partner: Deb. One is now two.

🐾 *A boy and his dog... I mean whale... I mean* horse! *But does it matter?* The Black Stallion *proves what "Buddy Love" movies are really all about: My life changed for having met another.*

6 BUDDY LOVE

Love is a many-splendored thing, or so the ballad goes. And aside from the fear of being eaten by sharks, the topic we most relate to, good cavemen that we are, concerns stories that deal with our primal need for this very special gift.

All stories are about transformation. Usually, a hero is changed by a key moment or event. But in the genre of movie I call "Buddy Love," the thing that most transforms the life of the hero is... someone else.

There are many variations on the "Buddy Love" story. Whether it's a traditional love match of "boy meets girl," two cops on the trail of a crook, or a couple of goofy pals who just like to hang out together, the same dynamics apply. Beneath the surface of all those Laurel and Hardy, Butch and Sundance, or Buddy Cop movies are the same elements found in *Bringing Up Baby*, *Pat and Mike*, and *Two Weeks Notice*. The only difference is that in the latter examples, one buddy is missing a Y chromosome. While sex is at the heart of a lot of these films, they are more about "completion," the slow realization the buddies are not as good apart as they are together. And though we often get confused due to the fact so many movies have a "love story" in them, the true "Buddy Love" is that film in which the main story is about two individuals whose lives are less without the other.

Be it a "Pet Love" fable like *Lassie*, *Air Bud*, or *The Black Stallion*; "Rom-com Love" like *You've Got Mail* and *When Harry Met Sally...*; "Professional Love" like that found in *Lethal Weapon* and *Rush Hour*; "Epic Love" in which sweeping events bring our lovers together, such as *Titanic* or *Gone with the Wind*; or "Forbidden Love" like that found in *Brokeback Mountain* — and even in the animated fairy tale,

Beauty and the Beast — what these stories have in common is a lesson we can all identify with:

My life changed for having known another.

Buddy Love movies seem vast and unwieldy but have three simple components: (1) an "incomplete hero," (2) a "counterpart" he or she needs to make his life whole, and (3) a "complication" that is keeping them apart — even though that force is actually binding them together!

I know that Danny Glover is the "incomplete hero" of *Lethal Weapon*. Why? Because despite the fact we probably all think of Mel Gibson as the star of that film, it's *about* Danny. What *I* remember is that scene at the movie's beginning: It's Danny's birthday and he's sitting in a bathtub depressed about his gray hair, imminent retirement from the police force, and general middle age exhaustion. Here is a guy who needs help he can't get from his loving wife and family — or his job. Danny needs something else to resurrect him.

He *needs* Mel Gibson.

Picture Danny in the bathtub (well, not for too long) and you have roughly the starting point for many a Buddy Love hero. The hip, slick, and cool Tom Cruise in *Rain Man* may be on top of his game as a Ferrari importer, but something is missing from the weigh bill of his soul. Likewise, when we meet her in *Titanic*, Kate Winslet is shackled to her mother and her fiancé without hope or a solution. Billy Crystal in *When Harry Met Sally...* is like this, too. Though Billy may not know that he's superficial in his relationships with women, we do — and so does Meg Ryan, the Sally who will fix his Harry and make him true. Yes, the adventures Tom and Kate and Billy go on are exciting, and you'll cite scenes of action and fun when you recount the movie to friends. But what these movies are "about" is the incomplete hero who can only be fixed by a special other, and who must have the other or "die." Despite all the cool scenes, *that* is our hook.

It's what all "love" stories teach us.

And who is that other? Odds are "the counterpart" is unique — and often bizarre. Think Katharine Hepburn in *Bringing Up Baby*, Dustin Hoffman in *Rain Man*, Mel Gibson in *Lethal Weapon*, a horse called Black, or a dog named Lassie. These are catalyst characters that shake the bathtub-sitters from their lukewarm malaise.

The prototypical catalyst character does not do much changing, but affects change in another. The perfect example is Dustin Hoffman in *Rain Man* who, by definition, is incapable of change. This is not to say the other half of the Buddy Love equation doesn't need help too, or does not have to evolve in order to fit into the life the two will find at the end. If both characters change and grow, the movie's called a **two-hander**, meaning that each of the buddies has a set-up and a pay-off. You will spend pages in the set-up to meet *both* buddies — and their problems — like in *Two Weeks Notice*, where smart and funny Sandra Bullock as an anti-capitalist lawyer meets Hugh Grant, as the foppish destroyer of the very buildings she's trying to save! We know right away that each of these opposites must take one giant step forward if they want to be together.

So what is keeping the two parties from doing that? Scratch the surface of most BLs, especially those of the "rom-com" (romantic-comedy) kind, and find "the complication" — often something bordering on the ridiculous. "For God's sake, Matthew," we yell at the screen during *How to Lose a Guy in 10 Days*. "You *love* Kate, just tell her about the bet!" But such are the requirements that must be crowbarred in by the screenwriters to keep our two lovebirds apart: geographic distance in *Sleepless in Seattle*; personal ethics in which two people believe in such different things that their core beliefs must change to be in love (*Two Weeks Notice*); and even a slowly sinking ship in *Titanic*. (talk about *romanceus interruptus!*) The ironic thing is: Each of these complications is actually what is keeping the two together!

The complication might also involve yet another person. Thus, the **three-hander** includes leaving the wrong guy or gal for the right one, as in most "triangle" movies like *His Gal Friday*,

Bridget Jones's Diary, and *Sweet Home Alabama*. There is even the **four-hander**, which dissects two couples, like *We Don't Live Here Anymore* and *Closer,* or the lighter — and certainly more fun by comparison — *When Harry Met Sally*.... But as in most BLs, it's all about that special other.

Like any story, the essence of a Buddy Love boils down to conflict, in this case between two people who don't know they have found "the one" they need. When you are writing a BL, make sure you take the couple in question all the way back before the starting line. If the two lovers don't hate each other on sight, you have nowhere to go. Even though you're rooting for the pair as much as the audience is, start them off as far apart, and in as much conflict, as you can.

And here's another little secret: Most of the time in many a romance, it's usually the girl who knows it's true love and the guy who doesn't have a clue. He is also the one who needs to do the most growing. Indeed, that's what many rom-coms of the screwball kind are really about. From the get-go in *Bringing Up Baby*, Katharine Hepburn knows Cary Grant is the one, and the entire plot — a leopard named Baby, the trip to Connecticut, the rocks thrown at the roof of Cary's benefactor — is about her stalling until he knows, too. In any situation you conceive, it is ever thus; someone has to change to be with the other and usually, gentlemen, it's us!

ARE YOU IN LOVE WITH YOUR BUDDY LOVE?

If you are considering a story about "completion" — be it with two, three, four, or more characters — here is a quick love note to see if your BL can get to the altar:

1. It's about an "incomplete hero" who is missing something physical, ethical, or spiritual; he needs another to be whole.

2. A "counterpart" who makes that completion come about or — in the case of a three-hander (story about a triangle) or a four-hander (story about two couples) — has qualities the hero(es) need(s).

3. A "complication," be it a misunderstanding, personal or ethical viewpoint, epic historical event, or the prudish disapproval of society.

The following Buddy Love movies span the definition of what makes a good "love" story work. Creating even a slightly different configuration can give you something brand new!

THE BLACK STALLION (1979)

The "boy and his dog" fable is one of the oldest and most meaningful to us cavemen. It can be traced to the story of Pegasus and to Jack London's *The Call of the Wild*. This sub-class of BL movie I refer to as "Pet Love," which includes *Lassie*, *My Friend Flicka*, and even a "boy and his whale" story like *Free Willy*, is about animals that have a special bond with man. There is something primeval — and forever fascinating — about the odd blend of feeling responsible to, and in awe of, a wild animal. In many such tales, man can learn more from his charge than vice versa. No film version of this relationship is more enchanting (or more beautifully shot by cinematographer Caleb Deschanel) than director Carrol Ballard's story of a boy and his horse.

When we begin this movie, the boy is on a ship at sea. Right off, his meeting with his friend, who'll be called Black, shows them as kindred spirits. The stallion is tied by ropes and being whipped by handlers; the boy is helpless in his own way, and in need of more guidance than his poker-playing father can provide. When boy and horse are shipwrecked, they share an idyllic life; once home, their friendship is challenged. Wonderful Mickey Rooney was nominated for an Oscar® for his role as the trainer who is also helped by the mysterious, four-hoofed Godsend.

BL Type: Pet Love

BL Cousins: *The Yearling, Lassie, My Friend Flicka, Air Bud, Andre, My Dog Skip, Free Willy, Beethoven, Benji, Black Beauty*

THE BLACK STALLION
Written by Melissa Mathison & Jeanne Rosenberg
and William D. Wittliff
Based on the novel by Walter Farley

Opening Image: A ship at sea. It's 1946, a transitional moment. A boy (Kelly Reno) stands alone on the deck of the mysterious vessel, *The Drake*. Loud voices and whinnies draw him to a wild horse being restrained by abusive handlers with ropes and prods. The boy observes and is immediately sympathetic to the animal.

Set-Up: The boy's father (Hoyt Axton) is an adventurer who plays cards as the boy watches. Dad rubs his son for good luck but is busy. An opponent bets a horse statue in the poker game, as the boy gives the real horse sugar cubes (Save the Steed!).

Theme Stated: Later that night in their cabin, Dad divvies up the spoils. He gives his son a pocketknife and the horse statue he won, and tells him a story. It's about Alexander, who tamed the wild horse Bucephalus. "Son, if you can ride that horse you can have that horse," Hoyt says, repeating the tale. To pursue the impossible even if no one thinks it can be achieved is our theme.

Catalyst: At Minute 13, panic. The ship is sinking and the passengers scramble for life preservers. Dad disappears to help others; the boy goes to help the horse and opens his stall.

Debate: What can the boy do to save the horse and himself? One of the passengers draws a knife on the boy — but only to steal his life jacket. Dad rescues the boy from the thief, and the horse escapes and jumps overboard. Dad and the boy are separated, and the boy falls in. He swims for his life as *The Drake* goes down.

Break into Two: In the water, the boy finds himself in danger from the ship's propeller when the horse swims by to save him.

The boy hangs on to the horse, choosing to go with the stallion instead of staying with the sinking ship. As morning comes, the boy wakes on an island. He has the totems his dad gave him. In a strange new world, with only his knife and horse statue to protect him, he must find a way to fend for himself. When he discovers the horse caught in his ropes on the island, the boy uses the knife to cut him free.

Fun and Games: The boy and the stallion play a game of flirtation on the island. Their dance of growing friendship is sensitively portrayed and photographed as each learns to adapt. To find food, the boy attaches his knife to the end of a stick and hunts along the shore, but discovers seaweed is edible, too. Later while asleep, the boy is saved from a poisonous snake by the horse, and rewards the animal by sharing his food. Slowly, the bond between them strengthens. Alone on the island, it is the "promise of the premise," as the boy tames the horse like Alexander, learning how to sit atop him and ride bareback in the surf. At night, they lay together in front of a fire. Finally, the boy is rescued by local fisherman and taken away; when the horse swims after the boy, he too is saved. The two are going home, but where's that?

Midpoint: Back in civilization, his schoolmates hail the boy, whose name we learn is Alec Ramsey, as a hero. The horse (called Black) is kept in Alec's backyard and looks confined. Alec's mom (the fabulous Teri Garr), a widow now, is glad to have her son home. One morning, the horse runs away and Alec follows. Told where Black is by an intuitive Junk Man (Clarence Muse), Alec finds the stallion is being kept in a barn on the outskirts of town.

B Story: The B story comes in late as Alec now meets the owner of the barn, Henry (Mickey Rooney). He is a former jockey retired from racing and from life. Picking up the lesson where his Dad left off, Mickey will take Alec on the final lap to believing in the impossible. When Mickey teaches Alec how to ride "scoot and boot" style, his own dreams have been recast in the boy.

Bad Guys Close In: The first sign of tension is between Mom and Alec when she picks him up from Mickey's. Alec's interest in racing will threaten his safety — and Black's. Mickey and Alec plan to race Black, but Mickey knows his "impossible" scheme will have detractors. "You and me, we have a secret," Mickey tells the boy. The secret includes taking a wild horse and turning him into a racehorse — and training Alec to be a jockey.

All Is Lost: The "complication" comes from the Junk Man: "Let the horse stay wild," he warns Alec. Is exploiting Black by racing him right? To get Black a race, Mickey calls in a favor with a race-track radio star, arranging for the man to come see the mystery horse run. On a dark, rainy morning, Alec rides Black with all his heart. The run is so strenuous, by the time they cross the finish line, Alec is unconscious ("whiff of death").

Dark Night of the Soul: The boy comes to and Mickey tells him Black did well. But should Alec ride Black in the big race?

Break into Three: A and B stories cross as Mickey waits outside while Alec tries to do the impossible again: Convince his mother to let him ride Black. To do so, he shows her the horse statue his father gave him and tells her about Alexander. Teri gives in.

Finale: The race. Alec will appear as The Masked Rider aboard the mystery horse. Pomp and ceremony at the track is a tense lead-up as three horses, including Black with Alec as his jockey, get into place. As we linger, we're wondering what the problem is. We know Black will win, right? Then, from nowhere, we see blood trickle down Black's leg. Alec sees it, too... just as the starting bell sounds. Out of the chute, Alec nearly falls off. But what we cavemen are thinking is: Will Black die? Will our impossible dreams kill what we love most? Far behind in the race, Alec and Black re-focus and charge forward. The crowd, including Mickey and Teri, watches in amazement as Black catches up. Approaching his goal, Alec feels

Synthesis of man and horse, flashing back to the island and the moment he first rode Black — and even to the more mythic story of Alexander. As Black and Alec win the race, they have captured what had seemed unattainable.

Final Image: Black's okay — his leg "strong as iron," as is Alec's friendship with Mickey. A change has occurred, however. Both boy and horse are free, thanks to having met each other.

LETHAL WEAPON (1987)

Let's face it: Shane Black is the coolest screenwriter of my era. During the "Golden Age of the Spec Script" in the 1990s when I thought I was hot stuff for selling screenplays to Spielberg and Disney, Shane Black outclassed us all. We'd hear tales of the days his specs went out, of Shane sitting in his backyard, reading, waiting by the phone, his price going higher with every bid. In addition to many great scripts (like *The Long Kiss Goodnight* and *The Last Boy Scout*), he turned writer-director in 2005 with the quirky *Kiss Kiss Bang Bang*.

He is a Hall of Fame scribe, for sure.

Legend has it that Shane, embarrassed by the over-the-top nature of his first screenplay, tossed out *Lethal Weapon* and had to retrieve it from the garbage, dust it off, and send it to his agent. As an example of a "Professional Love" story, we're glad he did. For despite the crazy antics of Mel Gibson (no, I mean in this movie) and the fact that after 20 years of copycats (including me!) it feels a tad formulaic, this Richard Donner-directed, Joel Silver-produced hit is the progenitor of the "Buddy Cop" genre. What makes it work is the intertwining stories of Danny and Mel. It's about two guys who need each other to save their lives, and as such, the very definition of what Buddy Love is about.

BL Type: Professional Love

BL Cousins: *The Producers, Butch Cassidy and the Sundance Kid, The Front Page, The Sunshine Boys, Tapeheads, 48 Hrs., Feds, Tango & Cash, Wayne's World, Rush Hour*

LETHAL WEAPON
Written by Shane Black

Opening Image: Night. Atop a high-rise in LA, a girl does a line of coke and jumps out the window, plummeting to her death.

Theme Stated: Morning in a less glamorous part of town, home to Detective Roger Murtaugh (Danny Glover). His wife and kids bring him his 50th birthday cake while he takes a bath. His daughter says: "Your beard's getting gray. It makes you look old," making Danny feel worse. Since suicide is our running theme, Danny — and we — must ask ourselves: Is it worth going on?

Set-Up: Because it's a "two-hander," we meet Martin Riggs (Mel Gibson). Mel and his dog live in a trailer at the beach. Mel is distraught and clutches the photo of his dead wife. Back at Danny's place, he's shaved his gray beard. And we learn that a "Vietnam buddy" has been calling. His name: Michael Hunsaker. (NOTE: Always try to make names we must remember memorable.)

Catalyst: At the scene of the suicide, Danny learns the name of the jumper: Amanda Hunsaker. Nope. Doesn't ring any... hey wait a minute! Danny now knows that Amanda is his friend's daughter.

Debate: What does it all mean, and how will Mel play in? We see Mel in action buying drugs at a Christmas tree lot. We don't yet know he's a cop. Gunplay as the bust goes down among the Douglas Firs. Captured by a drug dealer, Mel begs the other cops to "Shoot me!" His antics so spook the crook, Mel subdues him. Back at the station, we learn his bosses think Mel's either acting suicidal to draw disability or is out of his mind (no, I mean in this movie). Should they relieve him of duty or reassign him? At Minute 26, Danny finds out he's getting a sidekick — the hard way. Mistaking Mel for a bad guy with a gun, Danny attacks, only to end up on the ground with Mel on top. "Roger, meet your new partner."

Break into Two: Walking into the parking garage at Minute 27, the two get to know each other, but aren't happy about the pairing. "I suppose we have to register you as a lethal weapon," says Danny of Mel's dangerous side. Mel is trained to kill.

B Story: We meet the bad guys, including Gary Busey as Mr. Joshua and Mitchell Ryan as The General. Gary is key, as he's Mel's counterpart. This is a great example of the fine line between good guy and bad guy, for Mel and Gary are the dark and light sides of each other. We also have a classic "how bad is the bad guy?" moment: To demonstrate just how evil he is, The General tells minion Gary to hold out his arm, and, G. Gordon Liddy-style, scorches his own henchman with a lighter as Gary twitches like he's crazy (no, I mean in this movie).

Fun and Games: Two partners: one suicidal, the other in a mid-life crisis. What better way to demo the "promise of the premise" than to have Mel stop a suicidal jumper by going to the top of the building, handcuffing himself to the guy, and leaping together onto a safety mat? Later, when Mel and Danny go to a suspect's house — the last to see Ms. Hunsaker — there's more gunplay as Mel shoots the man, who drowns in his pool. "You ever meet anybody you didn't kill?" asks Danny. More fun as Danny takes Mel home, where Mel interacts with Danny's flirtatious daughter. ("Mr. Riggs, would you like a tart?") Next day at the LAPD shooting range, the two think a hooker, Dixie, might know something. The "Fun and Games" end with a perfect bit as Mel shoots a happy face in Danny's target. Mel's **button** on the scene: "Have a nice day."

Midpoint: The "stakes are raised" at Minute 65 when Mel and Danny go to Dixie's house and an explosion destroys it; they're almost killed. Kids describe a man they saw lurking there as having the same tattoo as Mel. Mel has a dark past — he was a Viet Nam Special Ops agent. Now we know the bad guys are Special Forces. A and B stories cross as Danny and Mel realize they have a common enemy; this "complication" is about more than a suicidal girl.

Bad Guys Close In: Conflict within the team as Danny and Mel confront Michael Hunsaker, who tells them what this is really about: His daughter was killed to keep him quiet. The General runs Shadow Company, an ex-CIA team now importing heroin. Suddenly we no longer have to remember his name, as Hunsaker is machine-gunned by Gary from a helicopter. Gary reports to The General "another problem exists": The police may know about the whole operation.

All Is Lost: While seeking more information from yet another hooker, Mel is "gunned down" by a drive-by Gary in a perfect "whiff of death" moment. Not really dead, Mel realizes he can fool the bad guys into thinking he is. Then Danny learns Gary kidnapped his daughter. Following the "All is Lost" rule, Danny is "worse off than when this movie started."

Dark Night of the Soul: Waiting by the phone, Mel tells Danny they're going to "get bloody" to get his daughter back.

Break into Three: They've been doing it pretty much Danny's way: now they do it Mel's way. "You're going to have to trust me," says Mel. A and B stories cross again as the call comes and the boys launch into action. By saving Danny's daughter, maybe Mel can get over the loss of the woman in his life, too.

Finale: There are three scenes of violence in the ending: (1) the desert where a rescue goes wrong; (2) back in Hollywood at the nightclub lair of The General, where Mel is tortured (he's tortured a lot, have you noticed?); and (3) Danny's house, where Mel has a showdown with Gary after Danny frees his daughter and dispatches The General. Mel beats Gary in a cool martial arts-fest; then Mel and Danny, guns blazing, kill Gary together.

Final Image: Having come to terms with his wife's death, Mel spends Christmas with Danny and his family. Danny is over his mid-life crisis, and Mel is no longer an insane person (no, I mean... nevermind!)

WHEN HARRY MET SALLY... (1989)

Of the romantic comedies featuring Meg and Tom, or Meg and Kevin, or Meg and Hugh, the imprimatur that made the world safe for the convenient use of Louis Armstrong tunes in lieu of actual screenwriting is director Rob Reiner's urban fairy tale about Meg and Billy. And no "complication" in the way of two lovers — geography in *Sleepless in Seattle*, an outrageous accent in *French Kiss*, or a time-travelin' portal in *Kate & Leopold* — can beat a man and a woman who are just too blockheaded to realize they're perfect for each other.

Created from the real-life experiences of screenwriter Nora Ephron, and enhanced by the matching dating tales of director Reiner, the set-up is simple: the claim made by Billy on the first day he meets Meg that men and women cannot be friends. Men, Billy states, just want to sleep with women and nothing more. But hazzah! After a few broken relationships, and the agony of having Bruno Kirby as his best friend, Billy slowly begins to realize that *When Harry Met Sally...* he found perfect love.

Despite eerie similarities to *Annie Hall* and *Manhattan*, and a few moments that suffer from "a case of the cutes," it's the touchstone we look to as the "Rom-com Love" that tops them all. For when Billy surrenders and races through the streets to confess to Meg he loves it when she orders salad dressing on the side, *somebody* has transformed — him!

BL Type: Rom-com Love

BL Cousins: *Pat and Mike*, *Pretty Woman*, *Sleepless in Seattle*, *You've Got Mail*, *French Kiss*, *Notting Hill*, *The Wedding Planner*, *Maid in Manhattan*, *Two Weeks Notice*, *Failure to Launch*

WHEN HARRY MET SALLY...
Written by Nora Ephron

Opening Image: A running bit (previously used in *Reds*) is the "real" couples talking to the camera about how they met. Their stories detail the odd chase through life we lovers make, and the wrong turns that ultimately lead to the perfect match.

Set-Up: Meet Harry Burns (Billy Crystal) and Sally Albright (Meg Ryan) on the last day of college, 1978. Billy kisses his girlfriend goodbye as Meg waits to drive with him from Chicago to New York. They are totally different types. She is straight-laced, organized, and perky. He is a slob, a front-seat philosopher, and by his reckoning, a ladies man. At a roadside diner, we introduce Meg's penchant for specific ordering of meals. They seem an unlikely pair. He's beer stein half-empty; she's champagne flute half-full.

Theme Stated: "It is impossible for a man and a woman to be friends." Can, as Billy claims, men not resist the lure of sex and see women only as objects of lust? We shall see.

Catalyst: "We are just going to be friends," states Meg and thus the gauntlet is thrown down. Meg and Billy part in New York City with a "thanks for the ride and nice knowing you." It seems like they may never see each other again... but we know better, don't we!

Debate: Is it over? Five years later: another departure, another shared trip. In a reverse of the first scene, a now older Billy sees Meg kissing her boyfriend goodbye at JFK. On the plane, we pick up where we left off: Meg is still naïve and Billy is still a Neanderthal — yet getting married, much to Meg's surprise. He proves he hasn't changed with talk about how long he must hold a woman after sex. Is five seconds enough? Meg is horrified. By the time they land back in Chicago, the two reunited collegians decide they are still not right for each other. And Meg, for one, is glad she has a nice boyfriend whom she's serious about.

Break into Two: Five years later, they are full-fledged adults, both looking again. Meg broke up with her boyfriend, who refused to marry her. Billy is in the process of a painful divorce. We are in the present and will remain here for the duration. Meg sees Harry in a bookstore ("Someone is staring at you in Personal Growth") and they agree to meet. Before they can be together, they must test the premise and see if men and women can be friends. They decide to give it a try.

B Story: The B story here is Billy and Meg's two friends, his best bud, Jess (Bruno Kirby), and Meg's galpal, Marie (Carrie Fisher). In a sense, this film is a bit of a "four-hander" as Bruno and Carrie will get together and be the push Meg and Billy need to get them into Act Three. But for now they are Meg's and Billy's mentors, the ones they talk to about the theme of the movie.

Fun and Games: Billy and Meg as friends. Two single people find solace talking about their exes, aerobics, yoga, food, and shopping. They go out to Chinese dinner, where Meg gets it her way as usual. OCD Meg and forever unhappy Billy do things lovers do, but do so as friends — watching *Casablanca* in their own beds while on the phone with each other, plus lots of afternoons at the museum — all the cute couple stuff without the complications of s-e-x. The two even root for each other when they have dates. During this part, Meg does her famous "orgasm in the deli" scene (what is more Fun and Games than that?), and both are free to be themselves. The whole time we know they are perfect together — why... don't... they?

Midpoint: At Minute 49 the stakes are raised at a New Year's Eve party when they realize they're falling for each other. They kiss as friends, trying to ignore the close call. To avoid this "complication," they set each other up with their best friends as A and B stories now cross. But the plan backfires: Carrie and Bruno fall for each other instead.

Bad Guys Close In: While out with Meg, Billy sees his ex-wife with her new boyfriend. Billy realizes his dating life is not getting better. At Bruno and Carrie's new place, Billy predicts their future — and it isn't pretty. He even fights with Meg, mad at her for not getting upset about anything. She fires back, saying his cavalier attitude about sex isn't helping. Now the "bad guys" include both Meg and Billy seriously dating others. But what else can they do?

All Is Lost: When Meg calls Billy because her ex is getting married, they make a fatal mistake and fall into bed. And though it all should be fine, the "death" is the death of their friendship — what are they now? The look on Billy's face post-sex tells all: He still has the problem of figuring out how long to hold her before leaving.

Dark Night of the Soul: Despite the joy of confessing the deed to Carrie and Bruno, Meg and Billy realize their error.

Break into Three: They both decide to tell each other they made a mistake. Over dinner they do just that. By rejecting each other, they hope to save their friendship — but can they?

Finale: A and B stories cross as the two attend Bruno and Carrie's wedding — and fight. Bruno and Carrie propose a toast to Meg and Billy: "If Marie or I found either of them remotely attractive, we would not be here today." It seems it's over. Billy calls her, but Meg won't answer. On New Year's Eve, the separated lovers realize they need Synthesis. The **chase to the airport scene** that ends most rom-coms, here is Billy running through NYC to be with Meg. Finally they kiss — this time as true lovers.

Final Image: A last couple: Billy and Meg tell the story of how they met.

TITANIC (1997)

The biggest movie ever made (at least when it was released) became the biggest hit of all time, and we would be remiss in our efforts if we didn't try to understand why. You have a great primal set-up: a sinking ship in the middle of an icy sea, the historic brand name of *Titanic* promising glamour... and death. But what makes this story work is that it's about two star-crossed lovers who yearn to be together whatever the odds.

And that *never* fails.

In the "Epic Love" category, the "complication" is bigger than the lovers. We're talking about *Gone with the Wind* and even more recent movies like *Mr. & Mrs. Smith* and *True Lies*. Whether there's a sweeping historic backdrop, or a globe-hopping adventure, the story is about a man and a woman who love and need each other — which is precisely what director and writer James Cameron understood when he took on this monumental project.

When we begin, the ill-fated nature of this relationship is seen in the differences between these two lovers. She is a pampered Victorian mama's girl about to marry the wrong guy, and he's a starving artist who wins his ticket to ride in a poker game before the greatest ship ever built takes off on its maiden — and doomed — voyage. Though we know the ending, and still hope for the best, we realize that a perfect love such as this often ends in tragedy — if we're lucky!

BL Type: Epic Love

BL Cousins: *Gone with the Wind, Dr. Zhivago, The Wind and the Lion, The Year of Living Dangerously, True Lies, The Last of the Mohicans, Mr. and Mrs. Smith, The Notebook, The Far Pavilions, The Painted Veil*

TITANIC
Written by James Cameron

Opening Image: Sepia-tinted footage of *Titanic* launching. Now in the present, an underwater sub explores the wreckage of the ship. In the sub, Brock Lovett (Bill Paxton) commands a robot camera into the ghostly hallways and staterooms. We will be cutting between past and present for the duration of the tale.

Set-Up: Up top, the crew salvages an old safe. They were looking for a diamond and are disappointed. But inside is something more important: a drawing. Dated the day the ship went down, it's a sketch of a nude girl wearing the very diamond they're looking for: the "Heart of the Ocean" necklace. On the other side of the world, a 101-year-old woman, Rose (Gloria Stuart), sees the portrait on TV and claims the girl in the drawing is her. As Gloria is flown in by helicopter to the excavation ship, all wonder if she is who she claims. "Are you ready to go back to *Titanic*?" Bill asks her. At Minute 20, Gloria begins her story: "It's been 84 years. *Titanic* was called the ship of dreams." Now going back into the past again, *Titanic* launches. An old car is loaded on board as passengers arrive, and we meet Rose (Kate Winslet), a perfect Victorian "dish." With her is her rich and pompous fiancé, Cal Hockley (Billy Zane). "To me," Gloria says, "It was a slave ship taking me back to America in chains."

Catalyst: Meet Jack Dawson (Leonardo DiCaprio), playing poker for tickets to *Titanic*. Since the A story is the love story, this game will directly affect both Kate and Leonardo. Leo wins passage for himself *and* a buddy — a "Save the Cat!" beat.

Debate: "Will Kate go through with her loveless marriage?" is dependent on "Will Leo get on board before *Titanic* leaves?"

Break into Two: Just as *Titanic* departs, Leo and friend leap onboard. Checking out the great liner, Leo stands at the bow watching dolphins and, James Cameron-like, proclaims: "I'm the king of the world!" But the true Break into Two comes when, after a stultifying dinner with her mother (Frances Fisher) and Billy, Kate runs to the back of the ship to commit *le suicide*. At Minute 41, Leo stops her, saying, "I'm involved now." When Kate slips, Leo saves her and is accused of rape by the sailors who find them. But his heroics get him a dinner invitation the next night.

B Story: I've wrestled with this one, which would make for a nice classroom discussion, but I feel that the B story is... *The Titanic*! If the A story is the "love story" between Kate and Leo, the thing that prods that forward, and in fact forces the theme of the movie (read ahead if you want to know now) is the ship hitting an iceberg and sinking. I could also be talked into calling the diamond the B story. But that feels more like a C story, as it really is the final mystery we need to solve.

Fun and Games: The fun here, the "promise of the premise," is two young people in love on the most amazing ship in the world. We see every inch of the vessel in the course of this movie. As they run from stem to stern, the two fall in love. We watch Kate discover Leo's talent for painting and for bringing out her hidden side. As they fight the prejudice of society that abhors first class/low class love, we are rooting for them.

Theme Stated: At the dinner, Leo says "Make each day count." Even Molly Brown (the Unsinkable Kathy Bates) is impressed.

Midpoint: After being tempted by Billy's offers of a diamond necklace and a life of ease, Kate goes with her heart and picks Leo. He paints her portrait, and like any two American kids, they make love in the backseat of the car we saw loaded onto the ship at the movie's beginning. Following this "false victory," we get an immediate "raising of the stakes" and an epic "complication": *Titanic* strikes an iceberg, in part because the lookouts were watching Kate and Leo. (Nice touch, James!) A and B stories cross as the on-coming disaster puts the theme to the test.

Bad Guys Close In: A "ticking clock" is introduced when the captain of *Titanic* asks: "How long have we got?" The ever-encroaching "bad guys" now include freezing water as the ship begins to sink. There are more complications when Kate and Leo return to warn Billy about the pending disaster, and Leo is accused of stealing the diamond. Kate's not sure what to believe, but the look in Leo's eyes as he's hauled to the brig convinces her he's innocent. What will she do? This is a nice "three-hander" as Billy, in his way, loves Kate, too.

All Is Lost: Passengers gather on deck as fear spreads, but no one knows of the real danger — except the ship's designer whom Kate has befriended. He confesses: "All this will be at the bottom of the Atlantic." Kate is pressured to stay with Billy, but realizes Leo is in danger below deck. In a breathtaking rescue, Kate courts the "whiff of death" and saves her true love from a half-submerged cell.

Dark Night of the Soul: As women and children head for the lifeboats, Billy and Leo put Kate onboard one too, along with her mother. Kate wears the coat Leo gave her — the diamond in its pocket. Briefly toying with a last chance to go back to her comfortable old life with her Mother and fiancé, Kate knows she must take a risk to be with the man she really wants: Leo.

Break into Three: A and B stories cross as Kate jumps back on the sinking *Titanic* to be with Leo and prove that one day with him counts more than all the days of a bleak future. She and Leo will now fight to survive together. After eluding Billy, and watching the chaotic mass of humanity struggle, they brace themselves for the ship's sinking. They're at the very place where they first met when *Titanic* upends and plummets into the icy sea.

Finale: Coming up to the surface, the two find debris and Leo puts Kate on a makeshift raft while he dangles in the freezing water. He makes her promise to live, then dies just as all romantic characters should! Finally rescued, Kate is pulled up to safety and asked her name. In a great moment of Synthesis, she says: Rose Dawson. She is a fusion of her true love and herself.

Finale Image: Back once again in the present, the mystery is solved, and her story verified, when Gloria drops the long lost diamond into the ocean. She then dies in her sleep surrounded by the images of a life transformed — thanks to epic love.

BROKEBACK MOUNTAIN (2005)

The buzz surrounding this Oscar®-nominated movie started early and often veered into the salacious, but after viewing director Ang Lee's cowboy love story, audiences realized that it had much more to offer. For despite its controversial subject, it's about the special world all lovers share.

Based on Annie Proulx's short story, and adapted by Western writer/icon Larry McMurtry (*Lonesome Dove*) and Diana Ossana, the film is the very definition of the "Give me the same thing, only different!" rule; it shows that putting a new twist on a cliché set-up adds new meaning. And as an example of "Forbidden Love," it proves the movie's premise: Expectation is often what causes problems in the first place.

The story, which begins in 1963 and spans 20 years, is about two men who, while working in the high mountains of Wyoming, fall in love. Because of the society they live in, their guilt, and the need to be "men" in the tradition of the Old West, their relationship is doomed from the start. Despite the shared memory of their time together, they can't overcome the obstacle of what this bond represents to their families and friends. Their secret life unravels amid anger and recrimination, but the BL rule holds true: Each man's life changed for having known the other.

BL Type: Forbidden Love

BL Cousins: *Lolita, Guess Who's Coming to Dinner, Romeo & Juliet, Harold and Maude, The Blue Lagoon, An Officer and a Gentleman, Dirty Dancing, Beauty and the Beast, Benny & Joon, Venus*

BROKEBACK MOUNTAIN
Screenplay by Larry McMurtry *and* Diana Ossana
Based on the short story by Annie Proulx

Opening Image: Car headlights on a prairie highway at dawn. 1963. Signal, Wyoming. One Marlboro Man is dropped off by an 18-wheeler. Another arrives by pickup truck. Both wait for the trail boss. What would be called a "meet cute" in a typical love story now involves two lonesome cowboys eyeing each other.

Set-Up: Sheep rancher Joe Aguirre (Randy Quaid) needs to send two cowboys up to Brokeback Mountain. Their mission: Outwit the forest service by illegally grazing the herd. In a bar before the two take off for their mission, Ennis Del Mar (Heath Ledger) and Jack Twist (Jake Gyllenhaal) get to know each other. Each has a tale of woe about his past. Heath is from "ranch people" and doesn't talk much; his shyness is caused mainly by the pain of his child-hood, which we'll learn more about later. Jake, for his part, "can't please my old man" and joined up with the rodeo.

Catalyst: At Minute 9, they are taken up into the hills to begin their stint watching the sheep, breaking the law, and being secretive.

Theme Stated: At Minute 12, Jake says to Heath: "Aguirre got no right making us do something against the rules." He is referring to his new boss's orders, but Jake is letting Heath — and us — know the theme: It's about keeping a secret vs. being true to oneself.

Debate: Can the two men do the job? One is to sleep with the sheep to ward off coyotes; the other will watch the campsite. Slowly the two men start to bond, and Heath starts to talk. He's getting married soon, turns out. Jake dreams of hitting the rodeo to meet girls and make money. Essentially, they are both "orphans." There is also an odd tension between them. When a bear spooks Heath's horse as he brings supplies, the two fight, then find a solution by hunting together. Duty to Randy says they should stick to the plan of sleeping apart. They do until...

Break into Two: ...at Minute 25, they decide to stay in camp together. Later that evening, the cold compels them to sleep in the same tent. And then in the middle of the night, we hear the sounds of sex. The next morning the two seem unaffected by what happened. Whether they admit it or not, they have crossed into a new world. As if a bad omen, Heath finds a sheep killed by a coyote. When the men finally talk, they agree: "This is a one-shot thing we got going on here, it's nobody's business but ours." But by Minute 32, they kiss again; it's something more.

Fun and Games: The two cowboys have fun together, enjoying their stay on Brokeback Mountain. At this stage, their relationship is "the promise of the premise." When Randy drops by unobserved and sees them wrestling playfully, he chooses not to intercede — but their business is not theirs alone anymore. When the season comes to an end, the two fight, but what about? Maybe leaving this place makes them realize they will have to face what happened in the "real world." At Minute 42, they drive away from each other.

B Story: After both men leave Brokeback Mountain, they try to resume their old lives, and now we follow twin B stories. Heath marries Alma (Michelle Williams). And though Jake will wrestle with his feelings for other men while out on the rodeo circuit, he eventually meets and marries Lureen (Anne Hathaway), whose father is a wealthy farm implement salesman. We continue to explore what "keeping secrets vs. being true to oneself" means in these B stories. During this period, Jake goes back to Randy to see if he can work for him again and hopefully see Heath. Randy tells him in few words that he knows about the relationship. Because of it, Jake is not welcome on Brokeback Mountain anymore.

Midpoint: Heath gets a postcard from Jake asking if he wants to meet again. "You bet," Heath says. Reunited, they hug and kiss — observed by Michelle. This is a back-to-back "false victory"/ "raising of stakes" one-two punch. The Forbidden Love "complication" is: other people. The two men go to a motel. Next day, Heath returns to Michelle, who remains silent.

Bad Guys Close In: Under the guise of "two old buddies going fishing three times a year," Heath and Jake try to maintain their relationship and lead a double life. Internal conflict continues to build, as do incidents of anger by both men, who occasionally lash out at friends and family. During an argument, Heath recalls how his father once showed him the body of a man who was killed for being gay: "My daddy made sure my brother and me seen it." On the domestic front, Heath finally divorces Michelle, who won't mention that she knows his secret until later. Heath moves into a dingy trailer, keeping to himself — even resisting attempts by his now 19-year-old daughter, Alma Jr. (Kate Mara), a "Booster Rocket" character — who wants to involve him in her life. For his part, Jake cruises for male substitutes in Mexico. Meeting for the last time, Heath and Jake both admit that "We could have had a good life and all we got was Brokeback Mountain."

All Is Lost: News comes that Jake is dead. When Heath calls Ann to learn the details, we see his imagined (or is it?) take on what happened: Jake didn't die in an auto accident, he was beaten to death by hate-mongers, like the incident in Heath's past.

Dark Night of the Soul: Jake's death leaves Heath with no hope of returning to Brokeback Mountain. How can he go on without the promise of love?

Break into Three: Heath visits Jake's parents. A and B stories cross as the "secret" Heath and Jake have lived is confronted.

Finale: Heath learns Jake wanted to bring another man up to Brokeback Mountain, but it never happened. He is allowed to visit Jake's room, and finds Jake's work shirt. Jake's Mom gives it to him. She knows that he and Jake had a special relationship.

Final Image: Heath keeps Jake's shirt together with his own in the closet of his trailer, a perfect Synthesis. And there is a last moment of hope when he accepts an invitation to his daughter's wedding. Perhaps he can still find love with his family? But the BL rule holds true: Heath's life changed for having loved another.

Why is this scene in Fargo *? Because it's that moment where the detective, in this case Frances McDormand, takes a "dark turn" when she meets an old friend at the Radisson.*

7 WHYDUNIT

I like to think of the narrative I call the "Whydunit" as a trip into the ever-smaller chambers of a nautilus shell. As we progress deeper into the secrecy that makes up the very best of this type of story, we begin to feel scared, claustrophobic, and in the dark. It's not evil we'll discover in that last little room... it's ourselves.

Who knows what madness lurks in the minds of men? If you are writing what is universally termed a "mystery," the answer must be sought in the darkness. While we're uncertain of exactly what we're looking for, what lies in wait is sure to shock us. And no amount of good intentions or righteousness on our part can stop us from being affected by what we find.

The model Whydunit involves the following: A man in a dingy office spies a woman through the frosted glass where we see his name: "EDAPS MAS" or "EWOLRAM PILIHP." But when *she* walks in, we not only have the feeling Lauren or Faye will get busy with our Detective, he may even have to "send her over" as part of his penance for having gotten involved when he knew he shouldn't. This is how we imagine the Whydunit — and in fact is the basis of them all! For whether it's a "private dick on a case," a robot bounty hunter, or a couple of journos chasing a hot lead, the story ends in the same surprise:

There is no mystery. There is only revelation.

The Whydunit can be of the "Film Noir" kind about a detective and his dark world as seen in classics like *The Maltese Falcon*, the Robert Altman take in *The Long Goodbye*, Roman Polanski's *Chinatown*, or the recent postmodern high school version, *Brick*. What makes these noirish is tone — and a shadow world only our hero can negotiate. There's also the "Political Whydunit," played out in the realm of governmental or corporate power

(*All the President's Men*, *JFK*, and *Missing*), or the "Fantasy Whydunit" where the "case" is set in another world (*Blade Runner*, *Who Framed Roger Rabbit*, *The Sixth Sense*).

This genre also includes the by-the-book (or not) police procedural of a "Cop Whydunit" where a lawman solves the crime — that turns out to be as much about *his* crime as anyone's (*Tightrope*, *Basic Instinct*, and *Fargo*). It might also be the amateur sleuth of a "Personal Whydunit," usually a "civilian" who is on the case out of curiosity or necessity to save himself or others — yet finds things about himself that are just as shocking, as portrayed in *Mystic River*, *Rear Window*, and *Dressed to Kill*.

Despite the wide-ranging canvases these Whydunits use, the gumshoe — whoever he is — and the case he gets involved in — whatever it is — have the same MO. As opposed to Monster in the House stories that are more concerned with stopping a supernatural bad boy than understanding him, Whydunits are about discovering the secret that prompted the crime in the first place. And unlike a typical Golden Fleece yarn whose hero, or heroes, seek a known goal — and the surprises that happen along the way to change that goal — the Whydunit is only concerned with **turning over cards**, those "reveals" writers can explode like time-bombs all along the trail.

The components of all Whydunits are the same: (1) a "detective" who starts out thinking he's seen it all, but is unprepared for what he'll find; (2) a "secret," the hunt for which is the raison d'être of the whole shebang; and (3) a "dark turn," the moment the hero breaks the rules in pursuit of the secret, his own or society's, which makes him a part of the crime.

The wide-ranging permutations of these basics cover the waterfront... and can be applied to almost any "case."

In terms of the "detective," a Whydunit lead is unique. The hero of a Whydunit is the closest thing to a narrator. He is, by proxy, "us," showing us the clues as he discovers them, and revealing their meaning. He will not be changed by what he finds — but we, most likely, will.

Isn't Jake Gittes the same guy with the same beliefs at the end of *Chinatown* as he is at the start? We don't yet know how this caper affects him, for he shows no sign of treating the next case any differently. The only difference is, we get the feeling if you asked him on his deathbed what case reinforced his cynical beliefs the most, it would be the one about the Mulwrays and the Water Department — and keeping it all in the family. Likewise, the detectives of any political mystery, e.g., the two journalists in *All the President's Men* and the DA in *JFK*, don't "change." We're doing that for them, based on what we are being shown.

The "secret" — and the need to know what that is — makes the mystery, which often starts with something very small or seemingly unrelated. A Whydunit means using all five Ws: Who, What, When, Where, and Why — and the lure to uncover every one is strong. In *All the President's Men*, Robert Redford and Dustin Hoffman portray young journalists just wanting a good story. "They're hungry! Remember when you were hungry?" Jack Warden asks their boss, Jason Robards. And soon their hunger propels them from a seemingly innocuous burglary all the way into the Oval Office.

Likewise in any number of tales, from the graphic murders in *Mystic River*, to fantasies like *Blade Runner*, to political mysteries like *Missing*, the need to know what's in that last little room is overwhelming — not just because the challenge of finding the answer is so great, but because we are unable to stop looking regardless. The secret that is driving us on grows in power throughout.

Inevitably, the "dark turn" comes when the hero gets so involved that he goes against his own rules, or the group's, to find the answer — and at some point realizes he is either setting himself up to be part of the crime, or has been guilty of a similar crime all along. Isn't Michael Douglas in *Basic Instinct*, while pursuing Sharon Stone, also on the path to being her next victim? Yet the attraction is so great Michael is literally dying to know.

Somewhere along the line, Whydunit heroes willingly become part of the darkness. "Of course, he has to swim in the same water we all do," says Jake Gittes in *Chinatown*. And that commonality does indeed include all of us.

At the end of the line, the trail doubles back on itself and onto those investigating the crime. This is why the set-up of many a detective story involves one case that seems to end — even end badly as in Altman's *The Long Goodbye* — and then has a reappearance as a new case with new players that brings the hero back to the initial escapade in a way we know will address the real problem. This Whydunit feature is called **the case within a case**, and often reveals the theme. By returning to the first caper, and discovering what it means to the detective, we learn what the real story has been about all along.

For those writers who wish to enter the dark world of the Whydunit, it's best to start with the crime and the criminals who engineered it. Though you should appear to *not* know what's happening as you begin to "turn over the cards" of evidence that lead to the evil, in fact you must know it all. Start by standing in the shoes of the bad guy and figuring out why he committed the crime and how he misdirected others to cover his tracks. Your job as the Whydunit's creator is to be brilliant in your obfuscation, then be just as brilliant as you uncover it — and do so fast, before the bad guy gets away! This two-part approach to writing your grim tale, if imagined smartly, guarantees a scary and revealing finale.

THE WHO, WHAT, WHEN, AND WHERE OF A WHYDUNIT

If you have a mystery on your hands and the overwhelming need to know what's in that last little room, get a clue:

1. The "detective" does not change, we do; yet he can be any kind of gumshoe — from pro to amateur to imaginary.

2. The "secret" of the case is so strong it overwhelms the worldly lures of money, sex, power, or fame. We *gots* to know! And so does the Whydunit hero.

3. Finally, the "dark turn" shows that in pursuit of the secret, the detective will break the rules, even his own — often ones he has relied on for years to keep him safe. The pull of the secret is too great.

So don't make me get tough with you, toots; take a gander at a few stories from my casebook, and trust me... they're doozies.

ALL THE PRESIDENT'S MEN (1976)

"I guess I don't have the taste for the jugular you guys have."

When a female reporter at the *Washington Post* says this line to Robert Redford and Dustin Hoffman, it shows the "dark turn" the two reporters have made. What begins when Bob is told to investigate a "third-rate burglary" at The Watergate is now a "compulsion." They have momentarily lost their way — and their confusion is what makes this "Political Whydunit" a winner. Director Alan Pakula knows that at the heart of any mystery, especially one about power, is a story about flirting with its dark side. And even though the visage of Richard Nixon is waiting behind the last little door, we must ask what we're willing to do to expose him.

If we are no better than our enemies, what are we?

In his Hollywood tell-all, *Adventures in the Screen Trade*, screenwriter William Goldman reports that writing this script nearly drove him mad. It was due to Pakula's mantra: "Don't deny me any riches" (meaning "let's wring every drop of story out of these events"). It's become a line I tell myself, and others, when working on a project. And the results here prove we writers are not always the best judges of when it's going well! It may not be the legendary Mr. Goldman's favorite script; it is certainly one of mine.

W Type: Political Whydunit

W Cousins: *Z*, *The Parallax View*, *Missing*, *The China Syndrome*, *JFK*, *The Insider*, *The Quiet American*, *The Manchurian Candidate*, *The Constant Gardener*, *The Interpreter*

ALL THE PRESIDENT'S MEN
Screenplay by William Goldman
Based on the book by Carl Bernstein *and* Bob Woodward

Opening Image: Like gunshots, the date "June 17, 1972" is pounded out by a booming typewriter as President Nixon's helicopter lands triumphantly; he is at the height of power.

Theme Stated: Burglars are arrested at the Watergate Hotel. On the story, *Washington Post* reporter Bob Woodward (Robert Redford) arrives at court where they're being arraigned. When Bob asks the burglars' counsel how he got there, the lawyer replies: "I'm not here." The theme is subterfuge by the men behind the men that govern us.

Set-Up: Bob digs into the case while another reporter, Carl Bernstein (Dustin Hoffman), realizes this is a big story and wants on it "bad." Bob learns that one of the men arrested worked for the CIA. Is there more going on than a break-in? Bob is assigned to the story, while Dustin dogs the edges, trying to be included. As the reporters attempt to work out their differing styles, Bob learns the phone number for the White House was in one of the burglar's address books, and finds out another of the President's men, Howard Hunt, was also in the CIA.

Catalyst: At Minute 23, the two are told they're both on the story. They begin in earnest to write their first byline together.

Debate: Are these two reporters too green to do the job? As the stakes keep getting raised, we always come back to this question.

Break into Two: At Minute 33, they file their first story and interact with boss Ben Bradlee (Jason Robards), who shoots it down. "Bury it in the back somewhere," he grumbles. And now the team must choose: Quit or re-double their efforts? They decide to go back to work and get the story right.

B Story: Twin B stories as Bob and Dustin find two mentors who inspire them to dissect the "subterfuge" that is our theme. One is Jason, whose "love" for the rookie reporters pushes them on when the going gets tough. The other is "Deep Throat," the real-life mystery man (revealed in 2005 to be Mark Felt) who provided Bob Woodward with inside information. We meet him (Hal Holbrook) in the underground parking lot scene this film is most noted for.

Fun and Games: Told by Deep Throat to "follow the money" (a famous line created out of whole cloth by writer Goldman), the boys have newfound direction. Jetting to Florida, Dustin tricks a secretary to see a local official (Ned Beatty). Armed with what Dustin dug up, Bob tracks down the Midwest Finance Chairman of CREEP (The Committee to Re-Elect the President), who reveals it was his check that wound up in the bank account of one of the burglars. This is the "promise of the premise." Like any great detective story, the first blush of the case and the assorted clues connected to it are exciting. The story — and this mystery — can go anywhere!

Midpoint: The flurry of stories "Woodstein" files (the boys are working so closely, they've earned the nickname) are all sweet victories; their coverage of "Watergate" is making the reporters famous, and even getting results as Nixon's finance team is audited. But at Minute 56, A and B stories cross as Jason "raises the stakes" when he tells them he wants more — and bridles at the idea of Deep Throat, whom he now learns about. We get a "false defeat" as the reporters hit bottom at Minute 70 when they reach the end of a list of Nixon employees they've been investigating. It looks like the clues have dried up. "We'll just have to start all over again," says Bob, as they go back to the top of the list.

Bad Guys Close In: Scrambling to get the information they need, the "dark turn" takes hold as Bob and Dustin start to play games with witnesses, tricking them into going on the record and using their own subterfuge to get accurate quotes and sources. The "secret," the pull of what's in that last little room, is overwhelming their sense of fair play. Pressure is applied by the "bad guys" too, when one story linking Attorney General John Mitchell to the case includes Mitchell threatening Dustin and the owner of the *Post*, Katharine Graham. Despite all the progress, when Bob meets Deep Throat for a second time, he's frustrated when told: "You're missing the overall." And it's even worse: This time, Bob thinks he was followed. For his part, Dustin visits his doppelganger, Donald Segretti (Robert Walden), who admits that he will not only lose his law license but will probably go to jail for his dirty tricks. The lawyer's tale foreshadows the penalty for failure.

All Is Lost: Because the midpoint is a "down," the All Is Lost is an "up" or a "false victory." After thinking Bob and Dustin have vetted a story that links the break-in to the Oval Office, Jason agrees to "go with it" — but the boys were double-crossed, and the story is immediately denounced by the White House. Threats by Nixon's team include a demand for a retraction. About to be fired, or worse — get their boss sued and his reputation destroyed — the rookies seem to have blown it.

Dark Night of the Soul: "What was our mistake?" Dustin asks.

Break into Three: A and B stories cross as Jason votes to "stick with the story" and "stand by the boys." As a result, Bob sets up another meeting with Deep Throat to find out how they goofed.

Finale: At the garage, Bob has finally had it with subterfuge: "I'm tired of your chickenshit games," he tells Deep Throat. "I need to know what you know." Deep Mentor decides to tell Bob all — the trail leads to the President. Bob rushes back to inform Dustin. Typing to each other out of fear of being bugged, Bob writes: "Our lives are in danger." The boys then rush to Jason's house to tell him. Jason lovingly says: "Go home, rest up, fifteen minutes." They are back on the case for real. As we go out, the two are feverishly typing more stories.

Final Image: A series of headlines spit out by a teletype machine reveal how the story unfolds in the next few years leading to Nixon's resignation. The press has triumphed.

BLADE RUNNER (1982)

How many times does the "director's cut" of a movie turn out better than the original? That's right: Almost never. While I appreciate any version of Ridley Scott's "Fantasy Whydunit," taking out the voice-over and leaving the ending a little more open-ended, as he does in his version of the story, to me works best. No matter what cut of this Harrison Ford-starrer we see, seeing is key. Not only are the visuals, imagination, and decor of the film its real high-points — and a cinematic milestone — but the running imagery of sight — eyes, eyeballs, death by having one's eyes pushed inward — is also a powerful motif.

For our purposes, this sci-fi detective set-up is like so many others over the years. In this case, Harrison is a "blade runner," a bounty hunter whose specialty is tracking down and retiring "replicants," androids so lifelike it takes a special test to make sure they're not human. And like so many "dark turns" a detective makes in a good Whydunit, this one involves a woman... kinda. When Harrison falls for Sean Young and discovers she too is "one of them," it's the start of his seeing life — and love — a whole new way. As the "bad guy," Rutger Hauer is truly inspired as the leader of the hunted, who teaches Harrison the meaning of being alive.

W Type: Fantasy Whydunit

W Cousins: *Total Recall; Who Framed Roger Rabbit; Cool World; Mulholland Drive; Ghost; The Sixth Sense; The Singing Detective; Minority Report; Sky Captain and the World of Tomorrow; I, Robot*

BLADE RUNNER
Screenplay by Hampton Fancher *and* David Peoples
Based on DO ANDROIDS DREAM OF ELECTRIC SHEEP?
by Philip K. Dick

Opening Image: Los Angeles in 2019, a smoggy cesspool of moral ambiguity and desolation. The flying cars tell us we're in the future — without them, what's new?

Theme Stated: At the Tyrell Corporation, Leon Kowalksi (Brion James) is given an odd eye test while asked questions. What is it to be "alive"? — that's our theme. Can you tell who is human and who isn't by looking into their eyes? At Minute 7, Brion kills his interrogator.

Set-Up: Meet Rick Deckard (Harrison Ford), one of the unlucky few still living on Earth. While ads promise "A new life awaits you in the off-world colonies," for some reason he's still here. He's not really "alive" himself — at least in a Stasis = Death way — and is waiting for a mission. Then the mysterious origami-making Gaff (Edward James Olmos) announces one.

Catalyst: Minute 12 (right on time!), Harrison gets his assignment. A cop, Bryant (M. Emmet Walsh), tells the specialist: "I got four 'skin jobs' walking the streets. You're going to spot 'em and you're gonna air 'em out." But Harrison hesitates.

Debate: Harrison reviews the tape of Brion's interrogation, marveling at how lifelike he is. The real mystery of all this: Why did the replicants come back to Earth from an off-planet base, and what do they want out of the Tyrell Corporation? We also foreshadow the other replicants, including Roy Batty (Rutger Hauer), the leader, and Pris (Daryl Hannah). The replicants were built to live four years; their life spans are almost over.

Break into Two: Harrison takes the case and arrives at the Tyrell Corporation, an Art-Deco-via-Hong Kong office space.

B Story: Harrison meets Rachael (Sean Young), who is the "love story" and the heart of the theme. We also meet founder Eldon Tyrell (Joe Turkel), who asks Harrison to test Sean just like Brion was — and we learn she is a replicant. At Minute 22, Harrison gives the punchline: "She doesn't know...." Tyrell tells Harrison the company motto: "More human than human." Even Sean's memories are fake.

Fun and Games: The case progresses as Harrison goes to his first stop, the hotel where Brion lived. Like the "promise of the premise" of any Whydunit, he digs for clues. He finds what seems to be a fish scale. Meanwhile replicants Rutger and Brion show up at the fresh-frozen lab of eye-guy Hannibal Chew (James Hong). Rutger wants to know where designer JF Sebastian (William Sanderson) lives. Learning Sebastian's address from Chew, Rutger sends Daryl to Sebastian's flat. We also see things heat up with Sean, for when Harrison gets home, she is waiting for him (kinda like in real life). "You think I'm a replicant," she says. Later, analyzing a photo (and exploiting the eye motif), Harrison finds more mystery. One clue leads to the next as he proceeds to a marketplace and, asking an expert with another microscope-like device (so many eye and lens images!), learns the "fish scale" is actually a synthetic snake scale.

Midpoint: Harrison goes to a trendy bar. A good detective story surveys the strata of the whole society — lower class, upper class, and in between — with our hero negotiating all. Harrison heads backstage where he pretends to be a nerd (the same guy Bogart posed as in *The Big Sleep* to get info at a bookstore). Zhora (Joanna Cassidy) is using a robot snake in her act (thus the scale). When she bolts, Harrison chases and kills her. The "stakes are raised," and A and B stories cross, when Harrison is told he has one more replicant to retire: Sean.

Bad Guys Close In: The vice tightens immediately. Brion grabs Harrison on the street. "Wake up, time to die," he tells the blade runner. That's when Sean rescues him by killing Brion. Having his life saved by a replicant, how can he *not* take a "dark turn"? At home, Sean watches him spit blood, fascinated. "What if I go north, disappear, would you come after me?" she asks. Alone with her, Harrison considers love with a robot (it *is* LA). They kiss at 1 Hour 12 Minutes. Meanwhile back at Sebastian's house, Daryl is donning her battle make-up and doing cartwheels; a clock chime is heard ("time clock" alert). Ironically, Sebastian has a genetic disease whereby he grows old faster than normal humans.

All Is Lost: Rutger visits Tyrell. When he refuses to help prolong their lives, Rutger kills him by pushing his eyeballs into his head. Sebastian dies too, and now the replicants know they are doomed.

Break into Three: A and B stories cross again as Harrison leaves Sean and goes to Sebastian's to face the other replicants. Daryl is a back-flippin' killer, but Harrison bests her.

Finale: Harrison's showdown with Rutger is brutal and poignant. In a way, they are two of kind — both are in love with a replicant. But robot saves human and in his final words, returns again to eye imagery: "I've seen things you people wouldn't believe. All those moments will be lost in time. Like tears in rain." (lines written on the set by Rutger Hauer himself!) As he dies, he releases a dove, and Harrison sees what's in "the last room": He too will die.

Final Image: Harrison goes home and finds Sean asleep, not dead. As he and Sean walk out to "head north," we see Edward left an origami unicorn, a sign he is letting Harrison off the hook and allowing him and Sean to "live" a while longer.

FARGO (1996)

What's inside the last little room of the nautilus shell in this Coen Brother's gem of a Whydunit is something truly horrifying. When very pregnant Sheriff Marge Gunderson (Frances McDormand) turns the handle and opens that final door, she confronts malevolence at its most blasé. There, a man with no conscience is feeding the limb of his latest victim into a wood chipper. But his expression is of one who's been interrupted doing the laundry. Marge began this journey in the warm bed she shares with husband Norm, who paints pictures of ducks for a living. Yet here on a cold Minnesota afternoon, she's found what she's looking for: Proof that evil is working overtime even while we sleep.

With a brilliant screenplay by Ethan and Joel Coen, and stellar performances from William H. Macy, Steve Buscemi, and McDormand (who won an Oscar® for this role), director Joel Coen's *Fargo* is an example of a type of "Cop Whydunit" in which the audience knows the "secret" and is waiting for our by-the-book detective to catch up. Despite her Midwest manners, penchant for smorgasbords, and awkward reunions at the Radisson, Marge is way ahead of us. She knows more that she lets on. She will take a "dark turn" herself — and is well aware of the power of its attraction.

W Type: Cop Whydunit

W Cousins: *The French Connection, Dirty Harry, Tightrope, To Live and Die in LA, Basic Instinct, City by the Sea, LA Confidential, Insomnia, Twisted, Narc*

FARGO
Written by Ethan Coen & Joel Coen

Opening Image: Out of a blowing snowstorm, a car and trailer pull into Fargo, ND, site of the planning for our sad crime.

Theme Stated: Late, due to getting the time wrong, mild-mannered car salesman Jerry Lundegaard (William H. Macy) arrives with a new tan Sierra for accomplices Carl Showalter (Steve Buscemi) and Gaear Grimsrud (Peter Stormare). He wants them to kidnap his own wife, but the kidnappers are confused. Why would anyone do that? Appreciating what you have, or not, is what this movie is about.

Set-Up: William needs money. His plan is to kidnap his wife and force her rich father to pay a ransom. Just how he lost the $320,000 loaned him, and for which he has borrowed on several cars used as collateral at the dealership where he works, is a mystery. When he arrives home to his wife and intended victim (Kristin Rudrüd), all seems normal. But we soon understand why he's harbored this plan. "Dad's here," his wife tells him. A bully, William's father-in-law, Wade (Harve Presnell), can do or say anything he wants in their home. William is the definition of the "little man" pushed around by life. We wish he'd stand up for himself. But that ship has sailed.

Catalyst: At Minute 13, William gets a call; Harve might go for a business deal he proposed that *we* know might save him — and eliminate the need for the kidnapping.

Debate: Can he stop the crime? William meets with a mechanic at the car lot where he works; Shep Proudfoot (Steven Reevis) arranged the kidnap, but the wheels are in motion. Harve cheats William on the deal anyway.

Break into Two: The two criminals break in and grab Kristin. William comes home and finds his wife gone, and seems almost surprised that his scheme is now in motion. He rehearses sounding upset and calls his father-in-law, saying his wife's been kidnapped. But the real problems begin when the kidnappers kill a cop, then chase down and kill witnesses to the crime.

B Story: At Minute 32, we meet Marge Gunderson (Frances McDormand), in bed with husband Norm (John Carroll Lynch) when the call comes. New to the case, she'll follow clues we've seen. She sounds more like a housewife than a hard-edged cop. "There in a jif, real good," she says. She and Norm are expecting. It is through Frances the theme of the movie will be discussed. Frances is satisfied with her life — but even she will be tempted.

Fun and Games: Frances is on the case; she shows her brilliance, and what a good detective she is, by reenacting the crime. "From his footprint it looks like he's a big fella," she says at the scene. She spots different tracks next to the dead trooper and realizes there's a team of killers. Frances is also kind when she corrects a fellow investigator: "I don't think I agree with you 100% on your police work there, Lou." Meanwhile, William continues his plan. In control, he's running the show, but this won't last; it's Harve's money. The kidnappers arrive at a cabin where they'll wait for the exchange, and Steve's partner acts insane. Watching TV that night, Frances gets a call. It's an old friend, Mike (Steve Park). Frances flirts with a "dark turn" by mulling his lunch invitation.

Midpoint: The "stakes are raised" as Steve calls William and tells him about the murders. "Circumstances have changed," he says. This is followed by a "time clock," when William is given 24 hours to send proof for his loan. There's a lot of eating in this movie, by people and on nature TV shows; while at another buffet, Frances is ordered to the Twin Cities on the case. Mike lives there — and now Frances' "stakes are raised."

Bad Guys Close In: As Frances arrives in the Twin Cities, Harve refuses to let William handle the pay-off. Frances shows up at William's work to interview Shep Proudfoot. At 1 Hour, Frances questions William for the first time. Then, making her "dark turn" — even if it's the Minnesota housewife's version — Frances dresses up and meets Mike for lunch. It's an awkward moment as Mike has a tearful breakdown. The scene revisits the theme: If Frances is satisfied with her life, why hasn't she told her husband she's here? That night, Shep finds Steve and beats him. Their plan is falling apart fast.

All Is Lost: Picking up the money, Steve's surprised by Harve, who acts tough. Steve kills him but not before Harve shoots Steve in the face. William, with no money or wife, is "worse off than when this movie started." Later, Steve opens the bag and sees the million dollars William got Harve to pay them. Steve buries the money; he has an idea how to keep it all.

Dark Night of the Soul: Packing to leave the city, Frances learns Mike has psychiatric problems. Isolated on the road, she tries to find comfort in fast food and prepares to take a last stab at cracking the case.

Break into Three: Frances returns to the car dealership and interviews William. She looks at a photo of William's wife on his desk; the woman's smiling face touches on the theme of "being happy with what we have" — Is Frances? Then she sees William fleeing the scene and knows he's part of the kidnapping. Meanwhile, Steve comes back to the cabin and finds William's wife dead; his cohort killed her. Attempting to escape, Steve is axed to death by his homicidal partner.

Finale: Frances finds the tan Sierra and discovers the bad guy putting Steve's body parts in a wood chipper. She shoots and arrests him. On the way home, she even lectures him and sums up the theme: "There's more to life than a little money. Don't you know that? And here you are and it's a beautiful day. Well... I just don't understand it." This is a reminder for herself, as well.

Final Image: William is arrested in a motel and Frances and her husband are back in bed. Frances' flirtation with the dark side has made her homecoming and home life all the more rewarding.

MYSTIC RIVER (2003)

In a great example of the "case within a case," director Clint Eastwood explores how the past affects the present in his adaptation of Dennis Lehane's best-selling novel. The incident at the heart of the story takes place 30 years earlier when the lives of three boys are changed when one is abducted by pedophiles — an event that seems buried. It will take a new crime — the murder of another man's daughter — to rouse old ghosts and confront the sins of the past.

The "detective" here is actually several characters, for even though one, played by Kevin Bacon, is the cop on the case, the real mystery-solving is left to "civilians," which is what makes this such a great example of the "Personal Whydunit."

Sean Penn plays the father of the murdered girl, who now has to dredge up his criminal past to avenge her. Likewise, the man who was abducted as a boy, Tim Robbins, must battle his own demons in a separate event that coincides with this new crime in ways that force his guilt into the open. As we will see by the film's ending, the rules are not the same for every community. The "dark turn" Sean makes to find the truth plays differently in this small town. A textbook adaptation by Brian Helgeland takes an unwieldy narrative and gives it a spine that shows the theme: Even the most innocent must face themselves and their sins.

W Type: Personal Whydunit

W Cousins: *The Third Man, Rear Window, Vertigo, The Conversation, Body Double, Final Analysis, Jagged Edge, Kiss the Girls, High Crimes, Disturbia*

MYSTIC RIVER
Screenplay by Brian Helgeland
Based on the novel by Dennis Lehane

Opening Image: 1975. Three boys play ball in a working-class Massachusetts neighborhood. Pausing to etch their names in wet cement, one is stopped mid-task by two men posing as police. They take the boy with them in their car.

Theme Stated: Days later, after being held and sexually abused, the boy escapes. Returned home, he is talked about by neighbors who refer to him as "damaged goods." Does the "damage" of the past mark us for life? That's what this movie will explore.

Set-Up: Now in the present, the three boys have grown up, each affected by this past event. Dave Boyle (Tim Robbins), the one who was abducted, is now a quiet, overprotective father and husband. Jimmy Markum (Sean Penn) has a teen daughter, Katie (Emmy Rossum), a new wife, Annabeth (Laura Linney), and a criminal past. He too is overprotective, not liking that Katie is seeing Brendan (Tom Guiry), son of Just Ray, a man Sean once committed crimes with. We also meet a third man, Sean Devine (Kevin Bacon), now a cop. One night, while at a bar, Tim sees Katie, drunk.

Catalyst: Tim comes home to his wife (Marcia Gay Harden) late. He is bloody, and cryptically tells her about being mugged and beating his attacker so hard he may have killed him. Next day, Katie's car is found abandoned; she's missing.

Debate: What happened? Is Katie dead or just a runaway? Brendan and his deaf brother, Silent Ray (Spencer Treat Clark), come into the store Sean owns, and we see Sean dislikes both. As luck would have it, Kevin gets the case, and arrives in his old neighborhood. After church, Sean sees police cars roar by, sirens blaring.

Break into Two: At Minute 23, Kevin works the crime scene, as Sean turns up with his old crew, the Savage Brothers, and yells to be let past the police barricade. Also involved now is Marcia Gay, who doesn't know what to make of her husband's wild story. Each "detective" will piece together the clues of the case as it relates to them, as past and present merge. At Minute 31, Katie's body is found. She has been shot.

B Story: Three B stories are in play in this film; the theme is discussed in each. Sean's B story is his criminal past, as seen through his involvement with the local thugs, the two Savage Brothers. Tim's B story concerns his trying to free himself from the pain of what happened to him. Is it enough to have made him kill Katie? Kevin's B story involves his wife who left him; he is patiently waiting for her to return. But whenever she phones Kevin, she cannot speak.

Fun and Games: As in most Whydunits, the cards in this case are now turned over. Brendan, the boyfriend, was taking Katie to Las Vegas; they were to be married. He loved her. Meanwhile Tim and Marcia Gay comfort Sean and Laura, but no story about Tim's mugging is in the paper. Kevin, meanwhile, seems to be hitting dead ends and runs afoul of his cop partner, Sgt. Powers (Laurence Fishburne), who doesn't get the rules of this burg.

Midpoint: Kevin's missing wife calls a second time and still isn't speaking. The inability to speak, and being held in place by events, complements the overall theme. But the "stakes are raised" when Tim is identified as a suspect. His own wife is questioning him, and his response to her is so odd she begins to doubt his story. At 1 Hour, Brendan passes a polygraph and at 1 Hour 5 Minutes, Tim is detained as a suspect.

Bad Guys Close In: Sean has been ruminating about Katie's death while the Savage Brothers interrogate suspects — often ahead of the cops. Now Sean begins to rage: "I'm gonna find him and I'm gonna kill him!" Kevin learns the gun used to kill Katie was also used to rob a liquor store years ago. The suspect: Sean's pal "Just Ray," father of the boys Sean hates. Is there a link between this second buried event and Katie?

All Is Lost: Marcia Gay tells Sean she thinks Tim killed Katie, sealing his doom. Kevin questions Brendan about his father's gun.

Dark Night of the Soul: With no proof, Kevin lets Brendan go. Just like Marcia Gay, he hopes he did the right thing.

Break into Three: The Savage Brothers pick up Tim, who gets in their car and drives away in a match shot of his 1975 abduction. Meanwhile, Brendan finds the hiding place of his father's gun; someone took it and used it. Brendan waits at home.

Finale: The Savage Brothers get Tim drunk at a local bar as Sean walks in. He now begins to question Tim. Staggering outside, Tim feels ill and realizes Sean thinks he killed Katie. At home, Brendan confronts his brother, Silent Ray. Ray didn't want Brendan to leave him; what's more, he's not even really deaf, but using the ploy to bond with Brendan. At the river, Sean pressures Tim to admit he killed Katie and Tim finally does, hoping Sean will take pity. Au contraire. Sean knifes, then shoots Tim. Weak is weak here on Mystic River. Only the tough survive and the breaks are the breaks. Tim dies, just as Kevin arrests Silent Ray for the murder.

Final Image: Turns out Tim was telling the truth: He killed a child molester that night. And Sean had killed Just Ray and has been sending his widow money all these years. Justice is also meted out for Kevin, whose wife comes back to him. By the end of the film, a parade in town shows only Marcia Gay is the loser. She ratted out her husband, and now she is a widow. Kevin and Sean nod to each other at the parade, knowing that justice has been served — maybe — but as we go out, we see the cement where the boys carved their names years ago. Only Tim's is incomplete, as was his life.

BRICK (2005)

The classic noir gets an update in 'tude when Philip Marlowe is reinvented for high school. Given the conceits of the form — the fast-talking gumshoe, the missing ingenue, the gimlet whore, and the DA bent on yanking our hero's license, this story is the same... only different. Writer/director Rian Johnson adds to the form begun with *The Maltese Falcon*, and tweaked in *The Long Goodbye* and *Chinatown*, setting his tale in the hardcore underground of San Clemente, California.

And it's a hoot.

Half-hilarious, half-ingenious, and written with mouth-watering dialogue that never disappoints, this is a story that inventively "steals" from its predecessors, with teens embodying the roles of noirs past. And it follows the rules of the Whydunit all the way — right down to the "dark turn" of the hero. Brendan (Joseph Gordon-Levitt) not only has a personal stake in finding his ex-girlfriend's murderer, he is drawn into her world for the same corrupt reasons that she was.

With the theme concerning whether or not we can possess another, every scene is about some form of control and owner-ship of someone else. Can our detective let go of his ex? Or did his inability to hang onto their relationship in the first place lead to her death? Brendan will discover he may be more responsible than he could ever imagine.

*Who*dunit? In his own way... he did.

W Type: Noir Whydunit

W Cousins: *Chinatown; The Long Goodbye; Farewell, My Lovely; The Big Sleep; Body Heat; Devil in a Blue Dress; Blue Velvet; Mulholland Falls; Hollywoodland; The Black Dahlia*

BRICK
Written by Rian Johnson

Opening Image: A dead girl lying in the spillway on the lip of a sewage pipe. A young man looks at the details of her body: her plastic bracelets, her blonde hair, and ponders... why?

Catalyst: Two days earlier, prompted by a note left in his locker at high school, the young man, Brendan (Joseph Gordon-Levitt), goes to a phone booth and fields a call from the girl we know will be dead soon. Emily (Emilie de Ravin) is his ex-girlfriend, now in trouble.

Set-Up: Brendan's world, and the reflection of every Sam Spade and film noir cliché, is San Clemente High School. Few parents or teachers appear in this world, and those that do are stand-ins for stock characters in detective stories. We learn Brendan dropped out of the social whirl for reasons having to do with Emily. We also see whom Emily got involved with post-Brendan. These are the "cool" kids that include drug-using jock Brad Bramish (Brian White) and his mysterious girlfriend Laura (Nora Zehetner). We also meet Brendan's other ex, sexy high school theater geek Kara (Meagan Good), who has a string of freshman fans on bended knee.

Debate: What's going on with Emily? Not yet on the case, Brendan sneaks into a party and sees Laura talking with tough kid Tug (Noah Fleiss), who drives a Mustang just like the one Brendan saw when he last spoke to Emily. Next day at snackshack "Coffee and Pie," Brendan rousts Dode (Noah Segan), Emily's new boyfriend, to set up an appointment with her.

Theme Stated: Finally, Brendan meets Emily and she asks him to let her go: "I don't want to be put away and protected." And later says: "You don't love me, you just want to keep me." Can one person possess another?

Break into Two: At Minute 24, we are back at the sewage pipe where this movie began. Knowing he must hide Emily's body to buy time until he can find the killer, Brendan decides to "take the case" wherever it leads.

Fun and Games: Brendan meets his Watson, "Brain" (Matt O'Leary), who will help him solve the mystery. He reveals to Brain four clues Emily mentioned when he last spoke to her: "Brick," "Tug," "poor Frisco," and "The Pin." Brain figures out that The Pin means "The Kingpin," the rumored town drug dealer. Into the fray, Brendan has a hard-boiled fight in the school parking lot with The Pin's underling, Brad Bramish. This gets him a meeting with The Pin (Lukas Haas), who lives with his apple juice-serving Mom and does business out of their basement. We also see Brendan get called on the carpet by Gary Trueman (Richard Roundtree), Assistant Vice Principal and a parody of the DA in every detective movie. By turning in a student months earlier, Brendan became a snitch but refuses this time, telling the authority figure: "I'm not your boy!"

B Story: The question of whether Laura can be trusted or not is at the heart of this case, and her interest in Brendan a reflection of the power of possession. Like all tough detectives, Brendan needs love, too. This "love story" is where the theme of this movie will be discussed, and where Brendan will seek solace.

Midpoint: Laura saves Brendan when he's in a tough spot as A and B stories cross in "false victory." And the victory is enhanced when Laura tells Brendan what's at the core of the mystery (and one of the clues): a missing "brick" of heroin. At school, after fending off a knife-wielding thug, Brendan dips into the "dark side" when he joins The Pin, posing as a snitch to gain The Pin's trust and learn more about Emily's death.

Bad Guys Close In: Brendan is brought into The Pin's world, and the "stakes are raised." Assistant Vice Principal Trueman shows up at Brendan's class, asking about Emily; Brendan is now a suspect in her disappearance. When he learns "poor Frisco" died by using poisoned heroin, Brendan knows the crime is about more than just drugs. At The Pin's house, he finds a brick of heroin and learns from Tug that one was stolen and replaced with a tainted substitute. Everyone suspects Emily. Now Brendan does, too. Brendan accepts Dode's invite to a meeting with The Pin and Tug, then gets the biggest shock yet when Dode reveals Emily was pregnant.

All Is Lost: At the sewage pipe, Dode is about to tell The Pin he thinks Brendan killed Emily. But Brendan is saved when Tug kills Dode before he says a word — because it was Tug who killed Emily, and he thinks Dode was about to turn him over. "Worse off than when this movie started," and complicit in not just one death but two, Brendan experiences the "whiff of death."

Dark Night of the Soul: Brendan learns Tug thought Emily's baby was his; that's why he killed her. Brendan knows all now, except for one key piece: Who told Tug it was his baby? To find solace, Brendan seeks out Laura who comforts him, but an idle remark makes him realize she played a part in Emily's death, too.

Break into Three: A and B stories cross as we return to the theme of possession: Laura tries to keep Brendan from going to the final confrontation between Tug and The Pin, but Brendan breaks from her influence and heads to the face-off.

Finale: The showdown turns violent as Tug and The Pin kill each other. Brendan escapes before the police arrive. Emily's body is found in Tug's car, and he is blamed. Laura is the only one of the group who's gotten off scot-free. Or has she?

Final Image: Brendan puts the case together: Laura did it. She manipulated everyone, and told Tug about Emily knowing he would kill her. It was all done to keep control. But we also learn the horrible truth: The baby was Brendan's. He turns Laura in to the cops, but is in no mood to celebrate. The "dark turn" he needed to take to solve the mystery has tainted him for good.

 The "Fool Triumphant" comes in all shapes and sizes. In Legally Blonde, *Reese Witherspoon brings* da pink *to Harvard Yard — along with values of fidelity, truth, and perms — that will help this "fish out of water" win big.*

8 FOOL TRIUMPHANT

The tale of the Village Idiot is a tradition going back to ancient times. Whether an actual knuckle-dragging dimwit or a savant whose skills are disguised, being disregarded is the power of this character — and the secret of his success.

Crafty Greek protags like Ulysses often play the fool. Puck in *A Midsummer Night's Dream* delights us with hijinks and wisdom. And the "jester" is a stock character in the King's court. These are heroes famous for come-from-behind victories, for while those around them don't know a wise man or woman when they see one, we do!

And that's what makes the "Fool Triumphant."

The key ingredient in setting up the "fool as hero" story is giving him an establishment to stand against. And while he does not set out to do anything but live his life, it's usually the establishment that's exposed as the *real* fool in the equation. Have no fear, our unlikely hero won't become a part of the system — or want to! The fool will lead no revolution, upend no government, nor promote himself or even a cause, but his presence reminds us that an individual can still make a difference. The fool is that side of us that knows the truth of what we speak, but may be unable to convince others. He represents our fondest hope: That even on our most idiotic day, we're making sense...

...and maybe everybody should cut us a damn break!

The latitude of the FT tale can be found in many such circumstances. The "Undercover Fool" purposely assumes the identity of someone else, often disguised as the opposite sex (*Tootsie, Mrs. Doubtfire*); the "Political Fool" is a clown in the king's court who others mistake as a sage (*Being There, Dave*); and the "Sex Fool" (*The 40-Year-Old Virgin, The Guru*) is one who seems to be a lothario — but who actually needs help. This genre also includes the "fish out of water" tale where an unappreciated *piscis ex aqua* crawls up to dry land where she will find her true place (*Legally Blonde*), and where her skills suddenly have new impact. These "fresh start" stories reveal that back home the locals we grew up with are unsure what we're capable of, but with a bit of luck — and a bus ticket out of town — we can finally show how great we are. Such is the curse and the blessing of being considered a fool, the out-of-the-blue, didn't-expect-it, not-paid-attention-to person we all love and root for.

The rule of the fool is simple, and the Fool Triumphant template has three very definite conventions: (1) a "fool," the overlooked man or woman who is often naïve about his own powers; (2) an "establishment" that the fool either rises to challenge or is sent in to engage, as in most "fish out of water" stories; and (3) a "transmutation" that is offered the fool by circumstances that seem divine. Often this includes a "name change" — a beat seen in quite a few of these tales.

So let's examine these elements. I mean, you're here, why not?

The most important feature of the "fool" in literature is that he must be disregarded at first — and his being unaware of what he's missing is the preposterous starting point for all: Reese Witherspoon in *Legally Blonde*, Peter Sellers in *Being There*, Dustin Hoffman in *Tootsie*, Geoffrey Rush in *Shine*, and even Tom Hulce in *Amadeus* all share this underdog quality — and being overlooked is both their disadvantage and their greatest power. For whatever reason, these sad sacks are deemed less-than or discounted entirely. And even though they know they have what it takes, or at least have the pure chutzpah not to care, no one else takes them seriously or considers them a threat at first. Well... almost no one.

For every fool there is often a character described as the **Insider**, and he and the fool are a matched set in many an FT tale. This is the "jealous brother" who "gets it," who knows the fool has magic powers, sometimes ones that — in the beginning — threaten him. These are the "smart guys" who often pay for their insight by getting the karmic backlash from trying to compete with the fool: Salieri in *Amadeus*, Lieutenant Dan in *Forrest Gump*, and Chief Inspector Dreyfus (Herbert Lom) in the old *Pink Panther* movies. This is also the difference between a Fool Triumphant story and a "Superhero" tale (Chapter 10); in the latter, the hero *knows* he's special and also knows the cost that being "special" will entail — that is, in fact, what makes him a Superhero. But in a Fool Triumphant story, only the Insider really knows, and that information both gnaws at and inspires him to thwart the fool wherever he can.

The "establishment" we send the fool to confront, or one that he finds himself opposing, makes the fool stand out. Yet when they finally square off face-to-face, it's usually the establishment that blinks. This is why so many "fish out of water" tales — the "fish," meaning the fool, and "out of water," meaning where he lands — present such a scary predicament. We fear for the FT hero, and assume he will flail and die. Often these stories are of the "Country Mouse Goes to the City" variety, where the bumpkin finds himself amid city slickers who berate him.

The combinations of these fish tales are amazingly varied — yet have the same rules. Isn't Reese Witherspoon as the fabulous Elle Woods the least likely to do well at Harvard Law? And isn't Goldie Hawn in *Private Benjamin* the same character, just wearing a khaki color scheme instead of pink? If there's one thing these new-comers all have in common, it's that the more the establishment makes fun of them, the more likely they will get the last laugh. The establishment's traditions, one-track mindset, and ignorance of its need to change makes the quick-to-grow-legs fish likely to win. And the victory is sweet for us too, for we confront those who doubt us all day long.

And isn't *that* a drag?

Finally, the "transmutation" that occurs for the hero goes beyond the usual. All stories are about transformation — how many times do I have to say it? — but in the FT tale, there may be a new persona born in the process. Part of this story tradition is a **fool assumes a new name** moment, as when Robin Williams becomes "Mrs. Doubtfire" (thanks to a newspaper headline), and Chance the gardener becomes "Chauncy Gardner" in *Being There*. There is also a beat in many a "fish out of water" story when the fool changes his mission once he arrives on dry land, e.g., in *Legally Blonde*, Elle Woods gives up on her fiancé mid-journey to become a great lawyer. Disguised too long, and overlooked by all, it's time for her to emerge. In many ways that is who the fool *really* is: a butterfly misidentified as a caterpillar far too long.

The FT is one story we cavemen love because we have all been there — sent off to a new school, or another cave, and told to fit in, only to be reminded that what we brought with us really does have value.

We identify!

So maybe we're not so foolish as writers to come up with an FT that has never been done before. Try it. Maybe you will prove that *you* are no fool!

DO YOU HAVE A FOOL-ISH NOTION?

A place to send him? A disguise for him to wear? A lesson for the group to learn from *le cretin*? Be smart:

1. A "fool" whose innocence is his strength and whose gentle manner makes him likely to be ignored — by all but a jealous "Insider" who knows too well.

2. An "establishment," the people or group a fool comes up against, either within his midst, or after being sent to a new place in which he does not fit — at first. Either way, the mismatch promises fireworks!

3. A "transmutation" in which the fool becomes someone or something new, often including a "name change" that's taken on either by accident or as a disguise.

From the variety of movies using the FT template, it shows even we fool-like screenwriters can one day rule!

BEING THERE (1979)

Nowhere is the arc of jester-to-king more clearly seen than in director Hal Ashby's take on Jerzy Kosinski's tale. Peter Sellers is the sweet-natured cipher whose odd accent of origin defies computer analysis — but to me sounds like Stan Laurel on Halcion®. When we meet Chance the gardener, he is living in isolation — as he has all his life — polishing the car of his employer (despite its flat tire), tending his trees, and viewing a *lot* of TV. Like a visiting alien, he copies the gestures of humanity by watching. And then one day this simple soul is cast into the "real" world.

Because this FT tale is set among the power brokers of Washington DC, the fool's naiveté and common-man grace give him a miraculous demonstration of power. Suddenly being honest, forthright, and adept at mimicking others allows him to succeed wildly — and we are rooting for him all the way.

The establishment this "Political Fool" pokes fun at is reminiscent of other Washingtonian films but echoes a more ancient political figure, too. Biblical references abound, with a final image that involves our hero walking on water that is best described as Christ-like. But whether godly or so pure of spirit he is simply at one with the universe, this fool has a particularly triumphant secret of success: Speak the truth, serve others without judgment, and embrace every season.

FT Type: Political Fool

FT Cousins: *Mr. Smith Goes to Washington, Meet John Doe, King Ralph, Protocol, Dave, The Distinguished Gentleman, Moon Over Parador, Bulworth, The Princess Diaries, Head of State*

BEING THERE
Screenplay by Jerzy Kosinksi
Based on the novel by Jerzy Kosinski

Opening Image: Chance (Peter Sellers) wakes to the ubiquitous television. He gets out of bed mimicking what's on TV, then moves a houseplant to give it light.

Set-Up: Peter continues his workday as live-in gardener and handyman. While waiting in the kitchen for the housekeeper, Louise (Ruth Attaway), to bring his lunch, this particular fool appears to be mentally deficient. But something has happened: "The old man" who owns the house has died. Curious, Peter goes upstairs and looks at the body of his benefactor, then sits down on his bed and turns on the TV. It's a "Sealy Posturepedic Morning" according to the commercial; TV clips will comment on the action in the film throughout, offering ironic counterpoint.

Theme Stated: When the housekeeper scolds Peter for not seeming to care that his employer has died, she tells him: "That old man is lying up there, dead as hell, and it just don't make any difference to you." Peter's slow awakening to be able to love another will be our theme and Peter's arc.

Catalyst: At Minute 12, a pair of self-important attorneys arrive. The unwitting Peter takes the two on a tour, then is informed that he has until noon tomorrow to move out.

Debate: What is Peter going to do? Having been told he is allowed to wear any of "the old man's" suits, he grabs a suitcase, packs, and — looking like a high-powered, pinstriped bureaucrat — appears at the door of the only place he's ever lived, ready to leave.

Break into Two: At Minute 20, he walks out of the house and is immediately plunged into the hardcore, urban world of Washington DC. Graffiti mars the walls; there's poverty and anger everywhere; and when one of a gang of street toughs pulls a knife on Peter, the

200 SAVE THE CAT! GOES TO THE MOVIES ~ Blake Snyder

remote control he brought with him to "change the channel" does nothing. We get a hint of how his "disguise" will work when Peter finds a sick tree near the White House and summons a Mall cop. Peter gets immediate action because of his manner and dress.

B Story: At Minute 27, while watching himself on TV in a store window, Peter is struck by a limousine owned by Eve Rand (Shirley MacLaine). This begins the "love story" where the theme of the film will be discussed and Peter will learn to care. Mistaking Peter for an upper-class gentleman, Shirley invites him back to the family mansion. When asked his name, Peter coughs while saying "Chance the Gardener" and Shirley thinks he says "Chauncy Gardener." This accidental name change disguises his identity.

Fun and Games: We have one logic hurdle: Why would Shirley and her very ill husband, Ben Rand (Melvyn Douglas), let Peter stay with them? We get over that by raising the possibility that Peter could sue for being struck by their limo; to avoid this, they need to be nice to him. Peter's charm now begins to work on those around him. His dim-witted honesty is mistaken for sage wisdom. This is why we came to see this Fool Triumphant movie: to watch an idiot confused for a genius. The Fun and Games include near misses of his identity leaking out. Only the Insider, Dr. Allenby (Richard Dysart), is suspicious.

Midpoint: At Hour 1, Peter is introduced to Melvyn's friend, the US President (Jack Warden). This is a high-powered victory peak/ bad-guys-close-in hinge point as pressure begins. The Secret Service opens an investigation of Peter. When the President leaves, and Melvyn retires to bed due to his illness, a clock chimes. This "time clock" tells us Melvyn doesn't have long; he is dying. A and B stories cross as Shirley takes Peter on a tour of the garden, and the love story between them begins in earnest.

Bad Guys Close In: When the President quotes Peter on TV, the Doctor decides to investigate on his own. The Secret Service has found nothing about Peter, but re-doubles its efforts. Now recognized as a member of the inner circle, Peter is invited to be a guest on a late-night talk show. A Secret Service agent goes to the show to collect his fingerprints — but they yield no match. We also see love bloom and Shirley risk her marriage when she is overwhelmed by Peter's "charisma" and kisses him. Meanwhile, the uptight lawyers who discovered him at the house see Peter on TV and, thinking he might know their secrets, fear for their careers. The fool has outwitted them all, all but one — the Doctor, who now discovers who Chauncy Gardener really is.

All Is Lost: While Melvyn goes over his stock portfolio in preparation for his death, the Doctor (good Insider that he is) appears to tell him the truth about their houseguest. The end of Peter's ruse is nigh, but before the Doctor breaks the news, Melvyn confides, "Since he's been around, the thought of dying has been much easier for me." The Doctor says nothing.

Dark Night of the Soul: As Melvyn fades, Shirley and Peter "make love." ("I like to watch, Eve.") Waking to learn death is near, they look out at the bleak landscape of trees in winter.

Break into Three: Melvyn's dying wish is for Peter to stay with Shirley. "She's a delicate flower," he tells Peter. Melvyn dies as Peter watches. Unlike when his benefactor passed away, a tear appears in Peter's eye. He is changing — and one reason for the change is Shirley. Despite the Doctor confronting Peter, he too is charmed. "I love Eve very much," Peter tells him. A and B stories cross again, as we get the promise of a new Eden.

Finale: At Melvyn's funeral, as his own words are read, his pallbearers talk of Melvyn's empire being overseen by Peter.

Final Image: Peter drifts away from the funeral, pauses to right a sapling, then walks out on the water as Melvyn's last words are recited by the President: "Life is a state of mind."

TOOTSIE (1982)

There are moments in director Sydney Pollack's sex-swap comedy when Dustin Hoffman so becomes his female alter ego it's a little spooky. Beyond "exploring his feminine side," he's channeling another being. In a scene early on, Dustin, as out-of-work actor Michael Dorsey, tries on Teri Garr's clothes in a mirror and *becomes* "Dorothy." In a glimmer, he is transformed. Then again, disguise is what the "Undercover Fool" story is about, the FT template where costume, false identity, or sex persona is key. Unlike other "man gets dressed up as a woman" comedies, this one stands out. Why?

Because Dorothy is real. And so is the message.

The oft-told tale about this movie is that it was mired in development hell with writer after writer until Larry Gelbart figured out what it was really "about." Yes, the premise was funny, and it made sense, but it wasn't until *Tootsie* got her themes straight that the story worked. This is about a guy "who becomes a better man for having been a woman" — and with that as the arc, the pieces, the bits, the jokes, fall into place. It's a lesson for storytellers with a great hook, but nothing to say: Make sure your story is *about* something. Only God and the WGA Arbitration Committee know who really put Hoffman in heels... but the results are magic.

FT Type: Undercover Fool

FT Cousins: *Some Like It Hot, Trading Places, Soul Man, Working Girl, Victor/Victoria, Mrs. Doubtfire, Miss Congeniality, Big Momma's House, Connie and Carla, She's the Man*

TOOTSIE
Screenplay by Larry Gelbart *and* Murray Schisgal
Story by Don McGuire *and* Larry Gelbart

Opening Image: Make-up, wig glue, and costumes cover a table as Michael Dorsey (Dustin Hoffman) puts on a fake mustache. In a series of moments, the joy and pain of Dustin's life as an actor are seen: auditions, teaching, arguing with British directors (join the club). Dustin is talented but difficult.

Theme Stated: At one point Dustin is told by a casting director: "We're looking for somebody else." Who is Dustin? And who does he need to become to "get the part" in art and in life?

Set-Up: After a day of tryouts and working as a NYC waiter, Dustin and playwright/roommate Jeff Slater (Bill Murray) go home. Bill surprises Dustin with a birthday party, and we "set up" Dustin's **Six Things That Need Fixing**. He recoils when someone hands him a baby. He scams women at the party to pick them up. He is selfish and insensitive. Stasis = Death.

Catalyst: Fellow actor Sandy Lester (Teri Garr) is up for a part on a soap opera. In a "Save the Cat" beat, Dustin helps her prepare. We see a flash of "Dorothy," the character he will become, when he does a line reading. Dustin goes with Teri to the audition. There, he learns an actor on the show got the lead in a play he wanted. He storms out to confront his agent.

Debate: Why can't Dustin get a part? Dustin's agent, George Fields (Sydney Pollack), has had it with his client. He names a list of directors who won't work with him, despite Dustin's proclaiming his talent: "I did an evening of vegetables off Broadway. I did an endive salad that knocked the critics on their ass!" Sydney tells him to get therapy. Then adds: "*No one* will hire you."

Break into Two: At Minute 20, Dustin walks down the streets of New York dressed as a woman. He gets an audition for the part Teri was up for. Fueled by the desire to raise $8,000 to mount Bill's play, and cast himself and Teri in it, Dustin is also inspired by his name change, achieved by inverting his own to create "Dorothy Michaels." At first, director Ron Carlisle (the amazing Dabney Coleman) tells Dorothy she's too passive. But she turns him when she protests: "Shame on you, you macho shithead!" Nailing the audition, Dorothy is hired.

B Story: Just after the fool has entered the "upside-down world" of Act Two, Dorothy meets Julie Nichols (Jessica Lange). Their love story will teach Dustin how to behave with women, and supply the missing skills he needs to succeed.

Fun and Games: Now that Dustin has the part, the ruse must continue. He's caught trying on Teri's clothes and to avoid having to explain himself, he sleeps with her. While Dustin thinks his cross-dressing adventure is all about acting, he has entered "Girl World," forcing him to avoid ogling a nearly naked actress, April Page (Geena Davis) — and dodge "The Tongue," lecherous John Van Horn (George Gaynes), who finds Dorothy to his liking.

Midpoint: While rehearsing with Jessica at her home, Dorothy learns the actress is dating Dabney and has a baby. Meanwhile, Dorothy's TV character becomes a star, a symbol of liberated women. It's a "false victory" because Dustin is the successful actor he wanted to be, but can't cash in. He is even invited — as Michael — to an A-list party by his agent, where he sees Jessica. A and B stories cross as he uses a pickup line Jessica had told Dorothy would charm her, but Dustin gets a drink thrown in his face.

Bad Guys Close In: Dustin is drawn deeper into trouble. He is lying to Teri, fending off George, and trying to hang in long enough to get the money he needs. He goes so far as to accept an invitation from Jessica to spend a weekend at her father's farm. Lying in bed with

Jessica, as Dorothy, he is privy to her secret thoughts. And holding her baby, he begins to realize what's missing in his life. It's exactly what he needs as a man. But when Jessica's father (Charles Durning) develops a crush on Dorothy, everything starts to unravel.

All Is Lost: At Dorothy's urging, Jessica dumps Dabney. Then, as Dorothy, Dustin gets carried away and tries to kiss Jessica. She is horrified and tells Dorothy to let her father down easily. But when Dorothy goes dancing with Charles, he asks "her" to marry him. Later when Dustin gets home, still in drag, he finds "The Tongue" waiting. "I'm an untalented old has-been," George admits, and we realize Dustin is looking in a mirror: George is the lecherous "nobody" Dustin was on his way to becoming when this adventure began. Dustin gets rid of George as Teri enters. Knowing he can't tell Teri the whole truth, Dustin admits he loves another.

Dark Night of the Soul: Dustin visits Sydney: "You've got to get me off the show," he begs. Sydney can't help. Dustin is stuck.

Break into Three: News comes that the soap, usually taped, has to be done live. Dustin delivers a gift to Jessica to apologize for making a pass at her; she is confused. As A and B stories cross, Jessica reminds him that Dorothy taught her how to stand up for herself. Now Dustin realizes he has to take his own advice.

Finale: In one of filmdom's great finales, *Southwest General* goes LIVE! and Dustin takes center stage. Suddenly off script, Dustin spins a yarn about his character's secret past — ending with a flourish as he rips off his wig to reveal he's a man. The cast and crew gasp as the show cuts to commercial. Thinking he will be applauded for his stunt, Dustin is surprised when Jessica slugs him.

Final Image: After apologizing to Charles, Dustin seeks out Jessica. He tells her what he learned: "I was a better man with you as a woman than I ever was with a woman as a man," he says. Synthesis Man walks into the sunset with Jessica. The fool has triumphed.

FORREST GUMP (1994)

Of the many mainstream FT movies over the years, the one starring Tom Hanks and directed by Robert Zemeckis is perhaps the most spiritual. Mixed in with a mass entertainment film is a debate — with characters representing differing views — that could be part of any theology class. Amid the great action and greater laughs are questions we all need answered: What is the meaning of life? And how should I live mine?

Meet Forrest Gump, a simpleton with an IQ of 75. Like other savants in this category, he can do many things, such as run real fast and play wicked ping-pong. And like other heroes in the "Society Fool" class of FT movies — where the "fool" exposes the prejudices of the "smart ones" in life — he doesn't mean to show up others, but is clearly the wisest, and especially adept at outsmarting the Insiders that oppose him.

The "establishment" here is 30 years worth of American culture and our overblown reverence for it. The '50s, the Hippie era, the Disco life, and even the me-worshiping joys of jogging and wealth-building, are shown to be of lesser value than quietly observing a sunset on the Gulf of Mexico, and, most important, expressing love for others. Forrest shows us that the fool has a bead on the truth. While we go dashing all over the world searching, he can find a whole universe sitting on a bench, waiting for a bus.

FT Type: Society Fool

FT Cousins: *Charly, Zelig, Shine, Awakenings, Sling Blade, Radio, My Left Foot, I Am Sam, The Other Sister, Mask*

FORREST GUMP
Screenplay by Eric Roth
Based on the novel by Winston Groom

Opening Image: A feather floats in the wind. It lights at the feet of a man with a bad haircut, parked on a bus bench.

Theme Stated: A woman sits next to the man, who introduces himself as Forrest Gump (Tom Hanks). Offering her candy, Tom says: "Life is like a box of chocolates, you never know what you're gonna get." Fate vs. self-will, that's our theme.

Set-Up: In flashback we set up Tom's background. He is physically handicapped and mentally deficient, gifted with a loving single mother (Sally Field). Isolated as he is in 1950s Greenbow, Alabama, this young man has an effect on history even early on: Thanks to his leg braces, he teaches Elvis a unique way to dance.

B Story: At Minute 13, picked up by the bus for school, young Forrest meets Jenny (later played by Robin Wright). The theme of the movie will play out through their relationship.

Catalyst: When our hero is picked on by bullies, young Jenny urges him, "Run, Forrest!" and he learns he can run really fast.

Debate: Is it true, as his Momma says, that his feet can take him anywhere? That's the A story, and it seems to be so: The adult Forrest (Tom) plays college football at Alabama under Bear Bryant. *Zelig*-like, Tom folds himself into history again as he stands next to Governor George Wallace at a speech opposing integration, and later when he visits JFK in the White House.

Break into Two: Tom graduates, joins the Army, and enters the "upside-down world." Floating like a feather, suiting up and showing up, and trusting fate, is Tom's MO. On leave before he's sent to Vietnam, he sees Robin performing as a singer at a nude club. She has much to learn. Trying to "will" her life to be better, she forever comes up short. At Minute 31, Tom meets Bubba (Mykelti Williamson), a great example of revealing character in dialogue: Every time he speaks, it's about shrimp. Tom also meets Lt. Dan (Gary Sinise). Both men will help guide Tom, and he them.

Fun and Games: For anyone who lived through the era, Vietnam was the touchstone and the source of the powerful moments of this movie. Both at home (where Robin becomes a folk-singing hippie) and in the jungles of Asia, the war defines the era. Gary, the Insider, thinks like Robin does and is certain he's in charge of his destiny. But when an ambush wipes out his platoon, Gary is rescued by Tom, who carries him to safety. Mykelti dies, Gary loses his legs, and Tom wins the Medal of Honor. Yet all he did was what Robin said: Run. Now Tom finds a new skill: ping-pong. Why? Because he does what's put in front of him without judgment.

Midpoint: After Tom moons President Johnson at a White House ceremony, he is part of a DC war protest. At 1 hour 4 Minutes, A and B stories cross and Tom experiences a "false victory" as he is reunited with Robin at the Washington Monument, in front of a cheering crowd. "It was the happiest moment of my life," narrates Tom. From here on out, things will get tougher for Robin as she descends into the dark side of drug use, bad relationships, and loss of spirit. Likewise, after being on *The Dick Cavett Show* with John Lennon — and giving him the lyrics to "Imagine" — Tom is reunited with Gary, now a wheelchair-bound miscreant. Gary's bitterness is due to his disappointment with his life. "Have you found Jesus yet, Gump?" he snarls.

Bad Guys Close In: Tom fulfills his bargain with Mykelti and becomes a "shrimp'n' boat captain." We also see Robin get further lost in the glitterlands of America, now doing hard drugs. Gary joins Tom and, while fighting a storm at sea, finally "makes his peace with God," and thanks Tom for saving his life. The storm also makes Tom and Gary rich. When Tom gets a message that his Mom is sick, he races home. On her deathbed, she tells Tom he has to find his destiny himself. With her death, Tom is alone.

All Is Lost: At 1 Hour 45 Minutes, Robin comes home and sleeps "like she hadn't slept in years." A "whiff of death" is nigh. She throws rocks at her old house and "breaks" like Gary. After confessing to Robin: "I'm not a smart man but I know what love is" (trust me, this line *never* works), Tom proposes to her. She says no, but sleeps with Tom and leaves the next day.

Dark Night of the Soul: With the shoes Robin gave him, Tom starts jogging, sadly criss-crossing the US. Against the backdrop of the Carter years and Jackson Browne's "Running on Empty," he is bereft, reflecting the national mood post-Vietnam as well.

Break into Three: At 2 hours, A and B stories cross again as Tom gets a letter from Robin and seeks her out. Now sitting on the bus bench, he asks directions to her house. This is why he's been telling his tale. He learns Robin's house is five blocks away.

Finale: Tom and Robin reunite. Having given up her selfish pursuits, Robin apologizes and Tom learns he has a son (that's Haley Joel Osment). Robin and Tom marry and Robin dies, but not before Gary shows up a changed man. He is walking and has a fiancée, all thanks to the transforming power of being pals with Forrest Gump.

Final Image: At Robin's grave, Tom synthesizes the film's theme: Life is both fate *and* self-will. "I don't know if we have a destiny or if we're floating around on a breeze. It's both happening at the same time," he says. The moments that count most are those touched by an awareness of a higher power. He puts Forrest Jr. on the bus, and we notice the feather at Tom's feet. Off it goes blowing in the wind, into the sky... and right to you.

LEGALLY BLONDE (2001)

One of my favorite FT movies is the one that made Reese Wither-spoon a star. As the iconic Elle Woods, Reese plays a fabulous "fish out of water," a sorority girl who, dumped by her college beau, pursues him to Harvard Law and discovers she's got something special beneath her golden roots: a brain.

Unlike the "Undercover Fool" who takes on a disguise as part of the trip, the "Society Fool" overlooked by the group due to a supposed deficiency, or the "Political Fool" whose "jester in the king's court" role is his cover for superior wisdom, the "Fool Out of Water" brings a fresh set of principles from her old pond up onto dry land — where suddenly, almost magically, they have greater meaning. Elle will prove that the code of her sorority, and its principles of honor, truth, and fidelity — plus her Girl Power work ethic — can win. With the help of twin mentors, a manicurist who teaches her as much as she teaches the mentor, and a helpful lawyer (Luke Wilson), Elle is on her way to victory.

Helmed by Robert Luketic, the movie boasts a "killer title" and one of the most powerful color themes ever. Pink is the tint of triumph for this "Fool Out of Water," worn by Elle Woods and Bruiser Woods, the Chihuahua sidekick Elle takes with her every-where — even into court.

FT Type: Fool Out of Water

FT Cousins: *Stripes, Beverly Hills Cop, Private Benjamin, Crocodile Dundee, My Blue Heaven, Mr. Mom, Coming to America, Daddy Day Care, Elf, The Pacifier*

LEGALLY BLONDE

Screenplay by Karen McCullah Lutz & Kirsten Smith
Based on the book by Amanda Brown

Opening Image: It's a "Perfect Day" on Sorority Row at fabled CULA, an LA-based college, as the girls of Delta Nu sign a card for President and Homecoming Queen Elle Woods (Reese Witherspoon), wishing her luck. Her beau's proposing tonight!

Theme Stated: Shopping for an outfit, Reese and bosom buddies Margot (Jessica Cauffiel) and Serena (Alanna Ubach) are almost tricked by the clerk. "There's nothing I like better than a dumb blonde with daddy's credit card," the counter maven says. But Reese proves she knows more about the merchandise than the sales lady and outsmarts her. Being discriminated against for being blonde is the film's thematic hurdle, established here.

Set-Up: The Harvard Law School-bound Warner (Matthew Davis) turns up for their date. At Minute 7, he surprises Reese by dumping her. "If I'm gonna be a senator by the time I'm thirty," he says. "I need to marry a Jackie not a Marilyn." This variation on the "Save the Cat" scene is called **Kill the Cat**, and works exactly the same way: Until this moment, we think Reese is a tad plastic, but after seeing her smooshed, we feel for her. From this point forward, we'll root for her to get whatever she wants.

Catalyst: Moping at Minute 12, Reese goes to a beauty salon with her pals and gets new info: Her almost-fiancé's brother is engaged to a girl in law school. *That's* what Reese needs to win her beau back! By being more serious, maybe he'll marry her!

Debate: Can she get into law school? As Reese's counselor tells her: "Harvard won't be impressed that you aced History of Polka Dots." Fashion-major Reese begins to study for the LSATs, eschews

Greek Week, does a sexy video "directed by a Coppola," and gets approved by an all-male Harvard Law admissions staff.

Break into Two: At Minute 20, a pink-clad Reese arrives on dry land, a fish totally out of water, along with chihuahua Bruiser Woods and a Bekins truck in tow. Her goal is still getting a ring on her finger, so she's shocked to discover her ex is engaged to Vivian Kensington (Selma Blair). She's even more shocked when the unwelcoming Selma gets her kicked out of a class taught by the tough, *Paper Chase*-y Professor Stromwell (Holland Taylor).

B Story: Twin B stories as Reese meets Emmett Richmond (Luke Wilson), a seasoned law grad. But her guiding spirit is Paulette Bonafonte (Jennifer Coolidge), the "funhouse-mirror" twist on her sorority sisters, who has also been dumped by her ex. Both Luke and Jennifer will give Reese the push into Act Three she needs.

Fun and Games: Reese brings the pink to law school — and is rejected by the brown and gray-toned students who don't get her. Her attempts to blend in by dressing conservatively, bringing muffins to a study group, and using her CULA sorority-row ways in Harvard Yard are the crux of the "promise of the premise."

Midpoint: At Minute 42, we reach a turning point when Reese is tricked by Selma, who invites her to what she thinks is a costume party. Reese shows up dressed in a Playboy bunny outfit, and after running into her ex, is told she should give up her chase of him and law school. That exchange marks the end of one part of Reese's journey and the beginning of another, as Reese decides to redouble her efforts as a student. A determined Reese, still ala Bunny, is next seen in line at the student bookstore by Luke (as A and B stories cross). In her rebound rise, Reese and Jennifer reclaim Jennifer's dog from her ex-lover (a second A and B cross). There's even a nice FT moment as Reese dons glasses (her fool's disguise), so she can pose as Jennifer's attorney. As Selma (the Insider) watches in fear, Reese impresses Professor Callahan (Victor Garber) and presents him with a pink and scented resume. Finally Reese is chosen along with her ex and Selma to work on a big case with Victor, who's a practicing attorney.

Bad Guys Close In: The "stakes are raised" as Reese enters the world of the law firm. One of her Delta Nu sisters, Brooke Taylor (Ali Larter), is charged with murder; Luke is revealed as Victor's right hand man; and the pressure mounts for Reese to perform. While Reese coaches Jennifer in the art of wooing the salon's UPS Man and teaches her the "bend and snap" routine (that I *still* wish someone would explain to me), the case continues — and it looks bad for Brooke. Reese gets Brooke to reveal her alibi in private, but their sorority sister's code prevents Reese from telling anyone else. This honorable act shows Selma that Reese has character. Reese and Luke go to a spa to see the murdered man's ex-wife (Raquel Welch). On the way, Reese repeats the theme: "I'm discriminated against as a blonde."

All Is Lost: After Reese shines in court, the lecherous Victor calls her into his office and makes a pass. Devastated, Reese leaves as Selma accuses her of sleeping with the professor to get ahead. Reese realizes she will never be appreciated for her brain.

Dark Night of the Soul: Reese tells Luke goodbye, and packs.

Break into Three: Two A and B stories cross in fast order. First, Reese stops by Jennifer's beauty shop and is encouraged by Professor Stromwell, who tells her not to quit. Second, Luke and Selma (who's given up her Insider's distrust and become an ally) now confront Brooke, tell her the smarmy Victor hit on Reese, and convince her to fire him - and hire the Blonde!

Finale: All arrive for the final courtroom scene, including Reese's Delta Nu girlfriends and Jennifer with her UPS beau.

Reese enters wearing pink, a perfect example of Synthesis. And just as in the early scene when she bests the clerk by knowing the merchandise, Reese tricks the victim's daughter into confessing by understanding the rules of perms — and wins the case! Then true victory comes as her ex proposes and she turns *him* down.

Final Image: Big change from the opening image with caps in the air as Reese graduates Harvard Law — first in her class!

THE 40-YEAR-OLD VIRGIN (2005)

The risk of this movie is inherent in its title, for as clever as it is (it's also the pitch!), there is a sense going in that it might get, shall we say... sophomoric. And, yes, while this Judd Apatow-directed "farce of nature" does not disappoint in that regard, what we actually get is a sweet, sensitive, and in an odd way, inspiring comedy — and the very best of the "Sex Fool" sub-genre, those stories where the hero is confused for a lothario, but is quite the opposite.

Much of the successful finessing of this dilemma is due to the screenplay stylings of Apatow. In both *The Cable Guy* and *Knocked Up*, his approach is very Farrelly Brothers: Start with a broad concept and get more meaningful as the film progresses. It helps to have Steve Carrell (whose shy persona makes this silly premise believable) as co-writer and star.

Steve plays a lowly shipping clerk at a Circuit City-type store. His adventure begins when he admits that, though he is 40, he has never "done the deed." Into the breach rush his know-nothing co-workers, each considering himself an expert on sex. But it's not until Steve shows them how to do it that they all start to grow. And the fool has never been more triumphant than in the movie's final musical number, in which, to the anthem from *Hair*, the 40 Year-Old *Non*-Virgin celebrates the glory of patience.

FT Type: Sex Fool

FT Cousins: *I Love You, Alice B. Toklas; The Party; Play It Again, Sam; Bob & Carol & Ted & Alice; The World's Greatest Lover; Loverboy; Roxanne; Down with Love, Bridget Jones's Diary; The Guru*

THE 40-YEAR-OLD VIRGIN
Written by Judd Apatow & Steve Carell

Opening Image: Meet Andy Stitzer (Steve Carell) asleep in bed, looking kinda sad, and when he wakes, we know why: His morning erection reveals he's a little "backed up." Like a real-life Pee-wee Herman, boyish Steve makes breakfast and gets ready for his day, donning a helmet and riding his bike to work, but not before waving at the nice couple upstairs.

Theme Stated: The neighbor waves back and says: "That guy has got to get laid." It's the theme... but is it true? Do you have to have sex to have a fulfilling life?

Set-Up: Steve works in the stock room of Smart Tech. Sharing about his weekend, a co-worker, the bearish Cal (*Knocked Up*'s Seth Rogen), tells a graphic sex story while Steve can only talk about making an egg salad sandwich. We meet the others: David (Paul Rudd), who misses his angry ex-girlfriend, and shaved-headed Jay (Romany Malco), the player. The guys invite Steve to their poker game, assuming him a rube. Steve surprises them by winning. This won't be the last time Steve trumps his pals; it's a prelude to other lessons the "fool" will be dispensing. After the game has ended, the guys begin to tell sex stories. Steve is shy about his experiences...

Catalyst: ... and at Minute 13, it slips out: Steve's a virgin!

Debate: What should Steve do now? Embarrassed — and a little scared that the guys know — Steve considers quitting his job. In reviewing his life, we learn why Steve never had sex — although he came close. Like a 40-year-old boy, Steve collects comic-book action figures, paints soldiers, and plays video games. That life is now in jeopardy as Paul and the others begin to convince him to try again.

Steve can't escape a society consumed by sex — even ads for a sexy perfume called "Eruption" seem to be following him everywhere.

Break into Two: At Minute 22, Steve agrees to go out with the guys and enter the world of "men" — or at least the world these fellow boys he works with consider manly. The range of advice on how to "become a man" is hilarious. First idea: Find a drunk girl. At a club, Steve does just that and is sent home with her by the other guys, but his wild ride with *this* drunk girl mostly involves getting thrown up on. Steve has tried, but he is still a virgin.

B Story: At Minute 33, Steve meets Trish (Catherine Keener) — not only more age-appropriate, but actually attracted to him. Catherine works nearby, yet even when she gives him her number, Steve's too shy to call. Catherine will be his agent of change.

Fun and Games: Almost from the get-go, we realize Catherine is "the one" for Steve, but the "promise of the premise" includes showing just how far this fish is out of water. His buddies initiate Steve into their world, and lock him in the store with a porn tape playing in the front window. The guys also take him to get his chest hair waxed in a painful and hilarious scene. ("We gonna need more wax!") At Minute 46, telling Steve to "Be David Caruso in *Jade*," Seth takes him to meet Beth, a wild blonde. Beth confuses Steve's "virgin in the headlights" stare as "cool." The fool has a fan who's sure he's a lothario. Later, Paul drops by Steve's house with a box of porn, and pulls Steve into speed-dating, where we meet Paul's angry ex.

Midpoint: After the guys send Steve to a hooker (who turns out to be a man), the "Fun and Games" are over. Fed up with the guys' idiotic plans, Steve "raises the stakes" and A and B stories cross as he asks Catherine out. The fool is now teaching the "men."

Bad Guys Close In: Steve's date goes well but the "bad guy" closing in is Steve's inability to tell Catherine he's a virgin — and the close calls when he is almost forced to confess. After failing at using condoms, and interrupted by Catherine's Insider daughter Marla (Kat Dennings), who hates Steve on sight, Steve and Catherine agree to have 20 dates until they are intimate. Another "bad guy" is Steve's randy boss, Paula (Jane Lynch), who suggests he have sex with her. Despite all this pressure, Steve is rising to prominence at work, going from clerk to salesman to floor manager. He learns to drive a car from Catherine, and starts to sell his action figures on eBay. He also gets close to Kat in a great scene at Planned Parenthood where, as Kat's surrogate father, he admits he's a virgin. In a roomful of adults trying to be "hip" with their kids, Steve's candor is heroic.

All Is Lost: As Steve matures, he begins to counsel the other guys, including Romany — who now turns to the virgin for advice! But when the 20 dates are up — and Catherine suggests they finally be intimate — Steve freaks, blaming her for forcing him to sell his figurines; he also proudly defends the fact he rides a bike, even though it's odd for a man his age.

Dark Night of the Soul: Confused, Steve gets drunk at a party for Romany, whose girlfriend is pregnant. Romany is finally settling down. Steve meets Beth, who takes him back to her house. Beth is a real "freak," but even drunk, Steve can't have sex with her. In a sweet and funny scene, the guys rescue Steve — and Seth stays behind. Back home, Steve finds Catherine waiting, but still can't tell her the truth. A and B stories cross as she storms out.

Break into Three: A fresh "chase to the airport" as Steve races to catch Catherine via bicycle, leading to an accident when he busts through a billboard for "Eruption." Catherine comforts Steve, who now tells her the truth: "I'm a virgin."

Finale: The wedding of Steve and Catherine and the rush to the hotel. "Three and a half minutes later..." the smile on Steve's face as he lies in bed after their session of bliss is hilarious.

Final Image: Singing "Aquarius," the cast celebrates sex.

 The age-old dilemma of "Institutionalized" stories — them or me? — is seen in the brilliant Office Space, *as desk huggers at Initech (like Stephen Root as Milton) wonder if hanging on to their jobs is worth selling their souls.*

9 INSTITUTIONALIZED

You are a caveman. And with your fellow Neander-thals, you are about to join in a great tradition: the Woolly Mammoth hunt! This will involve weeks of tribal ceremonies — including a pre-hunt ritual in which a "virgin" (the girl who won't sleep with the chief) is sacrificed to the gods, and a stalking technique used for generations that guarantees a third of the hunters will die. To not go along with your fellow meat-eaters is akin to betrayal, yet as you reach for your spear there's an uneasy feeling in your stomach and a nagging thought: *What about a nice salad?*

If any of this strikes a chord at the core of your DNA, you likely identify with stories marked "Institutionalized." That same feeling in the center of our gut is one we now experience sitting in our cubicles at work, lining up in a row at Army boot camp, or joining a bunch of friends who have a new weight-loss product they're selling. The difference between a "family" we can count on and a "cult" is not always clear, and the pros and cons of being one of the gang our eternal debate. Though we know the perils of going it alone, that queasy intestinal twinge is often a saving grace; it's what separates us from the others — and might even save them, too! While this story is a product of the post-Enlightenment age in which being an "individual" is an accepted right, the feeling is one we've had for all of time.

One reason I like this story type is that, as a creative person, it is my daily dilemma. We writers are the ones who tell the king he has no clothes, and often the only ones with either so much insight — or nothing to lose — we can dub the group "wrong." The name I've given this genre has added meaning as it touches on a key question we ask when opposing an establishment:

Who's crazier — them or me?

Wherever a group gathers, a business booms, or a family re-unites, you'll find this conundrum. To join or not join, to stay with the rest or do it our way, this is the Institutionalized story. And it must be important, because there are so many examples!

We see the "Military Institution" in *Gallipoli*, *Full Metal Jacket*, *M*A*S*H*, and the best, Jean Renoir's *The Grand Illusion*. We also have the "Business Institution" tale of which *9 to 5*, *Office Space*, and Paddy Chayefsky's *Network* are a part. There is the "Family Institution," typified by movies like *Goodfellas* and *The Royal Tenenbaums*, and the "Issue Institution," where an ensemble cast deals with a specific theme (*Crash*, *Babel*, *Short Cuts*). And because one's indoctrination into the "machine" is such a common tale, the "Mentor Institution" story includes *Wall Street*, *The Devil Wears Prada*, and a John Lithgow TV-movie, *Traveling Man*, a pip about a mentor-mentee battle between two salesmen.

The rules of this story are constants, so if you rigidly adhere to my doctrine you'll see how all sagas of the "I" kind have: (1) a "group," (2) a "choice," and (3) a "sacrifice."

There's also a moral to most of these: Look before you join!

The number one indicator of an Institutionalized tale is: It's about the many. Anytime words like "ensemble," "group," or "multiple stories" show up on your yellow pad, you know what genre you're in. Often these concern work situations or closed societies with their own rules, ethics, and bonds of loyalty. I love learning about unique jobs, and movies like *Pushing Tin* (about air traffic controllers), *Tin Men* (about aluminum-siding salesmen), and *Boogie Nights* (about '70s-era adult film stars) give us an up-close look at the inner workings of these occupations.

There are a variety of characters that appear in tales of the "I" kind. One is the **Brando**, who stands opposed to the system by his very nature and reveals its flaws. Named for Marlon Brando in *The Wild One* (who, when asked what he is rebelling against, says: "Whaddya got?"), anti-heroes like Donald Sutherland in *M*A*S*H*, Jack Nicholson in *One Flew Over the Cuckoo's Nest*, and Kevin Spacey in *American Beauty* exist solely to reveal the system's flaws. In many an

"I" tale there is also a **Naïf** who may be the hero — eventually! He is the character the audience identifies with most — he's us — for we know nothing of the rules, like Jane Fonda in *9 to 5*, Tom Hulce in *Animal House*, and even Al Pacino in *The Godfather*, who is on the fringes and still a "virgin" until he is drawn into the group.

The "choice" for either or both these characters is the ongoing dramatic conflict in these tales. "Will he stick with the group or quit?" we ask of "Naif" Ray Liotta in *Goodfellas*, as the pros and cons of being "one of the guys" are shown to us. Through Ray, we must ask if we would be able to join in the tribal ceremonies that accompany his rise in the family — from "busting his cherry," when Ray is first arrested as a teen, to the dangers of going against the boss by running drugs, to the ultimate act of either betrayal or sanity (depending on your point of view) when Ray decides to turn state's evidence and rat out the men who were his brothers. Many times as the story progresses, the choice becomes harder, more difficult to understand, and the rules of the group — especially in regard to loyalty — more difficult to adhere to. The ongoing "choice" tells us what we know about groups: Either the rules are crazy, or we are for questioning them!

Another "I" character is the **Company Man**, an automaton entrenched in the system. Oddly, many of these characters suffer from sexual dysfunction... and insanity: Robert Duvall in *M*A*S*H*, Denzel Washington in *Training Day*, Humphrey Bogart in *The Caine Mutiny*, Jack Nicholson in *A Few Good Men*, and Louise Fletcher in *One Flew Over the Cuckoo's Nest*, display conformity that is sterility.

Finally, a decision must be made in an Institutionalized story, and it always comes down to: them or me? This is the "sacrifice," the act of surrendering our individuality to the group or destroying the institution when it proves to be less than advertised. You can see the result pretty clearly in the ending of *Goodfellas* — and even in comedies like *Animal House* with its final "Eat Me!" conflagration at the parade, or the inferno that ends *Office Space* literally burning down corporate headquarters! Often it is the sacrifice of the individual that is the finale of many such tales, and the cautionary end point to what we know about joining. Look at the endings of *Godfather 2*, *American Beauty*, and *One Flew Over the Cuckoo's Nest*, as these heroes' almost identical blank expressions tell us that their "sacrifice" has been... suicide.

The real lesson, and what these tales teach, is the peril of not paying attention to that voice inside. Like all good stories, this genre offers a deeper message: Our orders come from a higher source! Not tradition, not our parents, not the caveman in charge of the group. We who listen to our inner spirit are propelled by a power that can overcome all.

Tales of the many, of group dynamics, and stories about trusting the system — or overthrowing it — are some of the most primal ones we tell. Whenever a writer pitches me a story about a group, I always ask: "What would *you* do in this circumstance?" How long can you, the individual, believe in or trust others to have your best interests at heart?

If we look at our own experience, we can see how often in life the individual gets thrown overboard. These stories are our way of fighting back, and giving those who believe in the rights of the one as much as the rights of the many, a template for action. If you have a story that defies the rules, write it! Even if the rules you defy are found in this very book! "All screenwriters are bullheads," said a famous author we all know and love.

And aren't we glad they are!

DOES YOUR STORY NEED TO BE INSTITUTIONALIZED?

Are you convinced of your loyalty to the tenets of this cautionary tale? Then join us by knowing all its dictates:

1. Every story in this category is about a "group" — a family, an organization, or a business that is unique.

2. The story is a "choice," the ongoing conflict pitting a "Brando" or a "Naif" vs. the system's "Company Man."

3. Finally, a "sacrifice" must be made, leading to one of three endings: Join, burn it down... or commit "suicide."

If you want to write anything about the many, take a look at these tales of the "I" kind.

M*A*S*H (1970)

The good news is: You win the Oscar® for Best Screenplay. The bad news is: The movie your script is based on so veers from what you wrote, it is unrecognizable. Sound impossible? Nope. It's what happened to Ring Lardner, Jr. for *M*A*S*H*. And yet in the hands of director Robert Altman, who hijacked both Lardner's script and the production of the film, a work of genius — not to mention a huge TV franchise — was born.

For our purposes, it is a great example of the "Military Institution" tale about "regular Army clowns" trying to quash the individual. At first, finding its structure seems a fool's errand. Altman's improv style and the episodic nature of his films so go against the rules of structure, they seem not to have any!

But look again.

Altman uses the same storytelling tools we all do, and the familiar landmarks of Midpoint, Break into Two and Three, and Finale are here — just deconstructed as a jazz musician might a popular tune. Held together by the camp's PA announcements (a device Altman found in editing), the film is the story of a MASH-unit surgeon, Donald Sutherland, who challenges a series of "Company Men" such as Robert Duvall and Sally Kellerman. The former is sent to the loony bin, the latter brought over to "our" side in perfect Act Three Synthesis.

I Type: Military Institution

I Cousins: *Breaker Morant, Gallipoli, Paths of Glory, Platoon, A Few Good Men, Taps, The Caine Mutiny, Top Gun, Full Metal Jacket, We Were Soldiers*

M*A*S*H

Screenplay by Ring Lardner, Jr.
From the novel by Richard Hooker

Opening Image: The movie's theme song, "Suicide Is Painless," is heard as a military helicopter, with a wounded soldier strapped to a stretcher alongside, floats through the air. It lands at a war zone hospital that will be our setting. "Suicide" is the decision of those who surrender by choosing "the group."

Theme Stated: Meet Hawkeye Pierce (Donald Southerland). Waiting for a ride to a MASH (Mobile Army Surgical Hospital) unit, he's told by an official: "Just because you're a captain, don't think you run the joint." Who runs the joint? That's our theme. Hawkeye's iconoclast whistle tells us he's like his namesake, hero of James Fenimore Cooper's *The Deerslayer*.

Set-Up: "And then there was Korea…" To a war movie march, a **crawl** sets up the fact it's the Korean War, a tipping point in America's response to war generally. In charge of the MASH unit, Colonel Blake (Roger Bowen) and Radar (Gary Burghoff) wait for the new doctor, not realizing the "enlisted man" in their Mess Tent is Donald, who has removed his Captain's bars. At Minute 7, he meets Duke (Tom Skerritt), a fellow surgeon, and makes a beeline for the nurses. Everything is Army: silverware, regulations, even sex play is all according to rules. But not for long.

Catalyst: At Minute 12, Donald and Tom are ushered to their quarters and meet Major Frank Burns (Robert Duvall), teaching a Korean boy to read the Bible. In any other movie, this character would be applauded, but being a typical Brando, Donald suspects Robert from the jump. At Minute 17, Donald requests a roommate change and a new doctor: "We need a chest cutter." He is promised Robert will be out of "his" tent in 24 hours.

Debate: Will Donald get his way? And will the MASH get a better surgeon? It's the Army after all, and the conditions are hellish.

Break into Two: At Minute 20, Donald is pulled from a married nurse to meet his new roommate and fellow surgeon. "Trapper" John McIntyre (Elliott Gould) doesn't speak — until Donald offers him a martini and Elliott whips out his own jar of olives! A match made in heaven. At Minute 25, Donald finally recognizes Elliott. They have a shared past as both played football in college (a foreshadowing of the film's finale) and now have a shared future as well — and plans to get rid of incompetent doctors like Robert.

B Story: At Minute 27, Major Margaret O'Houlihan (Sally Kellerman) arrives. She is "regular Army" and immediately hates Donald and he her. It is their battle through which we will discuss the theme. Sally will have the biggest arc and be the way we chart how Donald is doing in his quest to de-Army the Army.

Fun and Games (Part I): In a movie with mostly trailer moments, this first batch begins as camp cut-ups Donald and Elliott grab martinis and nurses in an effort to stave off the inhumanity of their blood-spurting surgical sessions. When Robert makes a kid (that's Bud Cort!) think he killed a patient, Elliott decks the talentless doctor. At Minute 37, Elliott is elected Chief Surgeon, and at Minute 38, Sally and Robert write a complaint letter. Now the two camps are formed... and one draws closer as Robert and Sally negotiate sex. During this session, "Hot Lips" is born when a PA microphone catches the couple in the throes of passion. Next day, by egging on the Bible-thumping doctor, Donald causes Robert to go nuts and get hauled away in a strait jacket.

Midpoint: With Robert banished, a new problem arises... or doesn't. The camp dentist has sex trouble when he fails to perform. Thinking he's homosexual, a badge of shame in 1952, "Painless" (John Schuck) decides to kill himself. Assisted by the gang, complete with a match shot of "The Last Supper," he is cured in a "false victory" over death when he sleeps with a departing nurse at 1 Hour 5 Minutes.

Bad Guys Close In: Now in charge, the boys expand their good deeds and face more criticism. They operate on a prisoner of war and take blood from a sleeping Colonel Blake. And in a B Story "false victory," they strip Hot Lips of her last bit of dignity when they expose Sally in the showers. "This is an insane asylum!" she yells. Later in Fun and Games (Part 2), Donald and Elliott go to Tokyo and take their golf clubs, intent on getting in some R&R between operations. Joking they are the "Pros from Dover," they best another Army "clown" — an officer who doesn't think their act is funny — to save a US soldier's illegitimate baby.

All Is Lost: Returning from Tokyo, the boys find Tom and Sally together — she's coming around. But in a false "All Is Lost," news comes that a higher-up is visiting in response to Sally's complaint letter. In another movie, this would signal the potential "death" of Donald's anti-military run.

Break into Three: Instead, at 1 Hour 33 Minutes, the General challenges the MASH to a football game. As Sally organizes the nurses into cheerleaders, A and B stories cross, and Donald concocts a plan: They will get a "ringer."

Finale: There is no reason why this football game finale should or can work, but it does. Somehow, the MASH unit's anti-establishment team vs. the General's Patton-style team finalizes the conflict brewing all along. The MASH squad, with a "Booster Rocket" (Fred Williamson as "Spearchucker" Jones), represents the underdogs — and when they win, as Sally cheers, we win. All celebrate back in camp.

Final Image: Donald is called home, and as he breaks the news to Tom in surgery, we realize he hasn't changed a thing. His "sacrifice" is he did nothing. "They" won. The madness of war goes on. He is just no longer part of it.

DO THE RIGHT THING (1989)

Torn between wanting to belong and the need to "do the right thing," what is a more apt description of any dilemma of the "I" type than that found at the heart of writer/director Spike Lee's critic's fave. Featuring an all-star cast including such "unknowns" (at the time) as Martin Lawrence and Rosie Perez, and standout performances from veteran actors Ossie Davis and Ruby Dee, the film's about the pull of the group versus listening to the "little voice" inside us all.

At the center of the debate is Mookie (Spike Lee), poised between boyhood and manhood, old family and new family, peace (symbolized by Martin Luther King) and war (as represented by Malcolm X). He has loyalty to his proud boss and mentor Sal (Danny Aiello), but fears Sal's sons and an uncertain future.

On the hottest day of the year, a Bed-Stuy block will erupt in racial hatred. Despite the calming voices of Da Mayor (Davis) and Mother Sister (Dee), the friction creates sparks and finally fire. Setting it into motion are radical views represented by Buggin' Out and Radio Raheem. Told to "do the right thing," it will be loyalty to himself that changes Mookie's life.

I Type: Family Institution

I Cousins: *The Godfather, Boyz N the Hood, Goodfellas, Terms of Endearment, The Joy Luck Club, Liberty Heights, Avalon, American Beauty, The Royal Tenenbaums, Spanglish*

DO THE RIGHT THING
Written by Spike Lee

Opening Image: To Public Enemy's "Fight the Power," Rosie Perez dances. Beautiful and strong (Ernest R. Dickerson is the film's cinematographer and MVP), she soon wears boxing gloves. We're not just dancing; we're warming up for battle.

Set-Up: The forecast for New York's Bedford-Stuyvesant is HOT this summer morning, according to neighborhood DJ Mister Señor Love Daddy (Samuel L. Jackson). We meet Mookie (Spike Lee), counting money. Spike is alone at the start, but by the movie's finish (next morning), he is with Tina (Perez) and son Hector. Something will occur in the course of this day to make that trans-formation possible. We also see Sal (Danny Aiello) and sons, stalwart owners of Sal's Famous Pizzeria, a Bed-Stuy landmark — and soon to be ground zero for racial antipathy. We also meet the stuttering Smiley (Roger Guenveur Smith), selling a photo of Martin Luther King with Malcolm X. These two leaders' opposing views are the crux of Spike's dilemma — and his community's.

Catalyst: At Minute 11, Spike walks into work and is told, "You're late again" by "Company Man" Pino (John Turturro), Danny's bigoted son. Stress between Danny and John sets the tone for the day. We also meet the boom box-carrying Radio Raheem (Bill Nunn), a strong, silent man proclaiming "Fight The Power." He will spark the fire.

Debate: Where do Spike's loyalties lie? Spike's is a timeless "I" problem: being a Naif trapped in the system.

Break into Two: At Minute 19, after getting static from Danny about his pizza, a Brando figure, Buggin' Out (Giancarlo Esposito), looks up on the wall of Sal's Famous and sees nothing but Italian-Ameri-cans. "Why ain't you got no brothers up on the wall?" he protests. And since it's primarily an African-American community, Buggin'

Out wants answers. Instead, Danny kicks him out, with Spike assisting. For now, Spike is trying to keep his boss happy.

Theme Stated: At Minute 23, while on a delivery, Spike is told by Da Mayor (Ossie Davis) to "always do the right thing." As we'll see, this is Spike's choice: to listen to his inner voice or not.

B Story: Ossie is the spokesman for the neighborhood, its roving lifeguard and timeworn hero. His romance with Mother Sister (Ruby Dee), who hates him at first, is where we'll discuss the older values of this community and the film's theme. Like Spike, today will be a turning point for Ossie; he'll not be alone tomorrow.

Fun and Games: The city on a hot day is seen in "Fun and Games." When kids open up the fire hydrants and play in the water, the cops come by to shut it down, but for the moment, they are well-meaning defenders of the status quo. A bicyclist (John Savage) with a "Bird" jersey (for basketball star Larry Bird) gets grief from the kids for being a Yuppie renovator of a brownstone. We see more friction when Korean owners of a market get hassled by "Sweet Dick Willie" (Robin Harris). And at Minute 48, we get a close-up of hate as several citizens complain to the camera.

Midpoint: At 1 Hour 15 Minutes, the lines are drawn and the conflict looms: Danny tells John he's not moving, and Buggin' Out decides to organize a boycott of Sal's Famous. "Stakes are raised" more when Spike's sister visits and Danny flirts with her as John and Spike watch. There is a B Story "false victory" as Ossie buys flowers for Ruby. At 1 Hour and 19 Minutes, the sun is going down and Spike tells his sister: "I'll be making a move."

Bad Guys Close In: Tension increases between Danny and Spike over Danny's attention to Spike's sister. Later, Spike has a loving moment with Rosie but it seems to be the calm before the storm as the cops come by Sal's, acting a little more aggressively. John and his younger brother have a fight in the storeroom with John saying Spike is not to be trusted. Maybe John is jealous of Danny's relationship with Spike?

All Is Lost: About to close for the night, and pleased to have gotten through another day, Danny is confronted by Radio Raheem and Buggin' Out. With Radio Raheem's boom box cranked up loudly, Buggin' Out demands satisfaction, and the showdown boils over into violence. Danny grabs his bat and destroys the boom box. Raheem attacks Danny and the fight spills out into the street until the cops come. Arresting Buggin' Out, the cops grab Radio Raheem and violently put him in a choke hold. He dies while everyone watches. At 1 Hour 35 Minutes, all are in shock.

Dark Night of the Soul: Smiley wails while the cops take away the body. Danny pleads he had nothing to do with it. While Ossie tries to calm everyone, the neighborhood is about to tip. And the one who commits the "sacrifice" comes as a shock.

Break into Three: Naif turns Brando: Spike grabs a trashcan, throws it through the window of Sal's — and a riot starts.

Finale: The neighborhood kids burn Sal's Pizzeria down while A and B stories cross as Ossie whisks Danny to safety and comforts Ruby. The Korean market is next, but the owner manages to talk down the rioters by saying "Me black." The comment defuses the violence and the neighborhood watches as firemen come to put out the blaze. In a note of Synthesis, Smiley puts his photo of King and Malcolm X on the wall of Danny's burned-out restaurant.

Final Image: Spike wakes the next day with Rosie and their son, but leaves to get his back pay from Danny. Danny's business is destroyed, Radio Raheem is dead, and another day is starting — but has anything changed? Over credits we see quotes from both King and Malcolm X. Like the twin rings Radio Raheem wore — one saying LOVE, the other HATE — the conflict goes on.

OFFICE SPACE (1999)

In my opinion, Mike Judge is one of the great satirists of our age. When you think of the cultural malaise mixed with Jolt Cola that is *Beavis and Butthead*, and the good ol' boys who hang out — along with their beer guts — in *King of the Hill*, the nuance of his animator's eye is sharp. In his first live-action feature, which he wrote and directed, Judge proves that on film he can be just as cutting. With a few deft strokes, Judge captures a unique point in time: the cubicle-dwelling, commuter-numb, Fudruckers-plagued miasma that was the Silicon Valley '90s.

From the chirpy way the company receptionist greets callers, to the industrial-park dip in the grass when the three leads head back from a lunch spot where having "flair" is a part of the job, to the "Why don't you go ahead and..." patois of the office manager, Judge nails it in ways any caveman would get.

Ron Livingston has never been better than as mild-mannered Peter Gibbons, a guy who just doesn't want to work — and doesn't see why that's a bad thing. To find his bliss, he'll have to gather his fellow cavemen and lead a revolt against TPS reports, six bosses, and two Bobs. But with help from a hypno-therapist — and Jennifer Aniston — he'll be Synthesis Man by Act Three.

I Type: Business Institution

I Cousins: *One Flew Over the Cuckoo's Nest, 9 to 5, Network, The Hospital, Glengarry Glen Ross, Barbarians at the Gate, The Paper, Boiler Room, Pushing Tin, Ladder 49*

OFFICE SPACE
Written by Mike Judge

Opening Image: We meet our three wannabe "Brandos" stuck in traffic on the way to their corporate cubicles at Initech: Peter Gibbons (Ron Livingston) tries to changes lanes to get ahead, but finds it's a losing game; Michael Bolton (David Herman) defies his namesake and sings to rap music; and Samir Nagheenanajar (Ajay Naidu) vents by shouting in rage.

Set-Up: Ron sits in his cubicle as the receptionist answers the phone like a mynah bird. We also meet Milton (Stephen Root), the quiet worker (and the film's inspiration) who's been lost in the system, but at the moment he's just annoying. The day gets worse when "Company Man" and boss Bill Lumbergh (Gary Cole) tells Ron he's filling out his TPS reports all wrong. Ron, David, and Ajay go to Chotchke's, where waitress Joanna (Jennifer Aniston) is seen briefly. Ron's girlfriend (Alexandra Wentworth) wants him to see a therapist for his work avoidance, and David introduces his solution: a computer virus that would wreck the company.

Theme Stated: "What if we're still doing this when we're 50?" Ron asks his pals at Chotchke's in a Stasis = Death beat.

Catalyst: At Minute 11, on their way back from their coffee break, the guys learn two "efficiency experts" are coming to Initech. This can only mean one thing: a lot of firings.

Debate: How will Ron deal with this new threat? At his thin-walled apartment, he talks to neighbor Lawrence (Diedrich Bader), a construction worker who has the carefree life Ron wants.

Break into Two: At Minute 20, Ron is taken to the therapist by his girlfriend and asks: "Is there any way you can zonk me out so I feel like I'm not at work?" The shrink hypnotizes Ron and promptly has a heart attack — with Ron still under. At home the next day, Ron wakes up and has 17 messages from Lumbergh asking why he's not at work. He does pick up the phone for his girlfriend, who — frustrated by his zombie-like calm — admits she's been cheating and breaks up with him. But Ron doesn't care. He is a new man.

B Story: Still in a hypnotic state, and now a re-born Brando, Ron skips work and heads straight to Chotchke's to ask Jennifer out. While at work, the axe falls as we meet the "Two Bobs" (one played by hilarious John C. McGinley), who are revealed as down-sizers. On his date with Jennifer at Flingers, Ron's honesty is attractive but she will ultimately teach him what *real* honesty is all about.

Fun and Games: Back in the office, Ron wows the Bobs by admitting he does no work! Still in a daze, he knocks over his cubicle walls, pulls down a company motivational banner, and parks in Lundbergh's spot to the Geto Boys' "Damn It Feels Good to Be a Gangsta." This is truly the "promise of the premise." Ron is on a roll, and has even won Jennifer's heart. But his pals think he's crazy.

Midpoint: In a perfect "false victory"/"raising of stakes" one-two, Ron learns he's being promoted, but at a cost: His friends are being fired. We also find out poor Milton is going to be processed out; seems he was let go years ago, but a computer glitch kept him on the payroll. Starting to come down off his pink cloud, Ron tells David and Ajay the news of their firing, and they decide to fight back. "It's not just about me and my dream of doing nothing, it's about all of us," says Ron. "Human beings were not meant to sit in cubicles." At Minute 49, David vows: "Let's make that stock go down." Ron agrees: "I don't know about you, but I'm tired of being pushed around."

Bad Guys Close In: The plan to loose the computer virus on Initech and rob the company by an eighth of a penny at a time is set into motion. The trio loads the virus into the system and trouble begins almost immediately. In further insurgency, Ron steals David's archenemy, the office printer, and the three beat on it in a field, then celebrate by dancing in Ron's apartment. On the way to a company party, Ron tells Jennifer about the virus and she calls him on it: "So you're stealing." Despite Ron's explanation of eighths and quarters of pennies — she's right. Friction between them is furthered when Ron believes a rumor that Jennifer slept with Lumbergh. The party is for Ron's other boss, Tom (Richard Riehle), whose accident gave him a huge insurance settlement. Now a happy man, Tom advises, "If you hang in there long enough, good things can happen in this world." But Ron can't hang in... or forget Jennifer's alleged transgression.

All Is Lost: The plan begins to unravel and Ron and Jennifer break up. Ron has a dream about "Company Man" Lundbergh drinking coffee and having sex with Jennifer. Jennifer is so upset, she flips off her boss at Chotchke's and gets fired. To make matters worse, Ron discovers he and his buds have stolen $300,000 and there are only four days to put the money back.

Dark Night of the Soul: Milton's moved to the netherworld of the basement and is finally fed up. And Ron knows he's going to jail.

Break into Three: Ron writes a letter to the company taking the blame as his "sacrifice," then meets Jennifer, who's now working at Flingers. A and B stories cross as he apologizes. "I don't know why I can't just go to work and be happy," he says. "But I think that if I could be with you I could be happy."

Finale: Ron pushes an envelope under Lumbergh's door with the $300,000, but Milton goes into Lumbergh's office and finds the cash. While Ron packs, Milton blows up the building. Initech is destroyed as the "Cathy" cartoons go up in flames, along with evidence that could convict our heroes.

Final Image: The world after the inferno: Ron works construction and has Jennifer in his life along with his two friends, while Milton gets away with the money. They've accomplished what they wanted all along. Ron's been transformed. He and Jennifer are together. And Milton's on the beach in Cabo... but in a coda, we see things haven't changed for him — he *still* gets no respect.

TRAINING DAY (2001)

In a good example of the "Mentor Institution" tale, this Antoine Fuqua-directed slice-of-thug-life shows what happens when a student trusts a false teacher. It's one of the most primal stories we tell. We've all been there on our first day on the job, not sure what the rules are — or if we can make the grade. And the more eager we are to be accepted, the more open we are to manipulation from someone who means us harm.

Pity the sheep that meets a wolf in these circumstances.

Ethan Hawke plays one such ewe, an ambitious cop and Naif who lives in LA's San Fernando Valley. With a wife and baby to support, he wants to be part of a group of elite detectives, and puts himself in a position where his eagerness to succeed makes him vulnerable. When he agrees to learn at the feet of veteran narc and "Company Man," Denzel Washington, he finds there are no rules — except survival. Sanctioned by appearances from Dr. Dre, Snoop Dogg, and Macy Gray, the film is billed as a genuine look at LA's gang world. But for our purposes, Ethan's training of the "I" kind is about realizing any mentor can be corrupt... and insane. If he is to survive, he'll have to swear allegiance to a higher power: the inner guide that never lets him down.

I Type: Mentor Institution

I Cousins: *Wall Street, Dead Poet's Society, Swimming with Sharks, Mentor, Mona Lisa Smile, Apt Pupil, The Emperor's Club, In Good Company, The Devil Wears Prada, The Departed*

TRAINING DAY
Written by David Ayer

Opening Image: The alarm sounds and Jake Hoyt (Ethan Hawke) wakes, his wife and baby already up. They are his "Save the Cat" foundation; we are rooting for him because of them.

Set-Up: Ethan arrives at a coffee shop and meets new boss Alonzo (Denzel Washington makes this movie). At first, it's puppy dog Ethan versus big dog Denzel, as Ethan shows eagerness by interrupting Denzel's reading of his newspaper. But Denzel puts puppy in his place when he says...

Theme Stated: ..."Today's a training day, Officer Hoyt. You got today to show me who and what you're made of." Who is Jake? His mettle will be tested in the next 24 hours, and it will be life or death. We'll also see *who* gets trained — it may not be the puppy!

Catalyst: They roll. Ethan rides shotgun in Denzel's street car. From the start, it's obvious that Denzel's an undercover cop who skirts between legitimate and criminal behavior. "This *is* the office," he informs Ethan. At first Ethan is committed. "I will do anything you want me to do," he tells Denzel. Ordered to "take off your wedding band," he does so. Today will include a series of fraternity hazing-style tests to see if Ethan will obey (and make us wonder what *we* would do).

Debate: How far is Ethan willing to go? As if to press the point, at Minute 14, after watching a drug buy, they stop the buyers — a car full of suburban kids. Guns drawn, Ethan and Denzel relieve them of their cash, pot, and paraphernalia. Then Ethan is offered a new "choice," one of many that force him to question his decision to join the group. Denzel stops the car, pulls a gun on him, and says: Smoke the pot or quit. Ethan knows he'll be fired if drug-tested; what should he do?

Break into Two: At Minute 17, needing to belong, Ethan makes a big mistake and says: "Give me that thing." He wants to be "part of," and trusts his mentor. But as the effect hits Ethan, Denzel laughingly tells him the pot is laced with angel dust. Ethan has entered the "upside-down world" of Act Two.

B Story: Still high, Ethan is taken to the home of Roger (Scott Glenn), a drug dealer and Denzel's buddy. Though his actual screen time is short, Scott plays the B story role and is how Ethan will learn his real lesson. We also hear Scott tell a thematic tale of "the street" about a steadfast snail who refuses to give up.

Fun and Games: The "trailer moments" of two narcs on the beat. They leave Scott's house and cruise the city when Ethan spots a rape in progress. Making Denzel stop, Ethan breaks up the assault, gets beaten as Denzel watches, then is forced to let the bad guys go. But saving the girl will be crucial to Ethan. He's getting wise to his false mentor. And yet! As Denzel plays Ethan, even we can't tell if he is ultimately good or bad — it could go either way. Fun and Games end when Denzel takes Ethan to The Jungle, a gang neighborhood. The married Denzel has a girlfriend and illegitimate child there. As with the girl in the alley, Ethan befriends the boy, a caring act that pays off later.

Midpoint: The "stakes are raised" at Minute 55 as the two meet the "wise men," a corrupt group of LAPD brass. We learn Denzel owes the Russian Mob $1,000,000. This new information exemplifies a screenwriting trick I call the **lemon seed**. At mid-movie, think of new info such as this like putting a lemon seed between your thumb and forefinger and starting to squeeze until it… *squirts* out in Act Three. Every script should have a lemon seed in some way. From this point forward, it's on! — pace quickening, pressure building to the final pop! Armed with an illegal warrant — courtesy of the "wise men" — Denzel and Ethan meet a cop crew, dirty like Denzel. Ethan is the rookie, not trusted as they ready for a bust. Who's the target? Can you guess?

Bad Guys Close In: Yup. Scott Glenn. Denzel and crew burst in and rob him at gunpoint. Ethan refuses his cut of the money the crew steals from Scott. But "internal conflict" comes when Denzel murders Scott, then stages the scene to make it look like Ethan pulled the trigger. Ethan fights back, turning the gun on Denzel while the other cops threaten to shoot. Denzel tells Ethan he'll be drug tested. Denzel's been setting Ethan up from the start.

All Is Lost: Or has he? In some part of our soul we think, this can't be! But Ethan's "choice" is clear. "You guys are insane," he tells Denzel. Welcome to the "I" world, Ethan! Denzel drives Ethan to a gang house. Duped by Denzel, Ethan's taken hostage in a final betrayal. The "whiff of death" occurs when Ethan is wrestled into the bathroom to be executed. But when the gang members find a wallet on him belonging to their cousin, and learn Ethan saved her from being raped, they let him go.

Dark Night of the Soul: Riding the bus through the city at night, bloody but not done, Ethan plots the last "sacrifice."

Break into Three: Ethan, the "steadfast snail," walks into The Jungle looking for Denzel. What he was in Act One — an ethical cop — is added to by what he learned in Act Two — street toughness — for a dangerous combination in Act Three: pissed-off Synthesis Man.

Finale: The "time clock" has Denzel needing to get the money to the Russian Mob by midnight or be executed. It's why he got the warrant, why he robbed Scott, and why he set up Ethan. But Denzel has met his better. Helped by Denzel's son, who acts as a shield for him, Ethan battles Denzel and leaves him in the hands of the hood rats, who let Ethan walk out with Denzel's million bucks.

Final Image: Trying to make a getaway, Denzel is killed by the Russians, as Ethan walks in the door of his home — safe and much wiser.

CRASH (2005)

The "Issue Institution" is that story of the "I" kind that involves an ensemble cast, intersecting multiple story lines, and a theme. This style has returned to popularity of late and gives us ADD-afflicted lots o' stars to watch — and something to think about after the show. Like the spiritual forefather of this film type, Robert Altman, director/co-writer Paul Haggis uses this technique to dissect an Institutionalized problem — in this case, racism. But does *Crash* fit the structure of the BS2?

Answer: of course!

All stories are about transformation! And all good stories have beginnings, middles, and ends — with each story's lead character changing emotionally from + to − or from − to + at Opening Image and Final Image. This phenomenon is a result of entering Act Two's "transformation machine." In *Crash*, as in any ensemble film, each story has a Set-Up, Break into Two, Midpoint, Break into Three, and Final Image. And though each beat is compressed, the stories are woven together for maximum drama.

The ensemble forces the writer to intensify every beat of each story, so only the most relevant moments of the BS2 are shown on-screen. It is a technique that seems "hyper-real" at times, but supercharges the overall impact. And it's what makes any movie about "the many" so powerful — if executed well.

I Type: Issue Institution

I Cousins: *Nashville, The Big Chill, Short Cuts, Magnolia, Eating, Night on Earth, Thirteen Conversations About One Thing, Sin City, Friends with Money, Babel*

CRASH

Screenplay by Paul Haggis & Bobby Moresco
Story by Paul Haggis

Opening Image/Theme Stated: LAPD Detective Graham Waters (Don Cheadle) and partner/lover Ria (Jennifer Esposito) after a car accident. "In LA nobody touches you," he says. "I think we miss that touch so much, that we crash into each other, just so we can feel something." Jennifer is mad at Don, and when he gets out of the car, she gets into a racial-hate fight with a fellow crash victim that tells us Don may be right. What's stopping us from "touching"? Don finds a shoe at the scene as we cut to...

Set-Up/Catalyst/Debate: ..."Yesterday." We now set up our various stories, launching each into motion with a *Cat!*alytic moment, and with a "debate" about what the incident means.

- A Persian man, Farhad (Shaun Toub), and his daughter Dorri (Bahar Soomekh), buy a gun to protect their store. They argue with the gun shop owner. Bahar buys bullets.

- Two carjackers, Anthony (Ludacris) and Peter (Larenz Tate), fear being black on the white side of Los Angeles.

- Jean Cabot (Sandra Bullock) and husband Rick (Brendan Fraser) are Westside elites. He is the city DA; when they're carjacked, she will spiral into race hate.

- Don and Jennifer are called to a LAPD shooting incident.

- John Ryan (Matt Dillon) carps about his Dad's health to HMO worker Shaniqua (Loretta Devine). On patrol with Tom Hansen (Ryan Phillippe), Matt stops a black couple in their car. Cameron (Terrence Howard), a TV director, watches helplessly as racist Matt sexually frisks his wife (Thandie Newton).

- After a long day, and getting hate from Sandra, Hispanic locksmith Daniel (Michael Pena) gives his daughter an "invisible cloak" to protect her from stray gunfire.

Break into Two/Fun and Games: Less plot and more talk about racism as each of the stories deals with the theme.

- Afraid from the carjacking, Sandra chooses to deal with it by changing locks and yelling at Brendan and her maid.

- The interaction with the racist Matt makes Terrence and Thandie argue about his "blackness" and manhood. Why didn't he *do* something? More talk of race on the set when his boss (Tony Danza) tells Terrence how to coach a black actor.

- Ludacris and Larenz run over an Asian man and dump him at a hospital; they talk about the discrimination they face.

- After fixing a lock at Shaun's store, Michael is put down by Shaun as a Hispanic, and accused of cheating them.

Midpoint/Bad Guys Close In/All Is Lost: We see textbook "raising of stakes" on each story, and the melancholy that follows. In each case, the "bad guy" is internal turmoil.

- At Minute 46, Matt visits Shaniqua and apologizes for his racism, telling her about his Dad; she refuses to help.

- Don visits his Mom, a heroin addict. His brother is missing; she asks Don to find him.

- Shaun's store is robbed. The insurance agent tells him because of the Hispanic locksmith, they are not covered.

- Ryan tells Matt he's been reassigned. It's not stated, but Ryan doesn't want a racist partner. Matt warns him: "You think you know who you are. You have no idea."

- At Minute 58, police find cash in the car on the case that Don and Jennifer are working. The cop was corrupt.

- At Minute 59, Terrence watches a scene as cast and crew look on satisfied. This "false victory" makes Terrence seethe.

Break into Three/Finale: Now the stories reach a climax. We've seen set-up, raising of the stakes, tension — and now release.

- At 1 Hour 4 Minutes, Matt chooses to risk his life to save a woman who hates him (Thandie) from a burning car.

- At 1 Hour 13 Minutes, Terrence is carjacked by Ludacris and Larenz, who get separated when Terrence fights back. Recognizing Terrence, Ryan saves him and his carjacker from other cops who would have shot them. As Terrence lets Ludacris go, he tells him: "You embarrass me. You embarrass yourself."

- At 1 Hour 20 Minutes, Shaun goes to kill Michael, whose daughter jumps in front of the gunfire. Only later will we know Shaun's daughter bought blanks at the gun store.

- At 1 Hour 23 Minutes, Sandra realizes she's always angry, threatens to fire her maid, then slips on the stairs.

- At 1 Hour 29 Minutes, Ryan picks up Larenz hitchhiking and mistakenly shoots and kills him when he thinks he's reaching for a gun. Ryan dumps the body.

Final Image: At 1 Hour 30 Minutes, we are back to where this movie began, and when Don finds the shoe at the scene of the accident, we realize it belongs to Larenz, Don's brother! We sum up each tale by showing how each person has transformed.

- Ludacris returns to the spot where he hit the Asian man and turns in his van for cash — only to discover it holds illegal Asian immigrants. He could sell them, but in the course of this day, he's changed. He lets them go.

- Don's Mom ID's the body of her dead son, then blames Don for his death; he was "too busy" to find him. Jennifer understands what is troubling Don a little better now.

- Sandra's fall and revelation about her anger has had an effect: At 1 Hour 40 Minutes, she tells Brendan she loves him and hugs her maid, calling her "my best friend."

- Ryan burns his car to cover up his murder of a black man; his racist ex-partner was right about him.

- Thandie calls Terrence and he tells her he loves her.

- As snow falls on LA, Matt comforts his Dad with reborn compassion. In a button, Shaniqua, who did not help Matt, is in a "needed" accident. Crash bookends crash.

🐾 *Every "Superhero" must face a super bad guy, and Russell Crowe has met his match in one of the great Nemeses in movies: Joaquin Phoenix as Commodus, shown here in the Act Three crucifixion beat from* Gladiator.

10 SUPERHERO

Perhaps my favorite genre and one that's forever been the world's favorite is *le piece de resistance*… "Superhero"!

Somewhere up on Mt. Olympus is a special guy or gal who is on the way down here. Poor dope! Though imbued with amazing powers, and sent to save us dumb clucks from ourselves, he's the one who's stuck: Not quite human nor quite god, unable to date — or tell his plight to anyone who'll "get it" — Mr. Square Jaw must bear the brunt of the hostility, jealousy, and fear from us Lilliputians. He don't get no respect, he don't get no love — he don't get *nada*!

And yet he has no choice but to be our savior.

It's not easy being special. And the real bummer is the Superhero knows he is — and will pay a price for being so.

But what is he to do?

As long as we've been telling stories, someone is always coming to rescue us — Jesus, Moses, Hercules, Joan of Arc, and Spider-Man. And their legends are all the same. It isn't until later that we look back on these folks and say: "Thanks for stopping by!" 'Cause right at the moment, while in our midst, they're a little scary — which is why Dracula, Frankenstein, and The Wolfman fall into this same category. Truth is: There's a reason superheroes get no respect — because being special means they're not like us. It's why theirs are stories of triumph and of sacrifice.

And the range of these stories is Valhalla-like.

The "People's Superhero" is about a civilian rising from the ranks to meet a great challenge, like Robin Hood, Zorro, and the pre-fabricated kind, as seen in *Gladiator*. There is the "Comic Book Superhero," those we think of first from the genre's title, and very often with "Man" in their last name: Spider-Man, Superman, Batman… and Murray Silverman, my accountant. What about the "Real Life Superhero" like Jesus, Joan of Arc, Lawrence of Arabia, and true tales of biography shaped into the Superhero form, like the story of Jake La Motta in *Raging Bull*? Even made-up worlds need saving, so there's the "Fantasy Superhero" like those found in *The Matrix* and *Crouching Tiger, Hidden Dragon*. And since animated stories deal so heavily in this world, we get the "Storybook Superhero" in *The Lion King* and *Mulan*, tales for kids that are basically variations on the "chosen one"legend, but made palpable with funny songs and talking animals.

You know you have a Superhero story if you've got these three unique components: (1) a "power" the hero is imbued with, or a mission to be "super" that makes him more than human; (2) a "Nemesis," an equally powerful bad guy who opposes the hero's rise; and (3) a "curse" or Achilles heel — for every power there is a defect, one that can be used by the bad guy against our guy.

In terms of the "power" the Superhero is given, at first it seems like fun. Think of Superman as a teenager testing his speed and strength, Spidey flinging webs, or Jesus making the lame not so lame anymore. Whether it's New Testament or DC Comics, the appeal is the same; we watch as a special being gets to show off his specialness, demonstrated in the "Fun and Games" sections of these tales. The hero is not "us," but we can enjoy the fantasy by proxy. And it's great. It's magic. It should be! But we also know, deep inside, that the higher they fly, the harder they hit the pavement. For every superpower, there's a cosmic payback coming.

The Superhero genre is most like Fool Triumphant; there is a lot of crossover when dealing with stories of being special. One thing they share is the "hero changes his name" beat. In Fool Triumphant tales, the hero often sneaks into Act Two using his new name as a deception or as part of a disguise he needs to survive, while in SH tales the hero *proclaims* his new name, as seen when Colonel Lawrence, British officer, becomes "El Aurens" in *Lawrence of Arabia*, and Russell Crowe is dubbed "Gladiator." This tradition goes back to the "chosen one" tales in the Bible, as when Abram becomes Abraham and Saul is re-named Paul. The powers of the Superhero are different, too: Unlike FT tales, a Superhero knows power comes with a price. The Fool is unaware of his power's cost — and sometimes even unaware he is opposed!

What really makes the Superhero different from the Fool Triumphant is a Nemesis with matching or greater abilities. I say in the first *STC!* that what makes James Bond 007 is not the gadgets or the girls, it's Blofeld and Dr. No and Goldfinger. To be a Superhero, you must have a Lex Luther-y kind of bad guy opposing you: the Moriarity to our Sherlock Holmes, the Commodus to our Maximus, the Dr. Evil to our Austin Powers. These are the most fascinating good guy/bad guy match-ups in storytelling, because the distinction between good and evil is so slight. And what does the Superhero have that the Nemesis lacks?

The answer is simple: faith.

The Superhero doesn't have to wonder if he's special, he knows he is; the bad guy in these tales can only rely on himself and the little machinations he's created to prop up the image he has as the "chosen," which he secretly knows is false. Often the Nemesis is a "super genius," relying on his brain for his power — the very symbol of self-will run amok. While the Nemesis may best the Superhero for a time, in the end his lack of faith makes him need to kill his opposite, for only if he erases the real "chosen one" can he ever triumph. If the Nemesis were truly special, he wouldn't need to kill anyone, which is why in so many of these tales — the Christ story being the most obvious — there is a showdown where the hero is tested, facing his enemies essentially all by himself, and often killed or tortured for his trouble.

Finally, the "curse" is that thing in most Superhero tales that balances out the powers and makes us not hate the protagonist as badly as we might. From "The Immutable Laws of Screenplay Physics," we know that anybody who gets everything they want is unlikable, so to make them bearable, we stick our Superhero protags with some kind of handicap. Look at the "sexual sacrifice" of Jake La Motta in *Raging Bull*, Peter Parker in *Spider-Man*, Clark Kent in *Superman* — let alone the curse of having to keep one's identity hidden, leading to the duo-identities of these heroes. It's a pain being special is the message, and we have to give up something for the power. For every ounce of kryptonite for Superman, there is daylight for Dracula, and a full moon for the Wolfman, and on and on. And don't forget the Superhero, like Gulliver against the Lilliputians — forever tied down by a thousand annoying little threads — has us to contend with too. And yet we still identify. Though not super, we've also faced tiny minds.

Just try pitching your movie idea at Disney!

A character that pops up in a lot of these SH tales is the **Mascot**, that puppy dog nipping at the Superhero's heel and loyal to the end, such as the servants that Lawrence chooses in *Lawrence of Arabia*, Jimmy Olsen in *Superman*, Jake La Motta's brother in *Raging Bull*, and Simba's sidekicks in *The Lion King*. These are the characters who show the contrast between us and…them.

One interesting note in reviewing this genre is the absolute dearth of female-driven Superhero stories. Why?

No, really.

Of the very few that have been attempted — *Lara Croft*, *Elektra*, *Underworld*, *Aeon Flux*, and *Catwoman* — all seem to be pale imitations of their male Superhero counterparts, and like the historic Superhero tale of Joan of Arc, half the story is devoted to the people around the hero being unable to believe "a girl" can do the job. Of these, the best is a little indie called *Whale Rider*, but that story is more about prejudice than empowerment. So for those out there who like a challenge, let's see some more female Superheroes at the Cineplex! Perhaps this requires a reconfiguring of the rules, and a challenge to the group. Will you be "the one" to bring this change?

That's what being a true Superhero is all about.

IS YOUR HERO SUPER?

Does he deign to be among us? Know she's something special? Not afraid to face the forces that oppose? Shazam!

1. The hero of your tale must have a special "power" — even if it's just a mission to be great or do good.

2. The hero must be opposed by a "Nemesis," of equal or greater force, who is the "self-made" version of the hero.

3. There must be a "curse" for the hero that he either surmounts or succumbs to as the price for who he is.

If you feel the need to be super, take a look at these variations on one of our oldest story traditions.

RAGING BULL (1980)

What is "super" about Jake La Motta? The boxer on whom director Martin Scorsese based his landmark film don't seem all dat divine. When we meet him in the form of Robert De Niro (Best Actor Oscar®), it is 1964 and his "super" days are past. He is fat and full of himself, bloated by a life misspent, and dumb as a punch in the head. He's achieved much in the ring but years of battling his brother and his child-bride wife have left him with nothing.

What the protag of *Raging Bull* shares with others in the "Real Life Superhero" category, and the Superhero generally, is the price paid for being special. He has talent as a middleweight, raw drive, and an "up-from-the-street" urge to triumph in the name of family and neighborhood. But flaws of vanity, selfishness, and jealousy are the Lilliputian ropes that bind this Gulliver, taint his higher purpose, and finally pull him down to our level. Like many who descend from Mt. Olympus with a special gift, he's "cursed" by human weakness.

Animal imagery (from the title to sound effects in the ring) is used to show that the Raging Bull is less a boxer than a force of nature. And religious iconography, including his bloody "crucifixion" at the hands of one of his foes, reveals this movie is about a fall from grace. In the end, outside the ring that is his place to shine, we see how handicapped he is as a man.

SH Type: Real Life Superhero

SH Cousins: *Lenny, Gandhi, Braveheart, Malcolm X, Frances, Joan of Arc, Erin Brockovich, The Passion of the Christ, The Aviator, A Beautiful Mind*

RAGING BULL
Screenplay by Paul Schrader *and* Mardik Martin
Based on the book by Jake La Motta *and* Joseph Carter & Peter Savage

Opening Image: New York City. 1964. A fat and over-the-hill Jake La Motta (Robert "Bobby" De Niro gained the weight, dis ain't prosthetics) practices his "act" in a nightclub dressing room.

Set-Up: 1941. Bobby is in the ring in Cleveland. He is lean, mean, and hungry... but losing this fight. Despite his Mascot brother Joey (Joe Pesci), who tells him he needs a knockout to win, Bobby can't deliver — a foreshadowing of the near miss of greatness in his life. Back in the neighborhood, Joe meets Salvy (Frank Vincent), one of Bobby's Nemeses and the brains in this jungle. He and boss Tommy (Nicholas Colasanto) control boxing. Bobby is also in a loveless marriage. Joe and Bobby are underdogs who must work as one if they are going to win.

Theme Stated: Bobby complains to Joe about his small hands. He'll always be a middleweight and never fight the heavyweight champion. "What are you trying to prove?" Joe asks. Will needing to prove himself, and never being satisfied, be his undoing?

Catalyst: At Minute 17, Bobby sees a pretty girl, Vickie (Cathy Moriarty), and is smitten. She will fuel his desire to win.

Debate: Can he have her? His dream girl is not only 15 years old, she is Salvy's girl. No one to retreat from a challenge, Bobby dogs Cathy at a dance. Animal instinct is in the air as fights break out and Bobby sees Cathy get into Salvy's nice new car.

B Story: A Superhero should have a super mate. At Minute 25, Bobby drives up in his own car — just as nice as Salvy's — and asks Cathy out. Raising the ante, he woos her from the smarter animals in the jungle.

Break into Two: Bobby's rise to the top of the middleweight boxing world begins in a rematch with Sugar Ray Robinson (Johnny Barnes). In the ring, fighting with the boxing great, animal sounds and bird screeches are heard. Bobby is in his element; it is a world he understands. The drive to dominate boxing — and life — is on.

Fun and Games: The quest for the middleweight championship belt continues, as does Bobby's relationship with Cathy. But it takes odd turns, like when Bobby and Cathy avoid sex so he can stay strong. Part of the "curse" of the Superhero is his separation from the human race. In his rise to the top, Bobby's focus pays off. He starts to win, and in a montage, marries Cathy and has kids; Joe marries (Theresa Saldana) and has children of his own.

Midpoint: "False victory" at Minute 49, as no one else is left to fight Bobby. He has earned the nickname, the Raging Bull, and a reputation for stubbornness. He and Joe still haven't capitulated to Salvy, but have also failed to get a shot at the title. Before going out of town to train for a fight, Bobby, Cathy, and Joe go to a club. Bobby sees Cathy stop by Salvy and Tommy's table and decides to stop by, too. The "pretty" boxer Bobby is training to fight is mentioned by his Nemesis and Bobby becomes jealous when Cathy admits she thinks his opponent is attractive. Moments later, at Minute 57, Bobby pummels the boxer's face in the ring. The Raging Bull is at the height of power — king of his castle and the jungle — but jealousy and suspicion have entered his life as A and B stories cross. The "curse" of human weakness begins to corrode his mission.

Bad Guys Close In: Now it gets tougher for Bobby. There's trouble within the internal team when Joe catches Cathy at a nightclub with Salvy while Bobby is training out of town. We also see Bobby give in to Salvy, agreeing to take a dive to get a shot at the title. Bobby is suspended for this action and sobs after the fight for having looked like a coward to his fans. Though shameful, the loss will lead to a shot at being the middleweight champ. Bobby sees Cathy kiss Tommy on the cheek prior to the championship bout. Bobby wins the title, but jealousy is in full bloom. Though he has achieved his goal, he has nowhere to go… but down. Now, fat and out of shape, the disgruntled Superhero hangs around the house, and worries. Trying not to inflame his brother, Joe lies about the night he saw Cathy out with Salvy.

All Is Lost: Unable to leave it alone, Bobby continues to pester Cathy with his suspicions. Finally, he makes the outrageous claim that Cathy slept with Joe. A and B stories cross as Cathy, sick of the accusations, screams she had sex with everyone. Hearing this, Bobby beats his brother. It's over between them and now, without Joe, he is "worse off than when this movie started."

Dark Night of the Soul: It's not the same for the Raging Bull. In a final battle with Sugar Ray, Bobby knows he's done and allows his great foe to slug away at him — paying penance for a life now confused. But when he loses, Bobby gets the last word: "You never got me down, Ray." The blood on the ropes of the ring tells the real story — Bobby has been "crucified" for his human sins.

Break into Three: The slow slide into loserdom begins. Bobby moves Cathy and the kids to Florida and opens a nightclub.

Finale: Bobby is arrested for fostering sex with a minor. Forced to sell his championship belt, he knocks out the gems and destroys it. In the end, Cathy leaves and he's in jail. Reduced to MC-ing strip shows, he runs into Joe and tries to reconcile.

Final Image: Back in the dressing room where we began, Bobby works on his ironic "I could have been a contender" speech. He too could have been great but fell from grace. With a few winded punches at the air, Bobby goes out to face another crowd.

THE LION KING (1994)

In the sub-category of "Storybook Superhero," we get all manner of tales about princes, talking toys, and hunchbacks. As one who grew up in the elastic world of cartoons (and whose TV producer father had him stand up in front of a microphone to do the "kid" voices at age 8), I know and love this world. And though different from live-action writing... it's the same.

If I had my druthers, I'd start every screenwriting class with a study of animated movies. Why? Well, for one, they offer amazing lessons about how to write character in dialogue. Having worked with some of the great voice talents, like Gary Owens (voice of Roger Ramjet) and Sterling Holloway (voice of Winnie the Pooh), I saw firsthand how a good voice actor can pick up a script and infuse "Screwy Squirrel" with personality that informs the character ever after. But it must start on the page! Ask anyone in the Pixar/Disney/Dreamworks pantheon and they will tell you the same.

For our purposes, this 1994 animated classic overseen by Jeffrey Katzenberg (seriously, the best), and directed by Roger Allers and Rob Minkoff, concerns a Superhero kids can root for, but offers lessons adults, too, know are true. Like many a Disney feature, this journey of empowerment begins with the death of a parent. The movie is also a lesson about being "special" that includes learning about the needs of the common man or, in this case, the common warthog.

SH Type: Storybook Superhero

SH Cousins: *Peter Pan; The Hunchback of Notre Dame; Mulan; The Chronicles of Narnia: The Lion, the Witch and the Wardrobe; The Jungle Book; The Little Mermaid; Willy Wonka & the Chocolate Factory; the Harry Potter series; Happy Feet; Ratatouille*

THE LION KING

Written by Irene Mecchi *and* Jonathan Roberts *and* Linda Woolverton

Opening Image: In a stunning sequence, the animals of the African plain gather to witness the arrival of Simba, son of King Mufasa (James Earl Jones). The "Circle of Life" is introduced, as is the idea that as one generation passes away, it makes room for the next. The only lion not attending is the King's brother, Scar (Jeremy Irons). When confronted by Mufasa's bird domo, Zazu (Rowan Atkinson), Scar says a very Nemesis thing: "As far as brains go, I got the lion's share. But when it comes to brute strength… I'm afraid I'm at the shallow end of the gene pool." Scar is plotting to be king, but like many an SH story, this is about being the rightful — and the righteous — heir.

Theme Stated: As Simba enters young lionhood, his dad takes him on a trip around the kingdom. All this will be yours, Mufasa tells Young Simba (Jonathan Taylor Thomas). Then he adds our theme: "There's more to being King than getting your way all the time."

Set-Up: Simba is wet behind the ears and a little cocky, but eager to learn. Maybe too eager. When Dad is called away to handle "poachers" — the hyenas — Simba grabs his female ally, Young Nala (Niketa Calame), and takes her to the forbidden elephant graveyard. There they meet the hyenas (Whoopi Goldberg, Cheech Marin, and Jim Cummings) and are about to be lunch until Mufasa shows up, saving the cubs. Dad is mad at Simba, which sets up the poor little guy's undoing — and his father's death.

Catalyst: Scar now uses this incident to plan a takeover. In a deal with the hyenas (and a Hitler-esque review of their marching ranks), Scar sets his coup d'état in motion. Taking Simba to a dry wash, he tells him to wait for a surprise.

Debate: What should Simba do? And will Scar's plan work?

Break into Two: Suddenly the thundering sound of a wildebeest stampede is heard. Simba is stranded in the middle of it. When Mufasa is told, he rushes to his kid's aid. There, in a heartbreaking bit of Disneyana, Mufasa clings to the side of a cliff begging for help from Scar, who sends him falling to his death. By the time the stampede has passed, Simba finds his dad's body. Coming upon Simba, Scar tells the cub it was his fault. Frightened, Simba runs. Chased by the hyenas, he escapes, but Scar assumes the hyenas finished the job.

Fun and Games: The "upside-down version of the world" is represented by the new friends Simba meets: Timon the Meerkat (Nathan Lane) and Pumbaa the Warthog (Ernie Sabella). Outcasts who eat bugs, the two will befriend our hero and help him into Act Three. The fun of being away from his lion pride includes an idyllic life and singing "Hakuna Matata," a Swahili phrase that translates as "There are no worries here." The jolly song, which accompanies the fun and frolic of Simba with his pals, provides a therapeutic break from the responsibilities of being Mufasa's son. It's also a needed humbling for Simba to be among the common folk. But the break is only temporary.

B Story: Simba becomes an adult (Matthew Broderick), but he still hasn't learned his lesson. The "Fun and Games" peak when Pumbaa is chased by a lioness who turns out to be the adult Nala (Moira Kelly). Simba and the lioness who was once his playmate are reunited. In a romantic montage to the Elton John tune of "Can You Feel The Love Tonight" (nearly cut from the movie), they play, reacquaint, and fall in love.

Midpoint: Pumbaa and Timon lament the loss of their friend to a girl. A and B stories cross as the joy of being reunited with Nala turns serious. Simba has run away from his responsibilities, and Scar has become king, allowing the Pridelands to wither away.

Bad Guys Close In: Nala tells Simba he's the pride's only hope, but he won't accept the responsibility and they argue and separate. The struggle with his "internal team" — both his new friends and his old ones — shows even a Superhero can't ignore the "curse" of responsibility. Is Simba going to assume the leadership role as king as his father intended?

All Is Lost: Simba encounters the mystical baboon, Rafiki (Robert Guillaume), who was present at his birth and has been the soothsayer and Simba's silent mentor all along. In the most spiritual part of the film, Rafiki shows Simba his father is still alive… in Simba. "He lives in you," Rafiki tells the king's son. His father's ghost appears in the clouds and warns: "Remember who you are."

Dark Night of the Soul: Simba must decide if he should return and face his past.

Break into Three: A and B stories cross as — pushed by Rafiki and supported by Nala, Timon, and Pumbaa — Simba says: "I'm going back." "If it's important to you, we're with ya 'till the end," says Timon.

Finale: Simba returns to the pride and finds his homeland, once a lush veldt, now a burned-out ruin. Scar and the hyenas have run the kingdom into the ground. Scar says, "I'm the king. I can do whatever I want!" As we know, that's not what being king is about. When Simba challenges Scar, Scar calls him a murderer and Simba takes responsibility for his father's death. Then Scar reveals that he was there when Mufasa died, and was in fact the one who was responsible. A battle breaks out and Scar and Simba have their showdown. In the end, Simba triumphs, and Scar is left to the mercy of the hyenas he betrayed.

Final Image: Simba takes his place atop Pride Rock and finally lets out a deep adult roar. In a time lapse, we see the Pridelands have recovered and flourished under Simba's rule. He and Nala, now king and queen, are surrounded by friends and have their own lion cub. A new chapter in the "Circle of Life" has begun.

THE MATRIX (1999)

Sometimes the "average man" is called back to Mt. Olympus. That's the twist in the Wachowski Brothers' computer-game-driven meditation on reality that became the basis of a sci-fi mega-franchise. When we meet Keanu Reeves as Neo, he is the very definition of the average Joe. Joe job. Joe apartment. Joe life. And then the phone rings. And Joe realizes his Joe-ness is a plot — and that he may be "the one" Joe who can save the world.

Like other SH stories in the "Fantasy Superhero" category—those savior tales in a made-up world with little historic context — *The Matrix* became a breakout hit due in part to its use of mythology. With nods to the New Testament (Christ references galore), the Old Testament (the name of Morpheus' ship comes from a Babylonian king influenced by dreams), and even *Alice in Wonderland* (when Keanu "follows the white rabbit," a tattoo on a girl's shoulder), we too "go through the looking glass" and into the collective unconscious that seems so familiar. The movie also uses elements found in all SH stories: a sexual sacrifice, as when Keanu is tempted by the "Woman in Red," a Mascot as seen in the character of Mouse, and a host of Nemeses, the multiple enemies Keanu will face in the finale. The action is sci-fi martial arts and the special effects have become their own cultural reference.

But really, it's all about the sunglasses.

SH Type: Fantasy Superhero

SH Cousins: *Brazil, Hook, The Neverending Story, MirrorMask, The Nightmare Before Christmas, Antz, The League of Extraordinary Gentlemen, Van Helsing, V for Vendetta, Eragon*

THE MATRIX
Written by Andy Wachowski & Larry Wachowski

Opening Image: A computer screen indicating a call in progress. We hear two people talking about "The One." We'll soon know them as Trinity (Carrie-Anne Moss) and Cypher (Joe Pantoliano). One is a true believer, the other a traitor. (It's always Joe!) The point is made in this opening snapshot: There is a secret world connected via phone line... and a "savior" who is coming soon.

Theme Stated: After a great opening sequence of Carrie-Anne in action, including the breathtaking — and breakthrough — stop-time-float-in-the-air-spin-360° thing, she escapes the bad guys, including Agent Smith (the fabulous Hugo Weaving), via a ringing pay phone. We now meet Neo (Keanu Reeves), living in slacker squalor as the world's coolest computer hacker. When visited by a customer, Keanu says: "Do you ever have the feeling that you're not sure if you're awake or dreaming?" What is reality? That's what this movie is about.

Set-Up: Told, "You are my savior, man, my own personal Jesus Christ" by a visitor, Keanu goes to a club where he meets Carrie-Anne. At Minute 10, she introduces herself saying: "I know why you don't sleep, why night after night you sit at your computer."

Catalyst: Next day at Keanu's workplace, right at Minute 13, a package arrives. Inside: a phone. On it: Morpheus (Laurence Fishburne).

Debate: Should Keanu believe in the unseen world Laurence is telling him about? "They're coming for you, Neo," he is told, and indeed, here comes Hugo to arrest him. But what is Keanu to do? In a series of refusals to believe, Keanu drags his feet.

Break into Two: At Minute 25, after being de-bugged by Carrie-Anne and assorted hip-haircut-ed buddies, Keanu meets Laurence, and wow, his sunglasses *are* cool! "Do you believe in fate, Neo?" he is asked. Another thing to track in these movies: the hero who surrenders his sense of control to an unseen power in order to become great. SH tales are about faith. At Minute 29, Keanu is offered two pills. He chooses and begins his descent into the rabbit hole. At Minute 32, he wakes unplugged from the system and reborn, the painful and scary part of the "curse" of being special. "Welcome to the real world," Laurence tells him.

B Story: The B story is the "love story" between Carrie-Anne and Keanu. He and she are specially bonded. How? We'll see.

Fun and Games: On Laurence's off-world ship, *The Nebuchadnezzar*, debate is introduced about whether Keanu is The One. The "Mascots" hope he is. We also see Keanu's training begin, a common "Fun and Games" activity as the hero learns his fighting skills. Keanu is also told the truth: The world he knows as reality is really a Matrix of illusion, designed to imprison humankind. Only The One can save the slaves. And yet Keanu still resists. We also see another common SH dilemma: Is Keanu "too old" to be trained?

Midpoint: At Minute 59, Keanu's training ends as he is told he can eventually dodge bullets. And A and B stories cross when we learn Carrie-Anne has a special reason to be rooting for Keanu to be The One. We also learn Joe is a traitor who will swap out his friends to Hugo for the pleasures of being sent back into the Matrix as a movie star. When Keanu visits the Oracle (Gloria Foster) — complete with a waiting room full of other potential "Ones" (and a film clip of rabbits on the TV from B movie, *Night of the Lepus*) — he gets a "false defeat" from the soothsayer. Keanu is *not* The One.

Bad Guys Close In: The seeds of Joe's backstabbing come to fruition as the double-cross is set in motion, and the greasing of the skids that rockets us toward the finale begins to accelerate at a breakneck pace. "Mascot" Mouse is killed after ogling the "Woman in Red." And in a shootout with the agents, Laurence is captured by the bad guys and Joe is revealed as the Judas. Keanu and Carrie-Anne are trapped out in the world, their lives in the hands of Joe who — back on *The Nebuchadnezzar* — begins to unplug them.

All Is Lost: One by one, Joe kills the crew. A miracle saves Keanu when he is about to be unplugged. Maybe the Oracle is wrong; maybe he really is The One. Besting Joe, Carrie-Anne and Keanu are brought back aboard *The Nebuchadnezzar*, but their "father" and mentor, Laurence, has been taken prisoner by Hugo and tortured. What is Keanu going to do?

Dark Night of the Soul: In a perfect DNOTS moment, and a "whiff of death," the crew must decide whether to let Laurence die.

Break into Three: A and B stories cross as both Keanu and Carrie-Anne boldly choose to rescue their leader. As they lock in to the Matrix and the "false world" that Keanu has only just begun to master, they arm themselves with all kinds of cool hardware.

Finale: Carrie-Anne and Keanu burst into the building where Laurence is being kept. Bullets and bodies fly in the marble lobby, as Carrie-Anne and Keanu defy the laws of physics. Meanwhile, Hugo tortures Laurence and reveals his revulsion for the human race. Eventually, the two rescue Laurence — and Keanu dodges bullets on the rooftop. Keanu is "beginning to believe." In a final battle, Keanu not only defeats Hugo, he also has a vision of the Matrix. His faith in an unseen world is rewarded. He even experiences a crucifixion when he dies and is brought back to life by

Carrie-Anne, who reveals the Oracle told her she would know The One because she was in love with him. With metal monsters eating at the hull of *The Nebuchadnezzar*, Keanu is revived by Carrie-Anne's kiss and finishes off Hugo — at least for now.

Final Image: Back in the artificial world of The Matrix, an eyes-opened Keanu knows the battle for humankind is on. He flies into space proving he has mastered his new powers. The last image bookends the first: a computer screen and a phone call, as Keanu warns those listening that things have changed. Transmission ended. Transformation just beginning.

GLADIATOR (2000)

By now I'm sure you're asking, what is this Ridley Scott fixation? Well, including another fave, *Thelma & Louise*, El Rid is the master of storytelling for film in every genre. And when it comes to Superhero tales, none fits the "People's Superhero" better than the Ridmeister's "sand and sandal" saga, *Gladiator*.

With nods to *Ben-Hur*, *Spartacus*, and *The Fall of the Roman Empire*, in its simplest form this is the story of two "brothers" who, though not related by blood, are each vying for the love of a father. One man is a superior being called to service against his will, the other a jealous Nemesis — who may be one of the best examples of evil in movies. The bravura turn by Joaquin Phoenix, whose creation as the Nemesis occurs right before our eyes when he strangles his Emperor father (Richard Harris), horrifies us — and yet we understand, and maybe even sympathize! His headaches suffered during the story are the price of "super genius" to manipulate the world, and in direct contrast to the "chosen one" (Russell Crowe, Best Actor Oscar®) who, when first asked to rule, refuses.

The litmus test of greatness is knowing the price paid for being so, and taking on the task anyway. Though reluctant in the beginning, Russell puts things right in an epic showdown that proves the qualities of "strength and honor" can defeat even the most powerful forces.

SH Type: People's Superhero

SH Cousins: *Gunga Din, Ben-Hur, High Plains Drifter, Greystoke: The Legend of Tarzan, The Three Musketeers, Robin Hood: Prince of Thieves, The Mask of Zorro, Whale Rider, The Patriot, Casino Royale*

GLADIATOR

Screenplay by David Franzoni *and* John Logan *and* William Nicholson
Story by David Franzoni

Opening Image: A man's hand, with a wedding ring, touches a field of wheat. General Maximus (Russell Crowe) dreams of home. He smiles at a bird, a "Save the Cat" trifecta that includes his faithful dog and the respect of his soldiers. It is 180 AD. We are in Germania, edge of the Roman Empire. Emperor Marcus Aurelius (Richard Harris) mounts a final campaign. An update of the "sand and sandal" epic, we're surprised to see snow and The Black Forest. As usual, director Ridley Scott is visually fresh throughout.

Theme Stated: At Minute 4, an aide comments on their barbaric foe to Russell: "People should know when they're conquered." This is about the true meaning of "strength and honor" and not giving up.

Set-Up: Russell is fearless and a brilliant strategist, whose men will do anything for him. After the battle, Marcus lauds Russell, but is stopped by the arrival of son Commodus (Joaquin Phoenix) and daughter Lucilla (Connie Nielsen), who are incestuous and power mad. (The family that slays together, stays together.) Connie once loved Russell and is now a widow with a son. The emperor is to name his successor.

Catalyst: In a surprise, the emperor asks Russell to succeed him and make Rome a republic. But before Russell can agree, Joaquin strangles his father, furious that he was not chosen. The Nemesis has outmaneuvered the Superhero, and set their struggle in motion.

Debate: What should Russell do? He is told that the emperor is dead and Joaquin is Rome's new leader — and is asked to swear allegiance.

Break into Two: Russell chooses "strength and honor" over loyalty to Joaquin and knows the emperor's death was murder. For this, he is arrested and sentenced to be executed, as are his wife and child. Russell escapes in one of those really cool hero-avoids-execution beats and races to save his family — but is too late. He finds them dead and his farm burned. Wounded, he falls unconscious, then wakes in the "upside-down version of the world." He is sold as a slave — and doomed to die as a gladiator.

B Story: The "funhouse-mirror" reflection of the "normal world" of Act One: In place of a highly trained legion of soldiers, Russell now leads a group of misfit fighters; instead of the emperor, he now has Proximo (Oliver Reed), a moth-eaten impresario, consigned to the backwaters of the empire. Oliver has put "strength and honor" on hold, but as a former slave freed by the emperor, Oliver identifies with Russell's plight. Oliver and these misfits will teach Russell lessons in not giving up — and vice versa.

Fun and Games: Shades of *Spartacus* and *Ben-Hur* as Russell begins his long trek back from "death." No longer caring if he lives because his family is gone, he has to find a new reason to survive. His skills return when he fights for the best cause of all: service to others, including Juba (Djimon Hounsou), an Ethiopian who also misses his family. Russell is singled out as leader and the gladiators bond.

Midpoint: At 1 Hour 8 Minutes, Russell has beaten all challengers; there's no one's left to fight. Meanwhile, Joaquin has taken over Rome, and seems to have won the love of the people. He and a remorseful Connie rule, but the cost of killing her father weighs on her. The new emperor wants games in the Coliseum, little knowing that by calling up the best gladiators in the empire, he draws Russell closer. A and B stories cross as Russell and Oliver head to Rome. Russell is fueled by a new mission: revenge.

Bad Guys Close In: Oliver's gladiators look doomed in the first bout in the amazing CGI-rendered Coliseum. Disguised for fear of being seen, Russell returns to form as a commander and saves his men and wins the crowd — the key to survival, according to his new mentor. After the victory, Joaquin wants to know who this masked man is and Russell reveals himself — and his name Gladiator — to all, including Connie. Now the pressure is on as Joaquin realizes the threat and plots to kill Russell, while Connie sees Russell's "strength and honor" are what Rome and the people really need.

All Is Lost: The "whiff of death" includes Russell being challenged by an undefeated gladiator. Fighting him, and a series of hungry tigers secreted under the surface of the Coliseum, Russell eventually triumphs and asks the mob whether or not he should kill his helpless victim. He becomes "Maximus the Merciful" when he defies Joaquin and lets the man live. "You simply won't die," Joaquin taunts, describing how Russell's wife and son suffered as they were murdered.

Dark Night of the Soul: Wanting to be reunited with his wife and son, even in death, has been Russell's quest from the start. He is given religious statues representing them and longs to be together.

Break into Three: Plotting to escape from captivity, raise an army, and return to conquer Rome, Russell allies with Connie and some renegade senators in a conspiracy against Joaquin. But before the plan can be launched, Joaquin discovers it. (This is a typical reversal in many Act Threes: a plan is scuttled, causing the hero to dig down and find a new way.) This will be Russell's final test.

Finale: A and B stories cross again as Oliver re-discovers his soul and reclaims "strength and honor" when he sacrifices himself to help Russell escape. Yet the plotters are killed and Russell is captured. Back in full command, the crazed and jealous Joaquin stabs a "crucified" Russell, rendering him unable to fight, then brings him into the Coliseum to kill him in front of the crowd. But the duel turns when, with his last ounce of strength, Russell kills Joaquin.

Final Image: In a dream sequence bookend, Russell reunites with his family in the afterlife — his journey over, his earthly duty complete.

SPIDER-MAN 2 (2004)

We come to the end with one of my favorite movies, co-written by my favorite screenwriter, Alvin Sargent. Why? Because while others of Sargent's stripe are lauded and studied (e.g., the great Robert Towne), Sargent — much like the "Comic Book Super-hero" does in this film — continues to suit up and show up... and quietly save the day every time.

I get flack about which *Spider-Man* is the best so far, but I think 2 beats them all. Not only is director Sam Raimi firing on all cylinders, but the dilemma faced by Tobey Maguire deals with the problem of superpowers that's relevant to us humans. In a world where thinking only of our own wants and needs seems vastly smarter than "doing good," it is a quandary we too wrestle with.

What this movie is "about" is that selflessness and service to others are the greatest powers we have. That choice brings out "the hero in all of us" and proves it isn't the web-flinging or the adulation, but what we give back that counts most. *S-M:2* even shows how big studio fare can still have merit. Here we are at a summer "popcorn" flick, marketed all over the world, and yet within it is a lesson as powerful as any in storytelling: What is our purpose on earth — and how can we do a better job?

$10 plus parking and a Coke? I'm there. Forever.

Thanks, Hollywood!

SH Type: Comic Book Superhero

SH Cousins: *Batman, The Fantastic Four, The Incredibles, X-Men, Blade, The Hulk, Tank Girl, Catwoman, The Crow, Hellboy*

SPIDER-MAN 2
Screenplay by Alvin Sargent
Story by Alfred Gough & Miles Millar *and* Michael Chabon

Opening Image: Peter Parker (Tobey Maguire), late for work, ogles Mary Jane, aka MJ (Kirsten Dunst), who adorns a billboard. Tobey's human vs. Superhero dilemma is seen through his relationship with Kirsten. Can he have her *and* be Spider-Man?

Theme Stated: Blowing a pizza delivery, Tobey is told by his boss, "To you Parker, a promise means nothing." Holding true to what we promise — and putting others before self — is the theme.

Set-Up: Tobey is in multi-tasking hell. He works for *The Daily Bugle*, run by J. Jonah Jameson (J.K. Simmons), who pesters him for photos of Spider-Man. He's a gifted student but behind in his studies — and his rent. Home for his birthday, he learns Aunt May (Rosemary Harris) is being evicted. Yet Tobey can do nothing. The bright spot is Kirsten, whose attitude suggests she has a crush on him, too. Tobey can't tell her who he is — or why he can't see her — but promises he will come see the play she's starring in.

Catalyst: At Minute 18, Tobey is introduced to Dr. Otto Octavius (Alfred Molina), who's created a new form of energy. The doc likes Tobey and introduces wife "Rosie" (Donna Murphy). Alfred has found a way to have a "normal" life and still have a mission.

Debate: Can Tobey balance his life? Getting ready for Kirsten's play, Tobey opens his closet; there are two suits hanging there, his every-day clothes and Spider-Man's outfit. On his way, at Minute 25, Tobey is involved in a police pursuit and arrives at the theater late. Waiting for the show to let out, Tobey sees Kirsten kiss John Jameson (Daniel Gillies). Tobey is heartbroken. Angry, he takes to the sky as Spidey, only to be brought down by *arachtile dysfunction*. Seems his web-slinging skills are ebbing.

Break into Two: Tobey attends the demonstration of Alfred's experimental power source. As Alfred dons a robotic six-limbed contraption and seals it to his spinal chord, one of the coolest bad guys ever is about to be created. At Minute 38, when the public experiment goes awry, Spider-Man appears but can't pull the plug in time; Alfred's beloved wife is killed and he is knocked unconscious. Later, trying to remove his robot arms, Alfred's artificial limbs come alive, killing the surgeons. "Doc Ock" is born.

B Story: The "internal story" is seen through Tobey's battle with the mad Doc Ock. Alfred's life — without his wife — is now out of balance. Love gone, he crosses to the dark side. As metaphor for what Tobey's life might look like, Alfred's is a cautionary tale.

Fun and Games: We also get a brand new creature found in the "upside-down world" of Act Two: an eight-limbed criminal running amok in the city and Spider-Man's Nemesis. "Doctor Octopus," as Jameson calls him, is on a new mission, his serpent-head arms urging him to re-do the experiment on his own. Ock and Spider-Man battle when Ock tries to rob a bank to finance his mad dreams.

Midpoint: With Spider-Man blamed for the robbery and his powers failing, Tobey hits a mid-point bottom and a "false defeat." Assigned to cover a society event for his boss' son, the real low comes when Tobey learns Kirsten and John are engaged. The next day, Tobey goes to a doctor to get help for his lagging powers, and told he doesn't have to be a Superhero if he doesn't want to. At 1 Hour 2 Minutes, he declares: "I'm Spider-Man no more." A and B stories cross as, prompted by his stalemate with Doc Ock, Tobey will be a "civilian" and wear only his every-day clothes for a while.

Bad Guys Close In: Tobey tries to be "normal." He gives up crime fighting, keeps his promise to see Kirsten's play (*The Importance of Being Earnest*), and catches up on his homework. But we know it won't last. Crime keeps happening — and duty pulls at Tobey.

All Is Lost: Finally, when a fire breaks out at an apartment building, Tobey dashes in to save a little girl. But the "whiff of death" of this "false victory" (and the perfect opposite of the midpoint low) is that one person didn't get out — and died.

Dark Night of the Soul: Tobey tells Aunt May about his part in the death of his Uncle Ben, but she tells him: "There's a hero in all of us, even though we have to give up the things we want most, even our dreams." Called back by the "promise" of duty, Tobey tries willpower to be Spider-Man again. Atop a building, he says: "Strong focus on what I want" and leaps — only to fall to the ground and hurt his back. His attempt at "self-will" fails.

Break into Three: Kirsten meets Tobey. She is about to accept his offer to be together, and though he is on a new track to return to crime-fighting, she's not giving up on him. As they're about to kiss, Tobey sees Doc Ock hurl a car at them and saves Kirsten, then loses her as the villain grabs her to use as bait for Spider-Man. A and B stories cross, thanks to Doc Ock, as Tobey realizes his power is back. The missing component was love, and the "promise" to be with Kirsten now combines with the "promise" to be a Superhero.

Finale: Among the great moments in this finish: Spider-Man stops an out-of-control train by "crucifying" himself (we've seen the exact same beat in *Raging Bull*, *The Matrix*, and *Gladiator*) and saving all onboard. Spent and without his mask, Tobey is brought inside and laid on the floor of the train. "It's just a kid," says a passenger. (Love that beat!) Tobey saves Kirsten when he convinces Doc Ock to re-embrace his humanity and not destroy the city. Kirsten now knows who Spidey is and loves Tobey even more.

Final Image: Kirsten makes her own decision and runs from her wedding to be with Tobey, despite the danger of his being Spider-Man. By being willing to give up everything he loves, Tobey has gotten both. He has Kirsten *and* his mission, his life in balance. Opening and final image are opposites, the screenplay perfect.

 Is this the end of the tail? Not quite.

AFTERWORD
SO WHAT ABOUT *GHOST*?

Whew! That's one hell of a lot of movies!

And it's my bet that at some point in reading one or more of these chapters you've had an "A-ha!" experience.

A-ha! *Bad News Bears* and *Ocean's Eleven* really are the same movie!

A-ha! The Half Man is in A LOT of Monster in the House flicks! How about that!?

A-HA! The Dude with a Problem is a movie I thought I knew but I *never* saw that "eye of the storm" beat before!

WOW!

At which point the top of your head explodes, and your brains spill out all over Starbucks.

At least this is my hope.

And yet, while those fantastic coffeehouse employees we love so — Nancine, Micah, and Tifani — are mopping up the contents of your brainpan, a new thought creeps in: *So what?*

This whole genre thing may be an amusing parlor trick, but what does it really have to do with the job of sitting down and cranking out *your* movie? And btw, what about movies that seem to blend a bunch of these story genres together?

What about *Ghost*?

Well calm down there, Starbuckeroo. Ask Nancine for a refill, sit down, and let's kibbitz awhile. I agree it's a lot to digest. But looking at these movies in a new way is really going to help. And the good news is that while we're sitting here chatting — at least we're not writing!

First of all, welcome to the business of storytelling. No matter what level you're at — novice, skilled practitioner, or stratosphere-scraping genius — you are aware of the never-ending battle. Each of us goes about it in a different way and yet it boils down to the same question:

How do I write *my* story?

What chunk goes where? What does the audience need to know when? Is my hero heroic enough, and if not, why not? And the bottom line of any story: What am I trying to say?

What should be clearer after reading this book is that you are not the first to climb Mt. Everest. And yes, it *is* about tricks, storytelling sleight-of-hand, and tradition. And guess what else? As original as you think you are, you aren't. Sorry! Whenever I hear someone insist that his story is original, I have to laugh. Fresh, I hope. Original?

No such thing.

We have already heard every story ever told. Like little kids who ask for the same tale over and over again, told exactly the same way, we too respond to hidden patterns. The elements that vibrate in us like a tuning fork — the stories that truly resonate — are based on patterns deep in our DNA. What we're looking for as writers, and even as listeners, is an "internal balance," a story that satisfies some pre-thinking part of the soul. And connecting to the stories we've told forever is key to figuring it out.

I, and a lot of my friends, call it "breaking a story."

But really it's about finding it.

I personally love working out a story. And I love knowing that I am part of a long tradition of writers who have wrestled with the very same problems. I'm glad I know "making it fresh" has always been the job. But it really comes down to: Does the story work? And if not, what can I do to make it work?

Not every story I have broken down in this book does! I've given you some creaky old movies that are way passé to us modern urbanites. I've reviewed a few films that are not my personal faves. What I've hoped to do is show how I, like everyone else in this craft, am always in the process of honing my storytelling skills. This book, if nothing else, is a method to do this in a new way.

Now when you tell me the movie you're working on is "a road picture," you know it should include things that a Golden Fleece has: a "road," a "team," and a "prize." And if you're working on a love story, you know the number-one litmus test is its theme: "My life changed for having met another." Writing a mystery? You must ask: "What's the 'dark turn' of my hero?" because that's what Whydunits are about. And if you're not sure if it's a Dude with a Problem or a Monster in the House you're writing, you must ask: "Is my hero an 'innocent'? Is this story about survival?" If "yes" to both questions... you know. Right?

It's all about getting a little better grip on what makes that tuning fork in our souls hum. And also knowing that you have a bunch of stories to study that can help!

So what about *Ghost*?

When I was in the middle of writing this book, deep in my own "My, aren't I a genius!" megalomania, the Bruce Joel Rubin-scripted, Jerry Zucker-directed thriller came on TV. And as I watched Patrick and Demi cavorting *ex corpus*... suddenly *my* brain exploded!

Ghost is supernatural, which implies it's an Out of the Bottle; it's a love story, which means that "my life changed for having met another" is certainly in play; and it's also a mystery and a Rites of Passage, too — for God's sake, Patrick *dies* and can't go to the light until he overcomes his unfinished business on Earth! So? What kind of movie is it?

After I simmered down, I realized two things: One, it's a Whydunit, because solving the mystery of who killed Patrick and why — even though he is no longer operating at room temperature — *is* the story. Yes, it's magical; yes, it's a love story. But at the end of the day, it's a "Fantasy Whydunit" — in the very same league as *The Sixth Sense*.

When I figured that out, I was kind of pleased. My system worked! But the second thing I understood was that in cases where we're not sure what type of movie it is, the bottom line is we now have a language to talk about it. Just like the bullet points of the BS2, when I say "Fun and Games" or "All Is Lost" or "Bad Guys Close In," we know what parts of the movie we mean; and when I say "Buddy Love" or "Rites of Passage" or "Out of the Bottle," we suddenly have an overview of story type — and a set of terms to talk about those stories in a way we understand.

And a fun way too, if I say so myself!

Point is: This is one more tool. Knowing story and knowing how stories are put together — and what is satisfying — is our goal as writers. Being experts on all types, even those outside our genre, helps us be better in our genre. And identifying any story, even those answering: "What did you do at work today, Dad?" as one type or another — even seeing mythic elements in a commercial for furniture wax on TV — makes us more aware of story mechanisms. Let this book be a way to do just that, a new method to deconstruct old ideas.

So if you are trying to "stump the author" by thinking up movies that don't fit the paradigm... stop. Won't help you. What will help you is seeing how the gray, as yet unformed notion in your head can be fashioned into something that works for us all — and shaping it into a story that resonates is the job. Tapping into the primal nature of stories and why we tell them is magic. You have it in you already, and as I say in my lectures all over the world (who knew?!), the only thing stopping the stories from getting out is you.

So get out of the way! Let the stories bubble up from deep within, in patterns we've used to tell stories forever. Fact is the stories come from a higher source — that's why they keep repeating. They're being broadcast to us to remind us why we get up every day and hit it one more time, and we all carry the message. Stories are everywhere. Just look around Starbucks. From the primal campfire to the market square to here among the *coffeeati*, what resonates is truth.

Find yours. And pass it on.

GLOSSARY REDUX:

EVEN *MORE* TERMS FROM THE 310 AREA CODE

ALL STORIES ARE ABOUT TRANSFORMATION! – This is not a Hollywood term… it is our motto! It should be printed out and put on top of our computers as a reminder of why we do this job. No story is worth telling unless change occurs in the hero — or in us, the audience. The bigger the growth, the more epic the tale.

BRANDO – The rebel found in stories of the Institutionalized kind. Named for Marlon Brando, who portrayed motorcycle tough Johnny in 1953's *The Wild One*, this is the radical who defies the system and doubts everything about the family, business, or group that has stood the test of time.

BUTTON – A line or visual punctuation that ends a scene: an ironic comment, a joke, or a note of deep meaning. "We need a better button here" is a line we hear from execs, which means our scene ends with a whimper… not a POW!

CASE WITHIN A CASE – In a Whydunit, usually the initial or long-buried caper that for some reason is unresolved. By pursuing another case, the detective revisits the original — and cracks both.

CHASE TO THE AIRPORT SCENE – In any movie with a love story at its heart, invariably one lover will leave near the end, prompting a frantic "chase to the airport" to stop him or her, e.g., Woody Allen in *Manhattan*. This big finish is re-freekin'-quired according to every studio exec you will ever hear on the subject… so be prepared with yours!

COMPANY MAN — In an Institutionalized story, the one who has so bought into the establishment that he has sacrificed his humanity for it, resulting in robotic side effects that often include sexual dysfunction and a general crankiness, e.g., Frank Burns and Margaret "Hot Lips" O'Houlihan in *M*A*S*H*.

COMPLICATION — Typically in a romantic comedy or love story, the *sabot* in the machinery: the person, place, or event that stops the lovers from being together, e.g., the iceberg in *Titanic*, the bet in *How to Lose a Guy in 10 Days*, and the fact that Matthew McConaughey lives at home in *Failure to Launch*. Ironically, it is also the thing that keeps the lovers together — and is usually what your rom-com is "about."

CONFIDANT — In an Out-of-the-Bottle story, a person the hero can trust with the secret of his magic power — and sometimes the one who uses that information to harm the hero (so much for trust).

CRAWL — The moving text at the beginning or the end of a film that explains its context, giving background to, or a time frame for, a historic or futuristic setting that we need to know to understand what will happen next. It is usually slow enough for us maroons to read — and getting slower every year!

DOUBLE MUMBO JUMBO — In movies using "magic," the tendency of the writers to pile it on, or use several forms of it, and unwittingly make the story feel fuzzy or confusing. The rule is: We, the audience, are allowed to suspend disbelief once in a movie. You cannot be led to believe aliens *and* vampires exist in one world.

EYE OF THE STORM — In a Dude-with-a-Problem film, the break from the fast-paced, confusing, and dangerous situation our innocent hero suddenly finds his bad self in. It can be a friend or a love interest who also offer the hero a needed lesson.

FOOL ASSUMES A NEW NAME – In Fool Triumphant, when the hero enters Act Two and takes on a new moniker, e.g., when "Michael Dorsey" becomes "Dorothy Michaels" in *Tootsie*. The name change usually occurs as a disguise or by accident.

HALF MAN – In a Monster-in-the-House movie, the partial survivor who has had an interaction with the monster in his past and comes away damaged in some way because of it. This is the "false mentor" who can tell the hero — and us — the horror of what dealing with the monster will entail — and who is sure to die!

INSIDER – In a Fool-Triumphant movie, the jealous one who realizes the "idiot" is wiser than everyone and seeks to stop him before others see this too, e.g., Salieri in *Amadeus*.

KILL THE CAT – An alternate to having the hero do something nice — like save a cat — so that we're on his side, is to have someone do something mean to him, e.g., when Elle Woods is dumped by her beau in the beginning of *Legally Blonde*.

LEARNS TO DO IT WITHOUT THE MAGIC – Usually a beat found in any movie using "magic" that indicates a change in the hero in Act Three. Up till then the hero has been empowered — or cursed — with some form of magic spell, and now must choose not to use the magic in order to learn a lesson, e.g., in *Bruce Almighty* when Jim Carrey does good deeds without using any of his godly powers. But this is a general term, too, used for movies *without* magic. It can indicate any Act Three change where the hero "learns he had it in him all along" or "learns he already possesses the bravery or skill he needs to win."

LEMON SEED – The new "thing" introduced at the midpoint of a movie that indicates we are going to be heading for the finish at a faster pace — and with added pressure. Think of a slippery lemon seed between your thumb and index finger being slowly squeezed until it *squirts* out in the Act Three climax! It is introduced mid-movie at the "stakes are raised" point.

MASCOT — In a Superhero tale, the loyal and very human underling who looks up to the title character but can never be him, e.g., Jimmy Olsen in *Superman* and Timon in *The Lion King*. Often used by the Nemesis to threaten the Superhero.

NAIF — The character in an Institutionalized story that is "us," such as Jane Fonda in *9 to 5* and Tom Hulce in *Animal House*, who, by being brought into the system, helps explain its rules.

RIFF — Coming from the musical world, this term implies a sometimes improvised bit, routine, or off-the-cuff piece of "business" that springs from a particular set-up. For instance, if you set up the premise of a mom and her cop son who become partners in solving crime, I will riff on ideas such as: mom stops a mugger with her knitting needles; the two get into the "world's slowest chase" when she and her son pursue a bad guy and she is driving; or mom thinks her son's room has been rifled by intruders when it's just a mess. See? *Stop! Or My Mom Will Shoot* was funny when it left my hands! And these riffs prove it!

ROAD APPLE — In a Golden-Fleece movie, this is the thing that stops the team from gaining the prize. It's the set-back, surprise backstab, or bit of new information that makes the participants think they will never win the day, e.g., when Tom Hanks and company find Private Ryan — and he refuses to go home.

RULES — The magic in an Out-of-the-Bottle story needs these parameters, guidelines, or boundaries to keep what happens credible. State The Rules up front and stick to them!

SET PIECE — Whenever I come up with a good movie idea, my first question, and that of a lot of movie producers who might buy it, is: "What are the set pieces?" These are the "trailer moments," examples of the premise that demonstrate the essence of the movie.

SIX THINGS THAT NEED FIXING — Six is an arbitrary number, but should indicate there are a bunch of defects in the hero's life when we first meet him that will be healed during the movie. In the opening scenes of *Tootsie*, Dustin Hoffman as Michael Dorsey is shown as: (1) a difficult actor with (2) an uncaring agent. He is (3) insensitive to women and — not surprisingly — (4) an ineffective pick-up artist and (5) bad friend who (6) doesn't like to hold babies. All these things will get "fixed" by donning a dress and becoming a better man for having been "Dorothy Michaels." The journey would mean nothing if these problems weren't set up in Act One.

TIME CLOCK — "How long do we have?" asks the captain of *The Titanic* upon hitting the iceberg at the midpoint of the movie. Meet the "time clock" or "ticking clock," a way to let us know how much longer we've got and to put pressure on the heroes to solve, get out of, or triumph before it's too late.

TWO-HANDER — A movie where we follow two characters, each has an arc, and each grows because of the other, e.g., the rom-com *Two Weeks Notice*. **THREE-HANDER** — A movie where we follow three stories, each with its own arc of growth, most often a love triangle, such as in *Sweet Home Alabama*, *Titanic*, and *Gone with the Wind*. **FOUR-HANDER** — A movie where we follow four stories, most often a two-couple love story like *When Harry Met Sally...* as well as such darker studies as *Closer* and *We Don't Live Here Anymore*.

TURNING OVER CARDS — Describes any progression that reveals the plot points of a story. In a Whydunit, it's the series of clues leading the detective to a final secret.

TURN, TURN, TURN — This is the dictate (at least in my book) that a story not only moves forward but faster and with more energy — particularly from midpoint on (see "Lemon Seed," page 283).

WATCH OUT FOR THAT GLACIER! — My ironic cry of boredom while sitting through a disaster movie or revenge tale when the heroes know a showdown is looming, but which is so slow in coming (one inch a year!) that we in the audience must wait and twiddle our thumbs. Screenwriters, watch out for... this icy sensation!

ABOUT THE AUTHOR

In his 20-year career as a screenwriter, Blake has sold, optioned, or been hired to write dozens of scripts for film and TV. Best known as "one of Hollywood's most successful spec screenwriters," he also co-wrote *Blank Check*, which became a hit for Disney, and *Nuclear Family* for Steven Spielberg — both million-dollar deals. Blake sold his 13th spec screenplay, the horror-comedy *Granny*, in 2006.

Blake turned author in 2005 with *Save the Cat! The Last Book on Screenwriting You'll Ever Need*, now in its ninth printing. He is also a popular and enthusiastic speaker who has prompted "standing room only" lectures and workshops in New York, London, San Francisco, Seattle, Chicago, Vancouver, Toronto, Barcelona, and his hometown of Los Angeles.

The *Cat!* method has become the "secret weapon" of many development executives, managers, and producers for its precise, easy, and honest appraisal of what it takes to create and write stories that resonate. *Save the Cat! The Last Story Structure Software You'll Ever Need* has codified this method in an easy-to-use CD-Rom that is, like the book, a consistent best seller.

Blake has a B.A. in English from Georgetown University and has been a proud member of WGA, west since 1987.

For information, check out *www.blakesnyder.com*.

THE MYTH OF MWP

In a dark time, a light bringer came along, leading the curious and the frustrated to clarity and empowerment. It took the well-guarded secrets out of the hands of the few and made them available to all. It spread a spirit of openness and creative freedom, and built a storehouse of knowledge dedicated to the betterment of the arts.

The essence of the Michael Wiese Productions (MWP) is empowering people who have the burning desire to express themselves creatively. We help them realize their dreams by putting the tools in their hands. We demystify the sometimes secretive worlds of screenwriting, directing, acting, producing, film financing, and other media crafts.

By doing so, we hope to bring forth a realization of 'conscious media' which we define as being positively charged, emphasizing hope and affirming positive values like trust, cooperation, self-empowerment, freedom, and love. Grounded in the deep roots of myth, it aims to be healing both for those who make the art and those who encounter it. It hopes to be transformative for people, opening doors to new possibilities and pulling back veils to reveal hidden worlds.

MWP has built a storehouse of knowledge unequaled in the world, for no other publisher has so many titles on the media arts. Please visit www.mwp.com where you will find many free resources and a 25% discount on our books. Sign up and become part of the wider creative community!

Onward and upward,

Michael Wiese
Publisher/Filmmaker

FILM & VIDEO BOOKS

TO RECEIVE A FREE MWP NEWSLETTER, CLICK ON WWW.MWP.COM TO REGISTER

SCREENWRITING | WRITING

And the Best Screenplay Goes to... | Dr. Linda Seger | $26.95
Archetypes for Writers | Jennifer Van Bergen | $22.95
Cinematic Storytelling | Jennifer Van Sijll | $24.95
Could It Be a Movie? | Christina Hamlett | $26.95
Creating Characters | Marisa D'Vari | $26.95
Crime Writer's Reference Guide, The | Martin Roth | $20.95
Deep Cinema | Mary Trainor-Brigham | $19.95
Elephant Bucks | Sheldon Bull | $24.95
Fast, Cheap & Written That Way | John Gaspard | $26.95
Hollywood Standard, The | Christopher Riley | $18.95
I Could've Written a Better Movie than That! | Derek Rydall | $26.95
Inner Drives | Pamela Jaye Smith | $26.95
Joe Leydon's Guide to Essential Movies You Must See | Joe Leydon | $24.95
Moral Premise, The | Stanley D. Williams, Ph.D. | $24.95
Myth and the Movies | Stuart Voytilla | $26.95
Power of the Dark Side, The | Pamela Jaye Smith | $22.95
Psychology for Screenwriters | William Indick, Ph.D. | $26.95
Rewrite | Paul Chitlik | $16.95
Romancing the A-List | Christopher Keane | $18.95
Save the Cat! | Blake Snyder | $19.95
Save the Cat! Goes to the Movies | Blake Snyder | $24.95
Screenwriting 101 | Neill D. Hicks | $16.95
Screenwriting for Teens | Christina Hamlett | $18.95
Script-Selling Game, The | Kathie Fong Yoneda | $16.95
Stealing Fire From the Gods, 2nd Edition | James Bonnet | $26.95
Way of Story, The | Catherine Ann Jones | $22.95
What Are You Laughing At? | Brad Schreiber | $19.95
Writer's Journey, – 3rd Edition, The | Christopher Vogler | $26.95
Writer's Partner, The | Martin Roth | $24.95
Writing the Action Adventure Film | Neill D. Hicks | $14.95
Writing the Comedy Film | Stuart Voytilla & Scott Petri | $14.95
Writing the Killer Treatment | Michael Halperin | $14.95
Writing the Second Act | Michael Halperin | $19.95
Writing the Thriller Film | Neill D. Hicks | $14.95
Writing the TV Drama Series – 2nd Edition | Pamela Douglas | $26.95
Your Screenplay Sucks! | William M. Akers | $19.95

FILMMAKING

Film School | Richard D. Pepperman | $24.95
Power of Film, The | Howard Suber | $27.95

PITCHING

Perfect Pitch – 2nd Edition, The | Ken Rotcop | $19.95
Selling Your Story in 60 Seconds | Michael Hauge | $12.95

SHORTS

Filmmaking for Teens | Troy Lanier & Clay Nichols | $18.95
Ultimate Filmmaker's Guide to Short Films, The | Kim Adelman | $16.95

BUDGET | PRODUCTION MGMT

Film & Video Budgets, 4th Updated Edition | Deke Simon & Michael Wiese | $26.95
Film Production Management 101 | Deborah S. Patz | $39.95

DIRECTING | VISUALIZATION

Animation Unleashed | Ellen Besen | $26.95
Citizen Kane Crash Course in Cinematography | David Worth | $19.95
Directing Actors | Judith Weston | $26.95
Directing Feature Films | Mark Travis | $26.95
Fast, Cheap & Under Control | John Gaspard | $26.95
Film Directing: Cinematic Motion, 2nd Edition | Steven D. Katz | $27.95
Film Directing: Shot by Shot | Steven D. Katz | $27.95
Film Director's Intuition, The | Judith Weston | $26.95
First Time Director | Gil Bettman | $27.95
From Word to Image | Marcie Begleiter | $26.95
I'll Be in My Trailer! | John Badham & Craig Modderno | $26.95
Master Shots | Christopher Kenworthy | $24.95
Setting Up Your Scenes | Richard D. Pepperman | $24.95
Setting Up Your Shots, 2nd Edition | Jeremy Vineyard | $22.95
Working Director, The | Charles Wilkinson | $22.95

DIGITAL | DOCUMENTARY | SPECIAL

Digital Filmmaking 101, 2nd Edition | Dale Newton & John Gaspard | $26.95
Digital Moviemaking 3.0 | Scott Billups | $24.95
Digital Video Secrets | Tony Levelle | $26.95
Greenscreen Made Easy | Jeremy Hanke & Michele Yamazaki | $19.95
Producing with Passion | Dorothy Fadiman & Tony Levelle | $22.95
Special Effects | Michael Slone | $31.95

EDITING

Cut by Cut | Gael Chandler | $35.95
Cut to the Chase | Bobbie O'Steen | $24.95
Eye is Quicker, The | Richard D. Pepperman | $27.95
Invisible Cut, The | Bobbie O'Steen | $28.95

SOUND | DVD | CAREER

Complete DVD Book, The | Chris Gore & Paul J. Salamoff | $26.95
Costume Design 101 | Richard La Motte | $19.95
Hitting Your Mark – 2nd Edition | Steve Carlson | $22.95
Sound Design | David Sonnenschein | $19.95
Sound Effects Bible, The | Ric Viers | $26.95
Storyboarding 101 | James Fraioli | $19.95
There's No Business Like Soul Business | Derek Rydall | $22.95

FINANCE | MARKETING | FUNDING

Art of Film Funding, The | Carole Lee Dean | $26.95
Complete Independent Movie Marketing Handbook, The | Mark Steven Bosko | $39.95
Independent Film and Videomakers Guide – 2nd Edition, The | Michael Wiese | $29.95
Independent Film Distribution | Phil Hall | $26.95
Shaking the Money Tree, 2nd Edition | Morrie Warshawski | $26.95

OUR FILMS

Dolphin Adventures: DVD | Michael Wiese and Hardy Jones | $24.95
On the Edge of a Dream | Michael Wiese | $16.95
Sacred Sites of the Dalai Lamas– DVD, The | Documentary by Michael Wiese | $24.95
Hardware Wars: DVD | Written and Directed by Ernie Fosselius | $14.95